Defense Assessment Workbook

A product of truth and empowerment by

JONATHAN T. GILLIAM

IF FOUND PLEASE RETURN TO:

_____

NAME

_____

PHONE NUMBER

A POST HILL PRESS BOOK

Sheep No More Workbook #2:
Defense Assessment
© 2019 by Jonathan T. Gilliam
All Rights Reserved

ISBN: 978-1-64293-251-5

Cover Photo by Barry Morgenstein Photography, barrymorgenstein.com
Interior Design and Composition by Spiro Graphics, Inc.

Post Hill Press
New York • Nashville
posthillpress.com
Published in the United States of America

Dedicated to the defenders of freedom. Without you, tyranny would reign.

In remembrance of US Navy SEAL, Glenn Collins. He could squeeze 25 hours out of a 24 hour day. See you in Heaven, brother.

For the oppressed and poverty stricken children of the world. May hope and faith abound in them until they are able to overcome their adversity.

May God Himself, bless this workbook and the entire "Sheep No More" series, just like he blessed this world with His Son, Jesus. May that blessing touch every person that decides to use these books to empower their lives. Amen!

FROM ATTACKER TO DEFENDER

This workbook will forever change the way you defend your surroundings. If you have read *Sheep No More: The Art Of Awareness And Attack Survival* and completed the *Sheep No More Workbook #1: Threat Assessment*, you are now ready to step up and flip the switch from attacker to defender.

The knowledge you have gained targeting your sectors thus far from the attackers perspective has allowed you to identify how attacker's assess the critical times, critical areas, vulnerabilities and avenues of approach of your facilities. At the same time, your commitment to analysis of your life has also allowed you to identify standard operating procedures from the defender's point of view.

WARNING: I WILL REPEAT THE INFORMATION IN THIS NEXT PARAGRAPH OVER AND OVER (IT IS IMPORTANT SO DON'T GET FRUSTRATED.)

All 10 sectors in this *Workbook #2: Defense Assessment*, will coincide with sectors 1 through 10 from your *Workbook #1*. Here you will continue to utilize the information you put into *Workbook #1* and expand upon it to create daily defense SOPs and also plans of action for what to do when you cannot avoid a critical area and/or you are caught up in an attack.

You will be pushed to make more detailed sketches and/or collecting map pictures of your targeted areas and utilize them to highlight the critical areas in and around each sector. Also, you will be expanding on what type of behavior is normal and what is not for each sector, which will help in building your awareness of what might stand out if surveillance or an imminent attack is being carried out on you. These exercises are critical and will save your life by helping you develop plans of action long before an attack may occur.

It's time to transition into the mindset you will have when you actually find yourself in a situation, the defender's mindset!

Let's Roll!

To join in the conversation, go to Twitter@attackanddefend or www.jonathanTgilliam.com/attackanddefend

Key Terms

Attack—Aggressive action against a place or enemy forces with weapons or armed force, typically in a battle or war.

Attacker—A person or animal that attacks someone or something.

Attack and Defend—The back and forth technique of defending a person, place, or thing through the development of an attacker's mindset and utilizing it to gain target information that is compiled into an attacker's target package, which leads to awareness and attack avoidance.

Attack Probability—Statistical calculations that rate the most likely place for an attack by assigning a number percentage.

Attack Possibility—Statistical calculations that reduce the likelihood of an attack to either yes or no.

Attacker's Avenues of Approach—An air or ground route of an attacking force leading to its objective.

Awareness—Knowledge or perception of a situation or fact.

Criticalities—The five specific parts of a target (including Critical Assets, Critical Areas, Critical Times, Vulnerabilities, and Attacker's Avenues of Approach) comprised of the exploitable information sought after and utilized by attackers to build a target package and used by defenders to ensure proper defenses.

Critical Asset—Facilities, systems, and equipment which, if destroyed, degraded, or otherwise rendered unavailable, would affect the reliability or operability of operations.

Critical Area—Soft target areas considered to have a heightened threat and easy access for an attacker.

Critical Time—Specific times when a critical area is under the highest threat.

Criminal—A person who has committed a crime not in the furtherance of political aim.

Defense—The action of defending from or resisting attack.

Defender—A person or animal attempting to ward off attack from an attacker.

Deranged—Mad; insane.

Hard Target—A building, facility, or area (critical area) that has been secured, making it less likely to be attacked.

Plan of Attack—Ideas or actions intended to deal with a problem or situation.

Private Sector—The part of the economy involved with enterprise not controlled by the state.

Procedures—Established and approved order of actions.

Public Sector—The part of the economy concerned with providing various government services.

Shared Threats—Possible or probable attacks shared by multiple locations or people or threats that, if carried out as an attack, could affect other nontargeted locations or people.

Soft Target—A building, facility, or area (critical area) that is difficult to protect.

Strategy—The thinking process required to plan a change, course of action, or organization. Strategy defines, or outlines, desired goals and why you should go about achieving them.

Surveillance—Observation for the purpose of information collection. Can be carried out electronically, in vehicle, or on foot.

Standard Operating Procedures—The standardization of tactics, techniques, and procedures into a step-by-step process for streamlined operations.

Task Organization—The process of assigning operations, tasks, work in an organized fashion.

Terrorism—The use of fear, intimidation, and violence in the pursuit of a political aim.

Terrorist—A person who carries out or facilitates when, where, how, and why a terror attack is carried out.

Tactics, Techniques, and Procedures (TTP)—Particular standard operating procedures utilized by attacking forces.

Tactics—The specific actions you take in implementing your strategy.

Techniques—The specific style or form used or applied to tactics.

Target Package—Information collected in order to develop an accurate picture of a given target for the purpose of attacking or defending.

VBIED—Acronym for vehicle-borne improvised explosive device.

Vulnerability—Identifiable areas of a location, facility, or person being exposed to the possibility of being attacked.

Defense Assessment Workbook
TRANSFERING AND CHARTING
INFORMATION FROM WORKBOOK #1
TO WORKBOOK #2

The Technique of Attack and Defend
Flowchart #1

NOTE: The following diagram on this page will help you understand the correlation of the information collected and cataloged in the Threat Assessment Workbook, and how that information flows into this Defense Assessment Workbook you are completing now.

Nothing you will do in this workbook will be done without the consideration of the information populating *Workbook #1: Threat Assessment.*

The recognition of the arrows on the diagram is important, because they show you the information flow, but also how some key areas of information will flow back and forth from the attack planning. As you learned in the original book *Sheep No More: The Art Of Awareness And Attack Survival*, in order to stay ahead of the bad guys, you have to periodically go back and attack your defenses. The more you do this, the harder your defenses will be, and the more aware you will become. Technically this should make it impossible for the bad guys to keep up with your defenses.

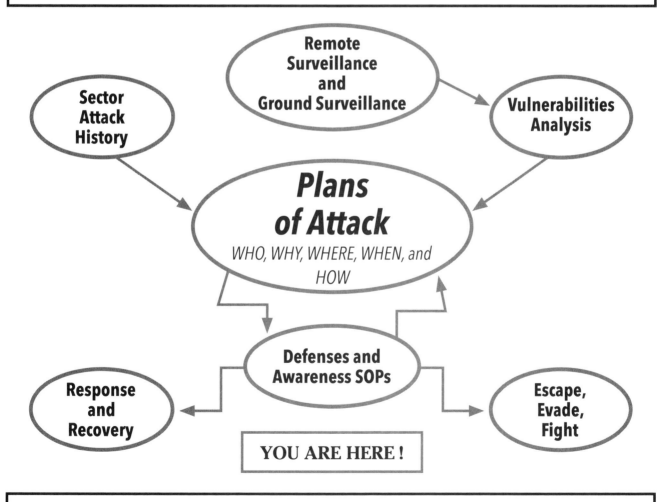

This fillable workbook begins with an overview of how the empty pages will be completed. Overall there are basically three types of fillable pages that will repeat in each Sector (1-10).

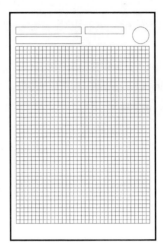

1. The Information Outline Sheet

All information that is to be charted, put in bullet statement, outline, or sketch format will be done on this type of page.

2. Threat Assessment Sector Overview

This will comprise of information transferred from *Workbook #1: Threat Assessment*, concerning first responders and other important information defenders will take into account when building defense SOPs

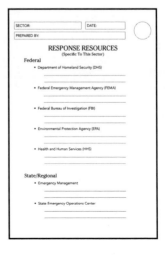

3. Response Resources Worksheets

This is where you will enter all the information you have collected into a brief overview of the different types of first responder resources and their contact information for each sector.

In order to perform a full assessment of your defenses, you will have to first read *Sheep No More: The Art Of Awareness And Attack Survival*, and also have completed *Workbook #1: Threat Assessment*. Once you have done this, you will have the understanding of the Attack and Defend technique as well as a thorough threat assessment on all your sectors, performed from the attacker's mindset.

If you have completed these first two requirements, then you are ready to transfer all the collected information into *Workbook #2: Defense Assessment*. As you are assessing the information transferred, you must put your main focus on the defender's mindset, while your secondary focus is continuously assessing your new SOPs from the attacker's point of view.

Read this   Fill this out   Transfer information into here

WORKBOOK #1: THREAT ASSESSMENT

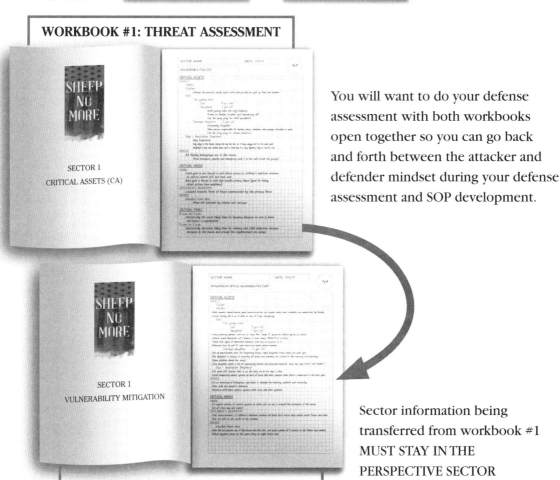

You will want to do your defense assessment with both workbooks open together so you can go back and forth between the attacker and defender mindset during your defense assessment and SOP development.

WORKBOOK #2: DEFENSE ASSESSMENT

Sector information being transferred from workbook #1 MUST STAY IN THE PERSPECTIVE SECTOR IN WORKBOOK #2

SECTOR

FIRST RESPONDER OVERVIEW

(example)

Sector and First Responder Overview
Example

SECTOR OVERVIEW SHEET (filled)
WORKBOOK #1: THREAT ASSESSMENT

Sector: HOME		Date: 01/01/2019

Prepared by: Jonathan T Gilliam

Situation: Five member family (including father, mother, two children and one teen-ager) living in a three bedroom, ranch style home, in a rural low crime area. House is occupied during the week from 5pm until 8am the following day except weekends when the family is usually around the house doing various individual things. Home is in the vicinity of a freeway exit and dry creek bed that runs behind the house.

Sector Overview: Little to no security precautions are set up and standard operating procedures are nonexistent and / or ignored by most family members. Neighborhood is considered low crime, middle income with one sexual offender registered three blocks away. Petty burglary of cars and dogs has been reported in the immediate area.

Note: Make sure you print out map and directions to pertinent police precincts.

Police Departments: Little Rock Police Department Pulaski County Sheriff's Office	PD Contact Information: SSS-SSS-SSSS SSS-SSS-SSSS	PD Response Times: LRPD 2-10 min PCSO 20-40 min
Crime Level: LOW	Possible Threat Level: MEDIUM	

Known Terror Threats: No known terror threats

Known Criminal Threats: Dog theft / Petty burglary of cars

Note: Make sure you print out map and directions to all trauma centers. Always make the effort to proceed to a level 1 trauma center if the injury is life threatening.

Trauma Centers: University of Arkansas for Medical Sciences (UAMS) Baptist Health Medical Center	Trauma Center Level (I, II, III): University of Arkansas for Medical Sciences (UAMS)	Response Times: 15 min

Weather Conditions:			
Spring Avg temp 80deg F Often rainy with thunder storms	Summer Avg temp 92deg F Often Dry	Fall Avg temp 70-85deg F Often rainy	Winter Avg temp 40deg F Some snow

Transfer the information from the SECTOR OVERVIEW SHEET's in *WORKBOOK #1: THREAT ASSESSMENT*, and populate this workbook's SECTOR OVERVIEW SHEET's at the beginning of each coinciding sector (S1 – S10).

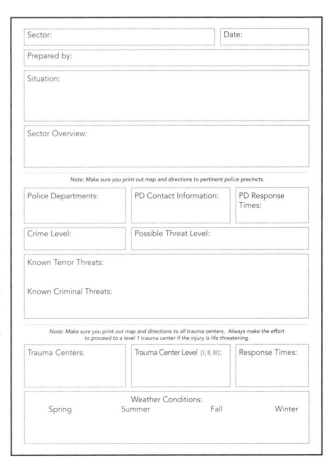

SECTOR OVERVIEW SHEET (empty)
WORKBOOK #2: DEFENSE ASSESSMENT

Sector:		Date:

Prepared by:

Situation:

Sector Overview:

Note: Make sure you print out map and directions to pertinent police precincts.

Police Departments:	PD Contact Information:	PD Response Times:
Crime Level:	Possible Threat Level:	

Known Terror Threats:

Known Criminal Threats:

Note: Make sure you print out map and directions to all trauma centers. Always make the effort to proceed to a level 1 trauma center if the injury is life threatening.

Trauma Centers:	Trauma Center Level (I, II, III):	Response Times:

Weather Conditions:			
Spring	Summer	Fall	Winter

This is the basic information that you will expand upon concerning the sector emergency responders, including information about true response times and the weather. Each sector in this workbook will start off the same way with this information.

This is the more detailed information you will collect concerning responding authorities and their contact information

---

Sector: *HOME*   Date: *7/4/19*

Pg #

Prepared by: *Jonathan T Gilliam*

RESPONSE RESOURCES
(Specific To This Sector)

Federal

Most of the federal addresses and phone numbers will be the same for each of your sectors.

- Department of Homeland Security (DHS)

  311 Federal Road, Little Rock, AR. 72301

  555-555-5555

- Federal Emergency Management Agency (FEMA)

  311 Federal Road, Little Rock, AR. 72301

  555-555-5555

This is where you will input **addresses** and **phone numbers** that you can find online concerning first responders. These lists will go into more detail than the single Defense Assessment Sector Overview.

- Federal Bureau of Investigation (FBI)

  311 Federal Road, Little Rock, AR. 72301

  555-555-5555

- Environmental Protection Agency (EPA)

  311 Federal Road, Little Rock, AR. 72301

  555-555-5555

- Health and Human Services (HHS)

  311 Federal Road, Little Rock, AR. 72301

  555-555-5555

State and regional authorities may vary sector to sector so make sure you do your research and put the proper phone numbers and addresses for things like police departments, fire departments and hospitals.

State/Regional

- Emergency Management

  1675 Barking Road, Little Rock, AR. 72301

  555-555-5555

- State Emergency Operations Center

  1675 Barking Road, Little Rock, AR. 72301

  555-555-5555

SECTOR

VULNERABILITY MITIGATION

(example)

As is always the case when assessing your defenses, a lot of the collected information will be utilized over and over. This is also the case when you analyze and mitigate vulnerabilities. Don't be upset if you find yourself copying the information about new SOPs over and over, because you are refining your understanding, awareness and overall, your SOPs as you flow through this workbook.

You will start to see how important simple sketches can be in helping you see where your vulnerabilities lie, and the highlighted areas of your sector that a bad guy will be attracted too.

As you perform the defense analysis, you will need your Threat Assessment Workbook side by side as the forms you filled out at the culmination of each sector in *Workbook #1: Threat Assessment* contain the plans of attack you will have to comb through in order to determine your counter attack and defensive SOPs.

Let's reflect back on the diagram from earlier which should make even more sense now.

INFORMATION COLLECTED

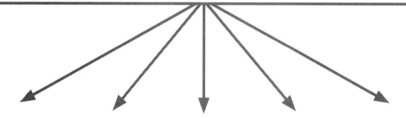

THREAT ASSESSMENT WORKBOOK
INFORMATION ASSESSED

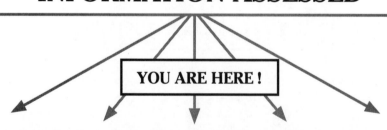

YOU ARE HERE !

DEFENSE ASSESSMENT WORKBOOK
INFORMATION UTILIZED

Vulnerabilities (V) Assessment
Information from Workbook #1 that will be entered into Workbook #2

As you can see this is where *Workbook #1: Threat Assessment* (example below) is used side by side with this *Workbook #2: Defense Assessment.* Regardless how you choose to use them together, remember that the Threat Assessment Workbook has all the information you'll need to complete your defense assessment and create SOPs. ***Just make sure it is coordinated sector by sector.*** The information below is from Workbook#1 and will be used to develop your lists of vulnerability mitigations in this workbook.

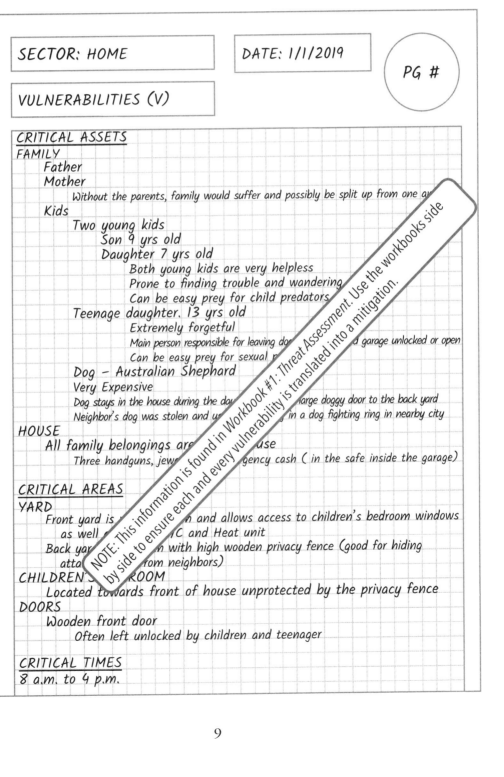

All of this information is found in your Threat Assessment Workbook

SECTOR: HOME   DATE: 1/1/2019   PG #

VULNERABILITIES (V)

CRITICAL ASSETS
FAMILY
    Father
    Mother
        Without the parents, family would suffer and possibly be split up from one a...
    Kids
        Two young kids
            Son 9 yrs old
            Daughter 7 yrs old
                Both young kids are very helpless
                Prone to finding trouble and wandering
                Can be easy prey for child predators
        Teenage daughter. 13 yrs old
            Extremely forgetful
            Main person responsible for leaving do...   ...d garage unlocked or open
            Can be easy prey for sexual p...
    Dog — Australian Shephard
    Very Expensive
    Dog stays in the house during the day...   ...large doggy door to the back yard
    Neighbor's dog was stolen and u...   ...in a dog fighting ring in nearby city
HOUSE
    All family belongings are...   ...use
        Three handguns, jew...   ...gency cash (in the safe inside the garage)

CRITICAL AREAS
YARD
    Front yard is...   ...n and allows access to children's bedroom windows
        as well...   ...C and Heat unit
    Back yar...   ...n with high wooden privacy fence (good for hiding
        atta...   ...rom neighbors)
CHILDREN'S...ROOM
    Located towards front of house unprotected by the privacy fence
DOORS
    Wooden front door
        Often left unlocked by children and teenager

CRITICAL TIMES
8 a.m. to 4 p.m.

NOTE: This information is found in Workbook #1: Threat Assessment. Use the workbooks side by side to ensure each and every vulnerability is translated into a mitigation.

Once again, this is where the rubber meets the road!!! Put on your defender glasses and identify EVERY possible Standard Operating Procedure (SOP) that can be created in order to counter vulnerabilities listed in the *Workbook #1: Threat Assessment*, (displayed on the previous page.) If you can identify the specific vulnerabilities about your life, then you can also find the mitigation strategies as well. Take your time, details are of the utmost importance here and the SOPs are only limited to your imagination!

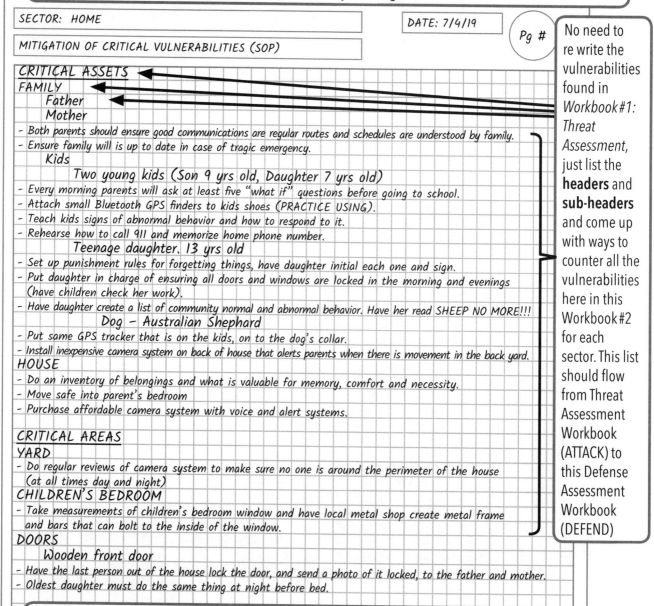

SECTOR: HOME

DATE: 7/4/19

Pg #

MITIGATION OF CRITICAL VULNERABILITIES (SOP)

CRITICAL ASSETS
FAMILY
    Father
    Mother
- Both parents should ensure good communications are regular routes and schedules are understood by family.
- Ensure family will is up to date in case of tragic emergency.
    Kids
        Two young kids (Son 9 yrs old, Daughter 7 yrs old)
- Every morning parents will ask at least five "what if" questions before going to school.
- Attach small Bluetooth GPS finders to kids shoes (PRACTICE USING).
- Teach kids signs of abnormal behavior and how to respond to it.
- Rehearse how to call 911 and memorize home phone number.
    Teenage daughter. 13 yrs old
- Set up punishment rules for forgetting things, have daughter initial each one and sign.
- Put daughter in charge of ensuring all doors and windows are locked in the morning and evenings (have children check her work).
- Have daughter create a list of community normal and abnormal behavior. Have her read SHEEP NO MORE!!!
        Dog – Australian Shephard
- Put same GPS tracker that is on the kids, on to the dog's collar.
- Install inexpensive camera system on back of house that alerts parents when there is movement in the back yard.
HOUSE
- Do an inventory of belongings and what is valuable for memory, comfort and necessity.
- Move safe into parent's bedroom
- Purchase affordable camera system with voice and alert systems.

CRITICAL AREAS
YARD
- Do regular reviews of camera system to make sure no one is around the perimeter of the house (at all times day and night)
CHILDREN'S BEDROOM
- Take measurements of children's bedroom window and have local metal shop create metal frame and bars that can bolt to the inside of the window.
DOORS
    Wooden front door
- Have the last person out of the house lock the door, and send a photo of it locked, to the father and mother.
- Oldest daughter must do the same thing at night before bed.

No need to re write the vulnerabilities found in *Workbook #1: Threat Assessment*, just list the **headers** and **sub-headers** and come up with ways to counter all the vulnerabilities here in this Workbook #2 for each sector. This list should flow from Threat Assessment Workbook (ATTACK) to this Defense Assessment Workbook (DEFEND)

REMINDER: If you haven't noticed, the SOPs on this page were created one for one with the vulnerabilities listed on the previous page which came out of Workbook #1 section SECTOR VULNERABILITIES (V) found in each sector (1-10). It is imperative that you go back and forth, one for one, building upon your already performed threat assessment. Otherwise, you will be playing a guessing game, causing this workbook to become incomplete. This is where the name for the technique ATTACK and DEFEND comes from!

READ *SHEEP NO MORE: THE ART OF AWARENESS AND ATTACK SURVIVAL*, COMPLETE *WORKBOOK #1: THREAT ASSESSMENT*, THEN USE THAT KNOWLEDGE AND INFORMATION TO COMPLETE THE ASSESSMENT PROCESS IN THIS *WORKBOOK #2: DEFENSE ASSESSMENT*!

Mitigation of Vulnerabilities (SOP Development)
Continued

SAME INSTRUCTIONS FOR THIS PAGE AS THE PREVIOUS PAGE!
You should expect the vulnerability mitigations to take up
more room than the lists of vulnerabilities in Workbook #1.

SECTOR: HOME

DATE: 7/4/19

Pg #

MITIGATION OF CRITICAL VULNERABILITIES (SOP)

CRITICAL TIMES

8 a.m. to 4 p.m.
- Ensure camera system can alert father, mother, and teenage daughter.

9 p.m. to 5 a.m.
- Make awareness a regular part of conversation, and play the "what if" game often.

ATTACKER AVENUES OF APPROACH

Freeway that exits into the neighborhood
- Purchase and install inexpensive camera system that alerts via telephone if someone approaches the house
  to ensure no one is approaching the house from the front or back

Dry creek bed behind the house
- Purchase and install motion sensor and light at the back of the yard overlooking the dry creek bed
  as a deterrent.
- Get a small dog that barks, that will alert the family if intruders are outside.
- Increase awareness of areas from where surveillance could be done.

    Get into the habit of performing counter surveillance of known areas where attackers could approach.
    Understand the behaviors, Normal vs Abnormal (list in section AWARENESS AND
    ATTACK INDICATORS)

Vulnerability Location (SOP Development)
Sketch Example

Draw a sketch of the area or include a map here. In many cases you can use the sketch and/or map to point out criticalities, including areas, times, vulnerabilities and avenues of approach. Use a red highlighter to point out critical areas and attack avenues of approach that you've discovered in Workbook #1.

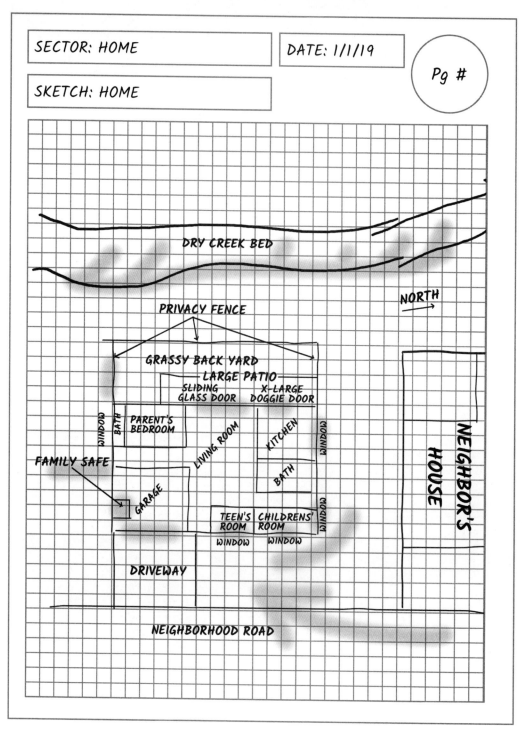

SECTOR

IMPLEMENTATION OF PHYSICAL DEFENSE AND TECHNOLOGY

(example)

Implementation of Physical Defense and Technology (SOP Development) Example

In this section you will be directing your attention to the sectors physical defense improvements which includes technology such as cameras and alarms if needed. With extreme discounts in this area along with advances in the relationship between cameras and their ability to notify you via cell phone, even your home can have real technological advances. Here is where you will list these needs and solutions for physical defense implementation.

SECTOR: HOME

DATE:

Pg #

IMPLEMENTATION OF PHYSICAL DEFENSE AND TECHNOLOGY SOPs:

- Purchase and install inexpensive camera system that alerts via telephone if someone approaches the house to ensure no one is approaching the house from the front or back.

- Purchase and install motion light at the back of the yard overlooking the dry creek bed as a deterrent.

- Get a small dog that barks when someone is outside the home.

- Buy inexpensive Bluetooth or GPS trackers for the kid's shoes and backpacks, as well as cars and other valuables.

- Start parking vehicles inside the garage.

- Collect old cellphones and plug them in and place them in each bedroom of the house.

Physical Defense and Technology (SOP Development) Sketch Example

Draw a sketch of the area or include a map here with focus on equipment changes or technology additions. In many cases you can use the sketch and/or map to point out mitigation SOPs, including areas, times, vulnerabilities and avenues of approach.

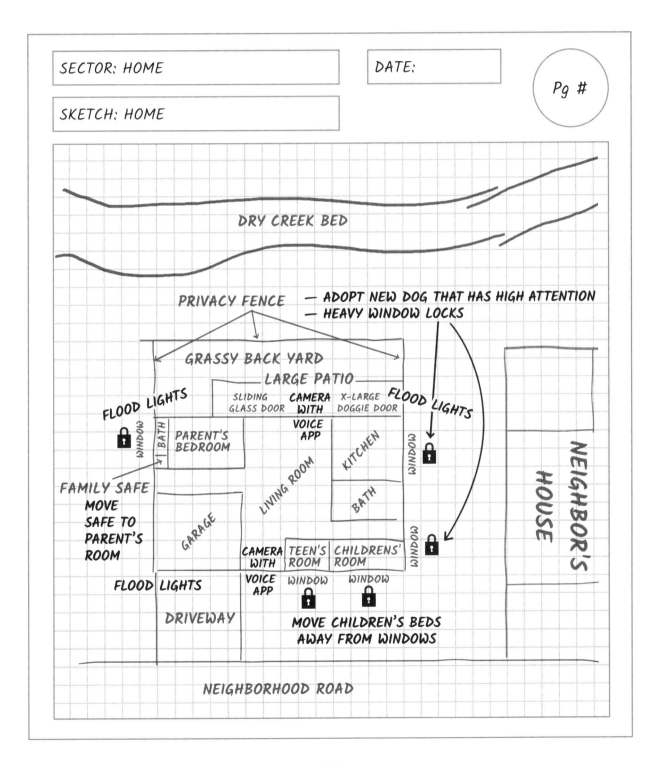

SECTOR: HOME

SKETCH: HOME

DATE:

Pg #

DRY CREEK BED

PRIVACY FENCE — ADOPT NEW DOG THAT HAS HIGH ATTENTION
— HEAVY WINDOW LOCKS

GRASSY BACK YARD

LARGE PATIO

FLOOD LIGHTS

SLIDING GLASS DOOR

CAMERA WITH VOICE APP

X-LARGE DOGGIE DOOR

FLOOD LIGHTS

WINDOW

BATH

PARENT'S BEDROOM

LIVING ROOM

KITCHEN

BATH

WINDOW

FAMILY SAFE
MOVE SAFE TO PARENT'S ROOM

GARAGE

WINDOW

CAMERA WITH VOICE APP

TEEN'S ROOM

CHILDRENS' ROOM

FLOOD LIGHTS

WINDOW

WINDOW

DRIVEWAY

MOVE CHILDREN'S BEDS AWAY FROM WINDOWS

NEIGHBOR'S HOUSE

NEIGHBORHOOD ROAD

15

SECTOR
BEHAVIORS AND ATTACK
INDICATORS
(example)

Sector Behaviors and Attack Indicators (SOP Development) Example

Behavior is one of the best indicators that surveillance is being performed or that an attack is imminent. All behaviors should be based on what is normal in your sector and what the attack history says of different attackers behavior on target. REMEMBER THINGS MAY CHANGE ON HOLIDAYS AND SUMMER VACATION DAYS.

SECTOR: HOME   DATE: 7/4/2019   Pg #

SECTOR BEHAVIORS AND ATTACK INDICATORS:

NORMAL:
- Neighborhood is isolated with no through traffic type roads,
  massive traffic or unfamiliar vehicles and pedestrian traffic is unusual.
- Only 8 regular walkers and/or joggers on a typical day.
    - 6am-8am
        - Two females and one male joggers
    - 8am-3pm
        - No known pedestrian traffic except moms and young preschool kids
    - 3pm - 10pm
        - This is the busiest time for the neighborhood. Lots of activity.

An important mitigation is simply taking time to observe all that you can daily.

ABNORMAL:
- Typically the same cars are parked on the street at specific times.
  Any lingering or slow driving cars are odd
- Almost no traffic after 8pm.
- Besides the individuals listed above, random walkers (ie. Unknown males)
  is highly unusual in this particular neighborhood.
- All street lights are usually well maintained by the city. Therefore,
  if a light is out, it should be reported immediately to the city.
  Always assume the worst for unknowns such as this.

ATTACK INDICATORS:
- Unknown males talking to children can be a behavior of a pedophiles
  slow approach to becoming familiar with a child in the neighborhood.
- Street lights could be a sign that criminals are targeting the neighborhood,
  especially if they are next to a house.
- Unknown cars patrolling the neighborhood late at night can be an indicator
  that criminals are casing the neighborhood to break into cars or
  unoccupied homes.

Actions to be Taken When Abnormal Behavior is Observed (SOP Development) Example

In this section, you are creating SOPs for how to react to abnormal behavior or an attack indicator. Do you do nothing? Do you approach? What do you ask? Or do you evacuate? Base your SOPs on historical behavior of attackers. Fluidity to maneuver is important, so you should also consider the different situations you could be faced with.

SECTOR: HOME **DATE: 7/4/2019** Pg #

ACTIONS TO BE TAKEN WHEN ABNORMAL BEHAVIOR IS OBSERVED:

- Take mental notes.

- Monitor joggers and walkers who are not known. Look for individuals making random, odd stops around children, homes or vehicles.

- If someone approaches a child, home or vehicle:
    - Immediately retrieve the child and call the police (depending on the situation)
    - If they appear to be attempting to gain access or just paying too much attention to homes or vehicles, call the police.

- If a vehicle appears to be patrolling the neighborhood, take a description of the vehicle and a license plate number if possible. Include known occupants of the vehicle, time, speed and direction the vehicle was traveling.

- If the vehicle is consistently patrolling the area DO NOT APPROACH, call 911.

- If you have a security camera that has voice ability, and if someone approaches your home, notify that they are being monitored via the speaker on the camera. If they persist in loitering, call 911.

SECTOR

SHARED THREATS

(example)

LIST OF SHARED THREATS (Sector specific)
Example

In this area you will list known shared threats that could potentially attract the attention of attackers. Is there an elementary school in your neighborhood? Is there someone in your neighborhood that collects cars? Remember the 1995 bombing of the Murrah Federal Building in Oklahoma City and how the attack that was targeting the federal building actually ended up destroying numerous surrounding businesses as well. That is why shared threats must be taken into account for any defensive security plan.

SECTOR: HOME

DATE:

Pg #

SHARED THREATS

- There is a strip mall located at the entrance of the neighborhood with multiple businesses, including a gas station, daycare and jewelry shop.

- Neighbor three doors down builds hot rod cars and owns an expensive motorcycle that are sometimes left out at night.

- There is a park in the middle of the neighborhood that often attracts teens hanging out on weekends.

SECTOR

TACTICAL PLANS OF ACTION
(WHERE VULNERABILITIES CANNOT BE MITIGATED)

(example)

TARGET EQUATION WORKSHEET

Sector: *HOME*

Date: *1/1/19*

Pg #

Type of attack: *Robbery*

Time of attack: *9 p___ 5 a.m.*

Avenues of Approach: *Nearby freeway allows fo___ of neighborhood, while the deep dry creek bed b___ lows for stealthy access to the neighborhood___*

Vulnerabilities: *Family sleeping, doors, ___ ___locked, easy access for criminals into the nei___ ___arby freeway and dry creek bed.*

Type of attack: *Burglary*

attack: *8 a.m. to 5 p.m.*

Avenues of Approa___ ___y allows for quick in and out of neighborhood, w___ ___creek bed behind the house allows for stealthy___ ___ighborhood and home.

Vulnerabili___ ___ome, easy access for criminals into the neighbor___ ___y and dry creek bed.

NOTE: *Use these Target Equation Sheets from Workbook #1: Threat Assessment, to augment your tactical plans of action. Remember that the concept of defense will also include actions such as Escape, Evade and Fight where elimination of all Vulnerabilities is not possible. Action beats reaction!!!*

Type of a___ ___: *Child*

Time of attack: *5 p.m. to 8 a.m.*

Avenues of Approach: *Nearby freeway allows for quick in and out of neighborhood, while the deep dry creek bed behind the house allows for stealthy access to the neighborhood and home.*

Vulnerabilities: *Helpless children, outside a lot, windows are located outside the privacy fence, windows unlocked, children's room on the opposite side house from parents' room.*

Tactical Plans of Action
Example

Not every sector will need tactical action plans because you may be able to mitigate the vulnerabilities to an extent you have eliminated most possibilities for attack. But every attack plan you discovered in workbook #1: threat assessment should at least be considered as needing a tactical action plan. Like the family plan listed below, public areas, work, vacation, places of worship and school are only some of the areas where you don't control the security procedures. This is where tactical plans of action are needed the most.

SECTOR: VACATION TRAVEL

3/15/2019

Pg #

TACTICAL ACTION PLAN

Our Family's Tactical Airport Plan

Step 1 — We will all wear clothing that does not require a belt.

Step 2 — Everyone wears shoes that are easy on/easy off.

Step 3 — One family member will carry all the electronics and valuables (wallets, purses, and so on) in a carry-on. Cell phones stay with each individual.

Step 4 — The person carrying the electronic items will be first in line so they can get through security with the important stuff if an issue arises. Also, this prevents our important and valuable belongings from being spread all over the conveyer belt. This point person will keep their phone with the other electronic gear, but every other person in the group will place their phone in their specific bin as they get ready to go through. The last person in the family line will keep their phone as long as possible until they are ready to go through the line. This will ensure that at least one phone is on either side of the security checkpoint as the family goes through. If the groups get split up, then communications can still be made.

Step 5 — Everyone will keep their shoes on until they are all at the conveyer belt. When everyone is ready, they will take their shoes off and put them in one bin that person number two will control.

Step 6 — One parent will be the first person through security and the other parent will be the last person through. [If you are a single-parent family, the adult goes last because you know through your research that the majority of people that have already passed through security will be able to escape an attack, so you want to send the kids through to the other side as soon as possible.]

Step 7 — The area of commitment is the critical area where we are committed to move through security. Our shoes are off, our carry-on luggage is moving through, and we are waiting for the X-ray and/or pat-down. If a shooting happens when we are at this point, we will act with the same procedures. If part of the group is through security, they will run to Gate 22. [This is a predetermined area in the terminal you've identified and selected beforehand. It should not be too far away, but far enough that a stray bullet can't hit you.]

Step 8 — During the attack, if something prevents you from getting through security to Gate 22, then you must assess the situation and run, opposite from the shooting if possible, to where we parked the car. [This is a location outside the terminal that's to be determined. Once you park the car, you send a text to everyone with the exact location so it doesn't need to be remembered under the tension of an emergency.]

Step 9 — If you can't run, and cover or concealment is not available, grab anything you can use as a weapon, reassess the situation, and strike the attacker(s) if possible and as the opportunity arises (i.e., when the attacker reloads a weapon or turns their back to you).

Step 10 — When the police respond, get ready to lie flat on the floor if they start shooting. If you are outside, and you have to lie down, remember that studies have shown lying in a depression in the ground 18 inches or deeper during a gun fight increases your survivability tremendously. Chances are that the attacker(s) will be standing along with the police so it is best to not be at their level, especially when the police respond with force. Lie low and flat and out of the way of the police.

> **NOTE:** this entire section must be completed utilizing all the information you have now compiled in this *Workbook #2: Defense Assessment*. If you have areas of uncertainty or vulnerability that cannot be mitigated completely, then you need to consider the tactics of escape, evade, or fight. The following example comes from chapter 11 in **Sheep No More; The Art Of Awareness And Attack Survival**.
>
> Fear is not a gift, but it is something that you can mitigate in any fluid situation if you use your defensive SOPs to pre-determine your actions in a possible crisis. Remember, action always beats reaction!!!
>
> If you run out of pages to complete these SOP tactical action plans, you can facilitate regular graph paper as additions to the workbook pages, and staple those pages to these sections.

LET'S

GET

STARTED

"Bottom line, building effective defenses requires your active participation! Otherwise your safety is just a gamble."

— Jonathan T Gilliam

Defense

Assessment

Workbook

S1

SECTOR 1

SECTOR 1
FIRST RESPONDER OVERVIEW

THREAT ASSESSMENT SECTOR OVERVIEW

Sector:

Date:

Prepared by:

Situation:

Sector Overview:

Note: Make sure you print out map and directions to pertinent police precincts.

Police Departments:

PD Contact Information:

PD Response Times:

Crime Level:

Possible Threat Level:

Known Terror Threats:

Known Criminal Threats:

Note: Make sure you print out map and directions to all trauma centers. Always make the effort to proceed to a level 1 trauma center if the injury is life threatening.

Trauma Centers:

Trauma Center Level (I, II, III):

Response Times:

Weather Conditions:

| Spring | Summer | Fall | Winter |

RESPONSE RESOURCES
(Specific To This Sector)

Federal

- Department of Homeland Security (DHS)

  _____

  _____

- Federal Emergency Management Agency (FEMA)

  _____

  _____

- Federal Bureau of Investigation (FBI)

  _____

  _____

- Environmental Protection Agency (EPA)

  _____

  _____

- Health and Human Services (HHS)

  _____

  _____

State/Regional

- Emergency Management

  _____

  _____

- State Emergency Operations Center

  _____

  _____

- State Police

  _____

  _____

- National Guard

  _____

  _____

- Joint Terrorism Task Forces (JTTF)

  _____

  _____

> Note: Make sure you print out map and directions to pertinent police precincts. Always make the effort to proceed to a level 1 trauma center if the injury is life threatening.

Local First Responders

- Police

  _____

  _____

  - Special Weapons And Tactics (SWAT) Teams

    _____

  - Explosive Ordnance Disposal (EOD)

    _____

- Police

  _____

  _____

  - Special Weapons And Tactics (SWAT) Teams

    _____

  - Explosive Ordnance Disposal (EOD)

    _____

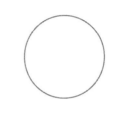

- Police

  _____

  _____

  - Special Weapons And Tactics (SWAT) Teams

    _____

  - Explosive Ordnance Disposal (EOD)

    _____

- Fire

  _____

  _____

  - Rescue / Emergency Medical Services

    _____

  - Hazardous Materials Response Teams

    _____

- Emergency Management

  _____

  _____

Note: Make sure you print out map and directions to all trauma centers. Always make the effort to proceed to a level 1 trauma center if the injury is life threatening.

Hospitals

- Level I Trauma Center

  _____

  _____

- Level II Trauma Center

  _____

  _____

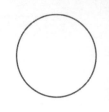

- Urgent Care

  _____

  _____

- Other Medical Center

  _____

  _____

- Other Medical Center

  _____

  _____

Known Threats

- Crime

  _____

  _____

  _____

  _____

  _____

  _____

- Terror

  _____

  _____

  _____

  _____

  _____

  _____

> *Note: If this sector is a special event or a vacation, take a screen shot of the weather report and attach here*

SECTOR 1
VULNERABILITY MITIGATION

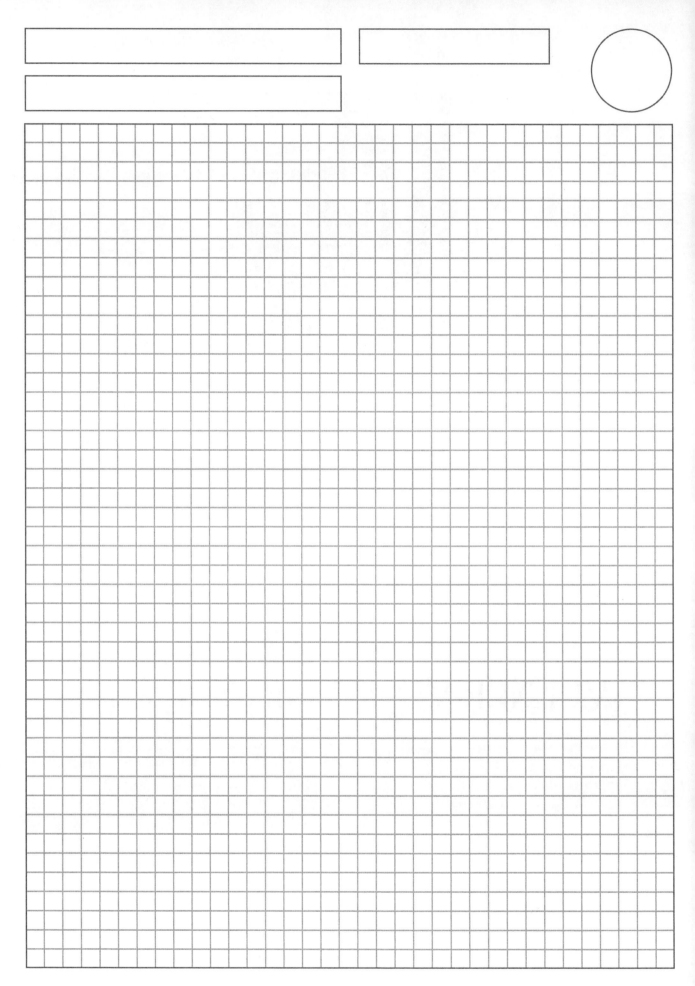

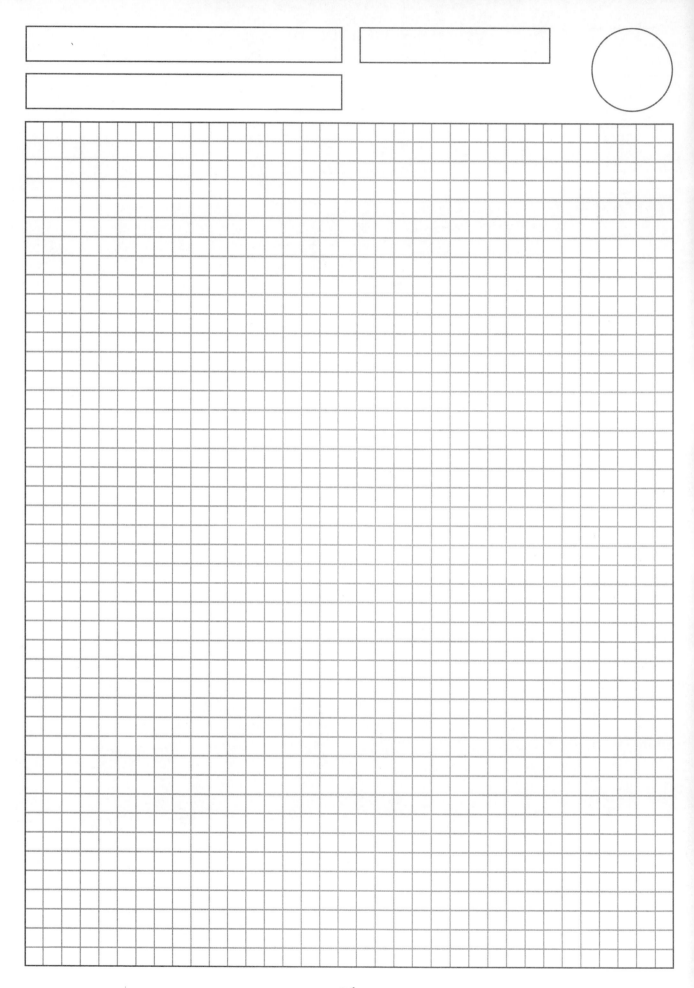

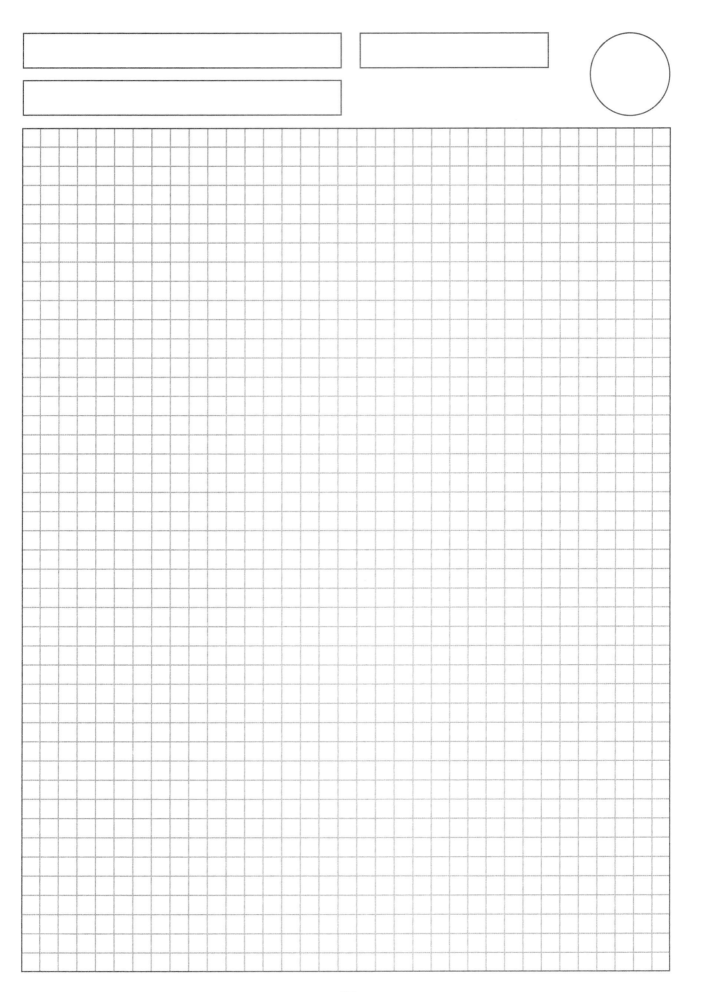

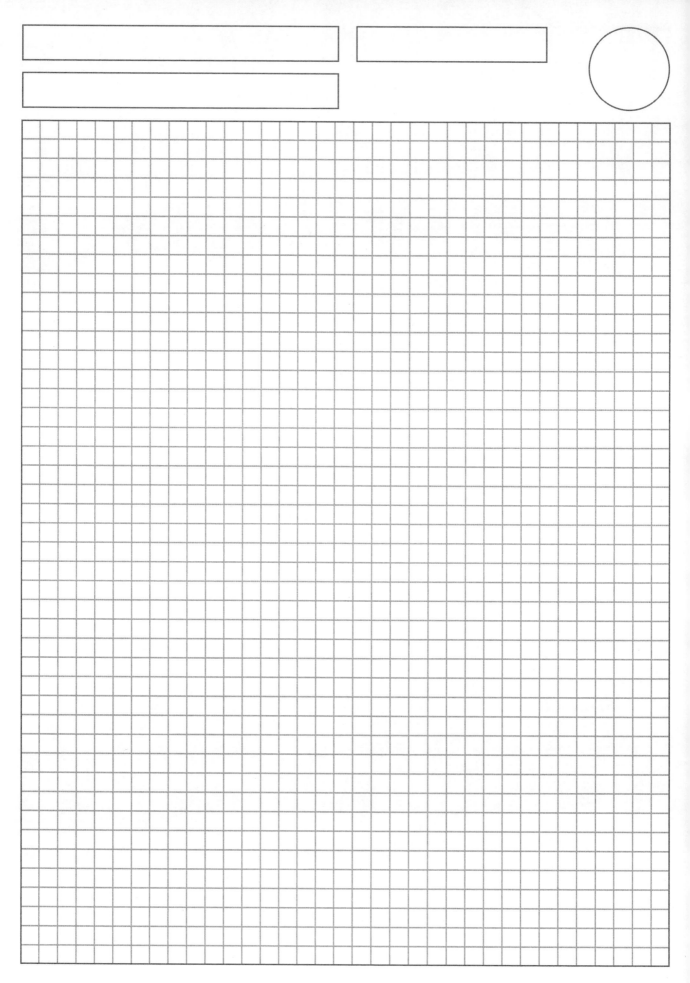

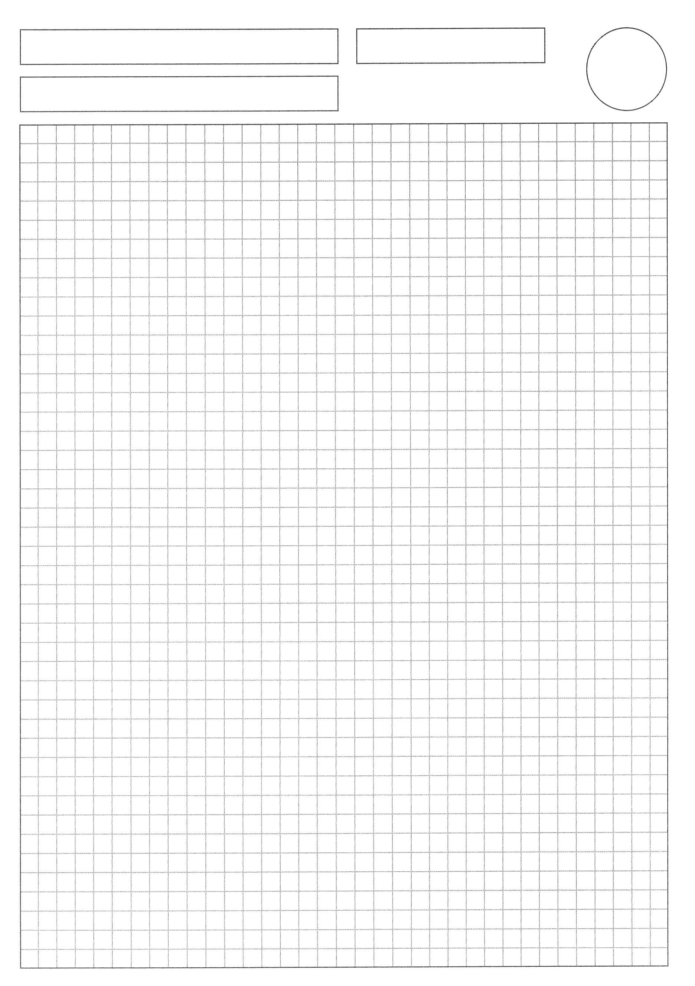

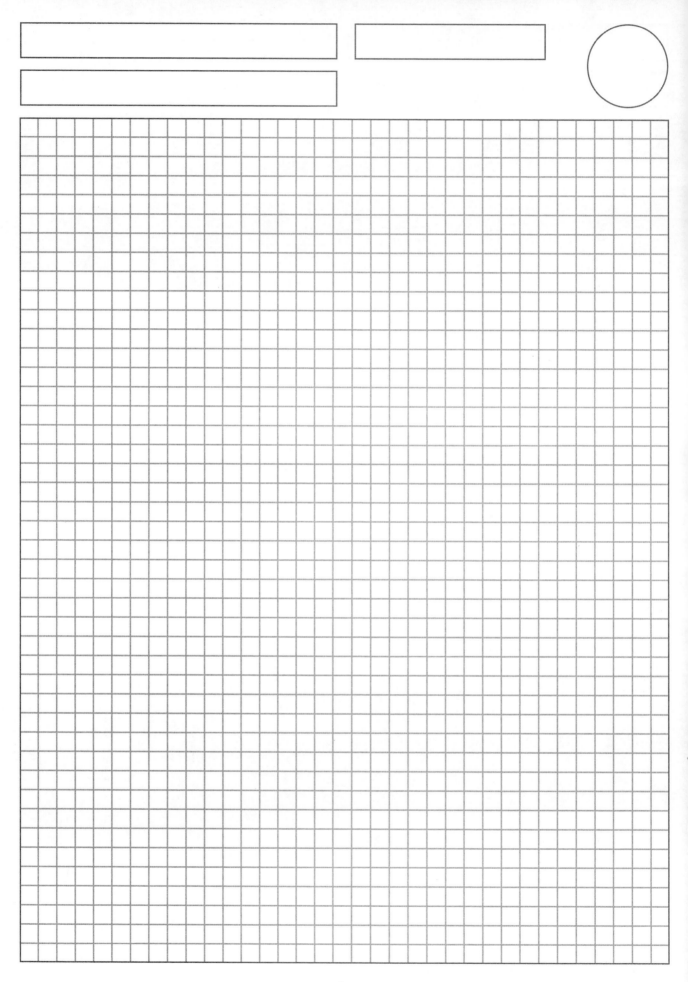

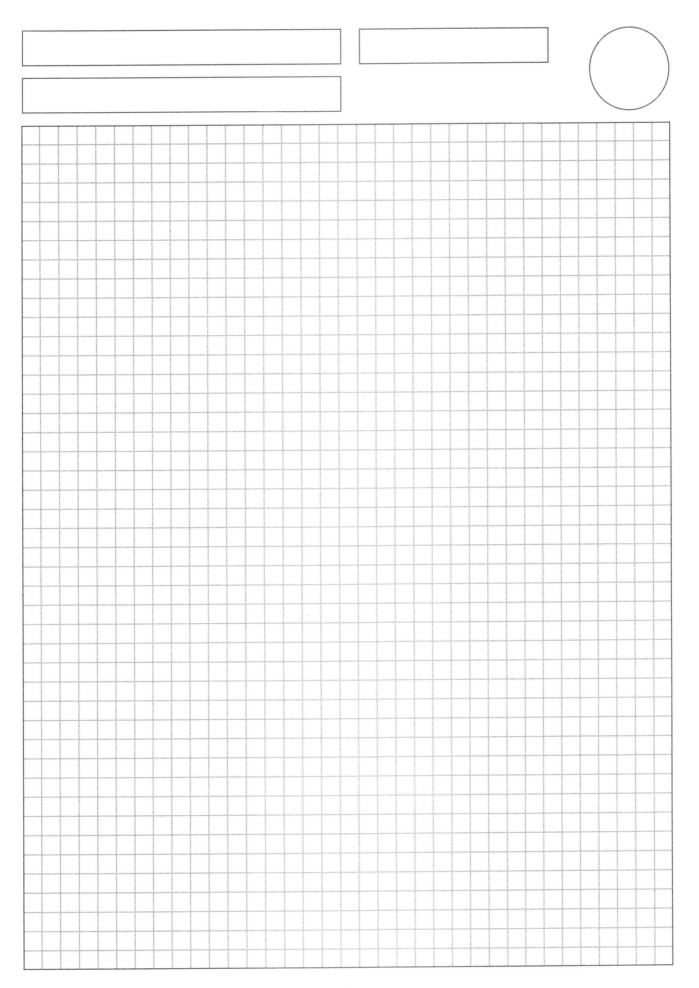

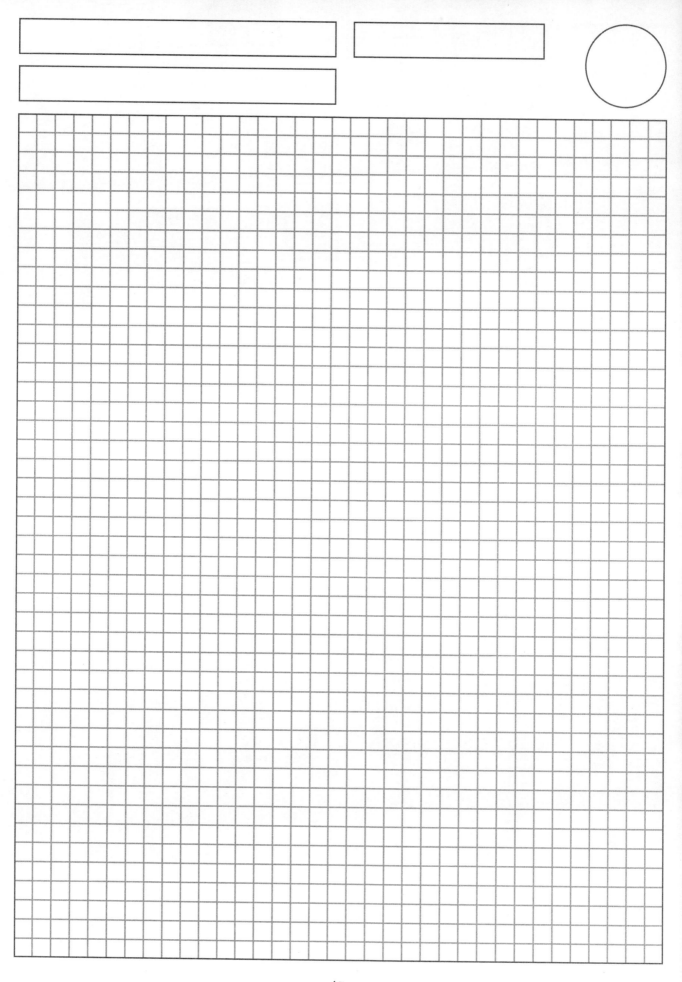

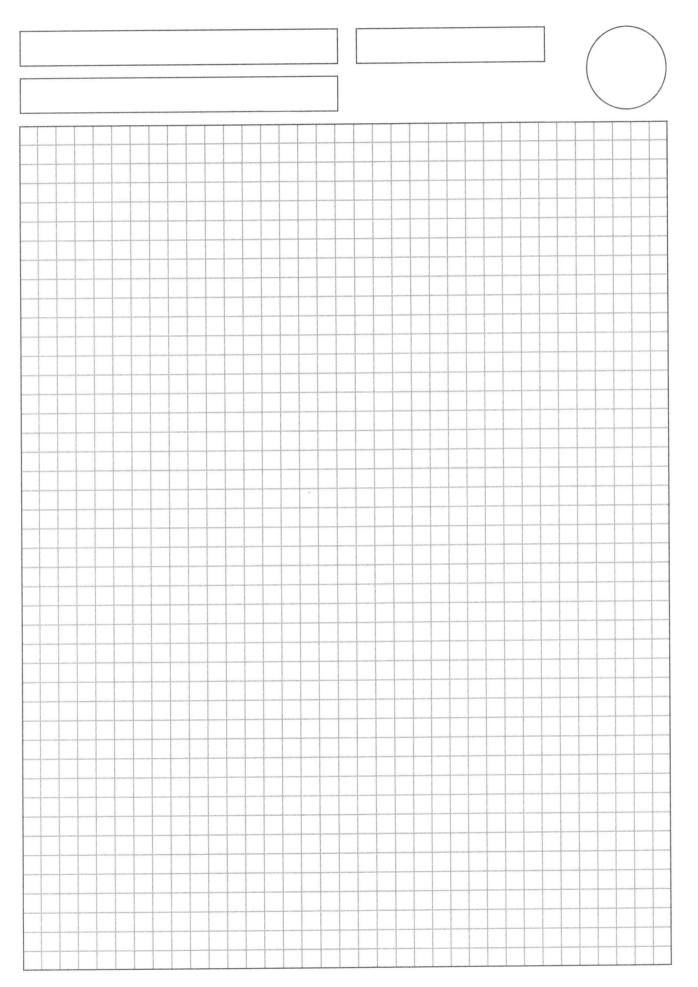

SECTOR 1
IMPLEMENTATION OF PHYSICAL
DEFENSE AND TECHNOLOGY

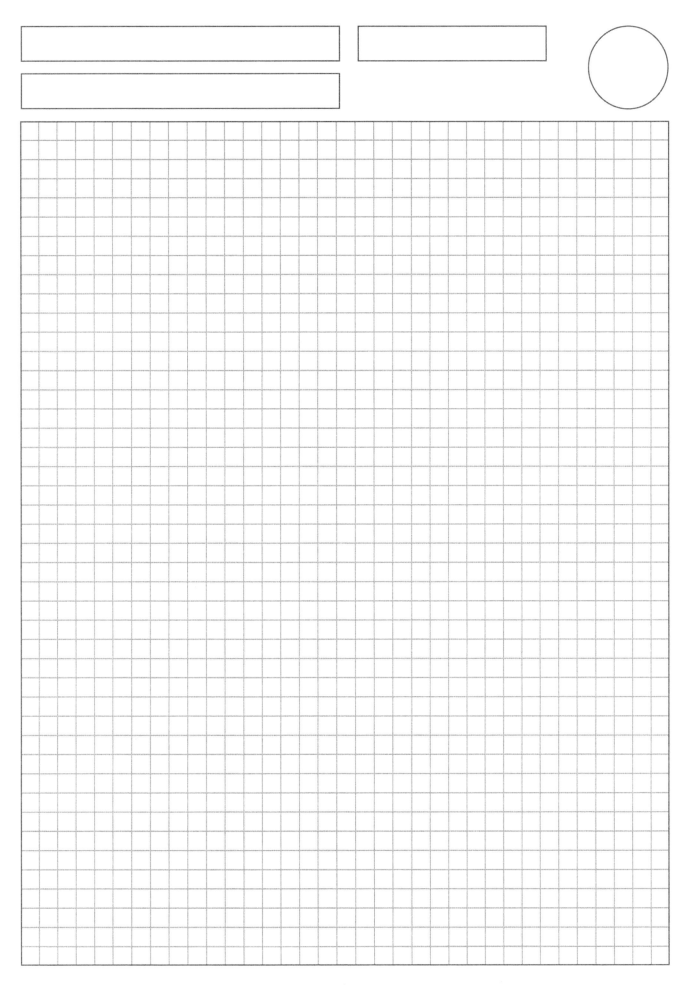

SECTOR 1
BEHAVIORS AND ATTACK
INDICATORS

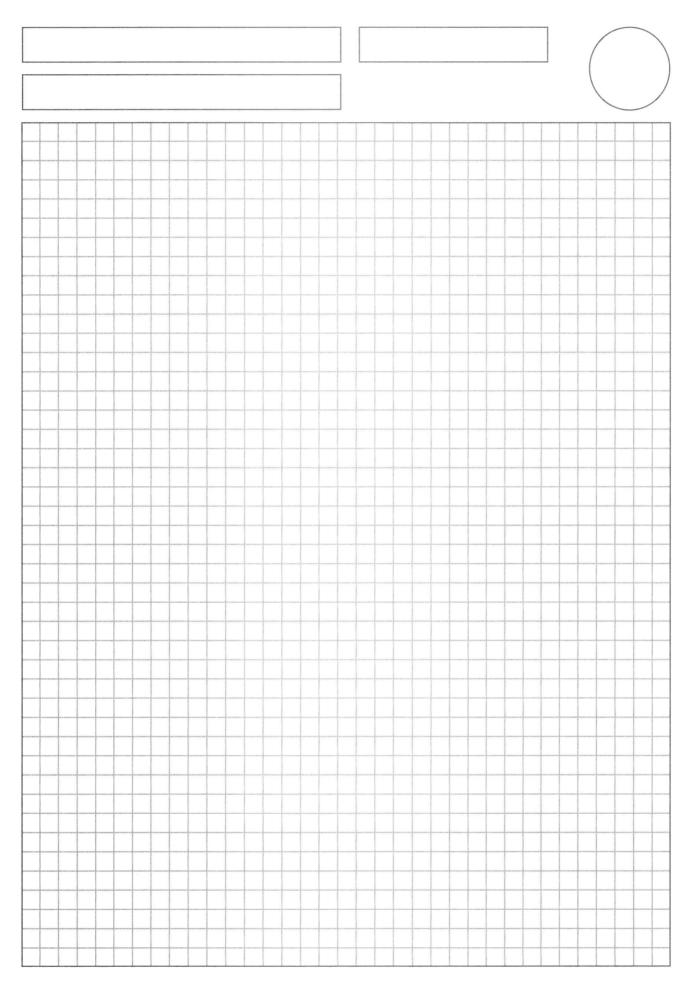

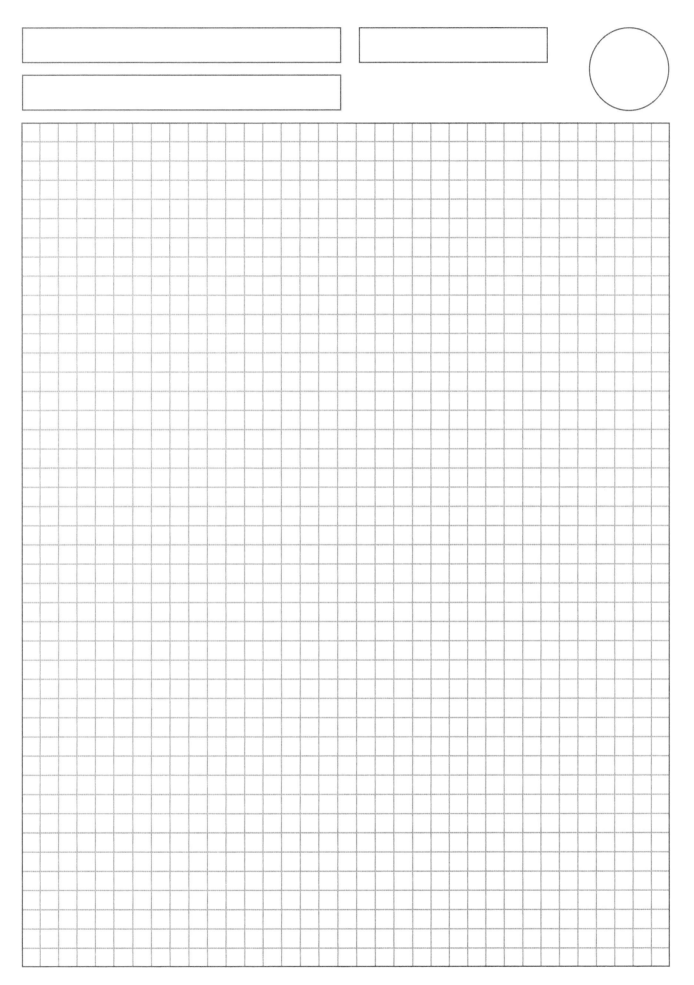

SECTOR 1
SHARED THREATS

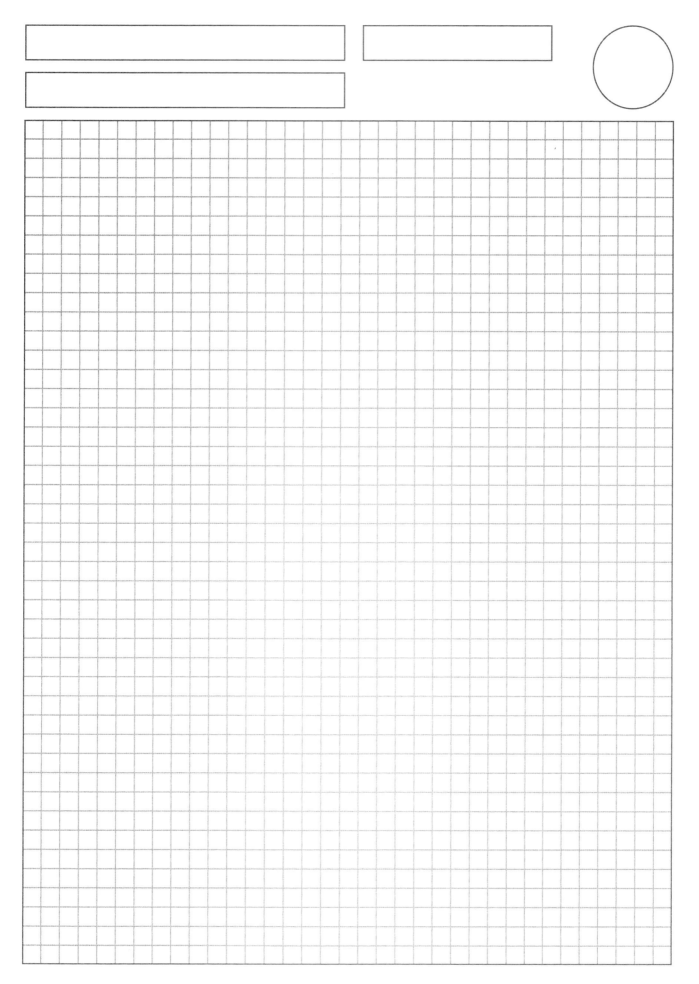

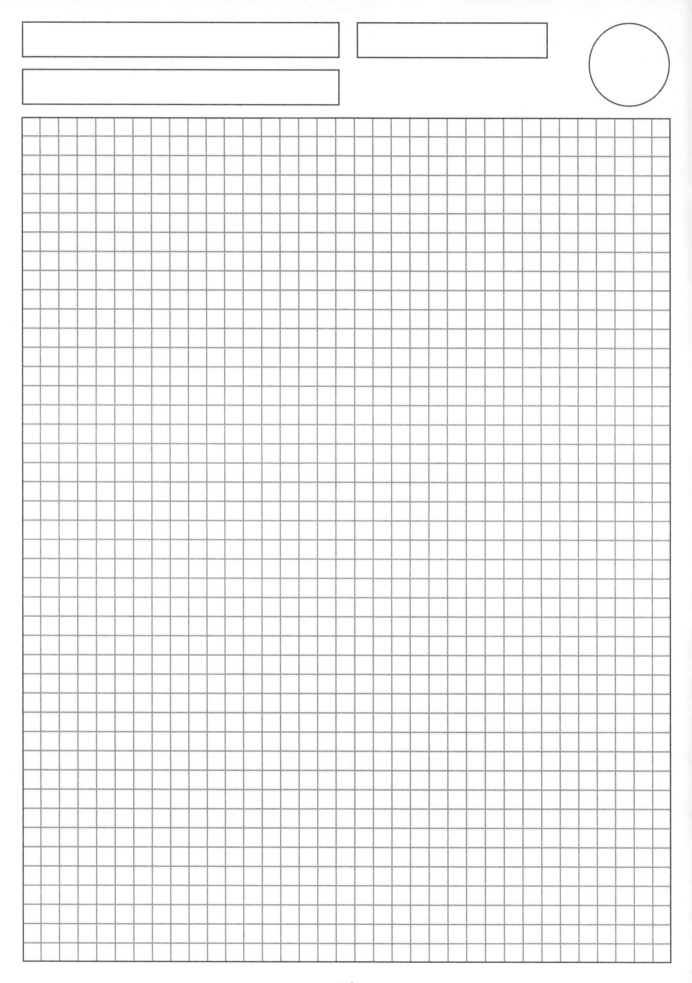

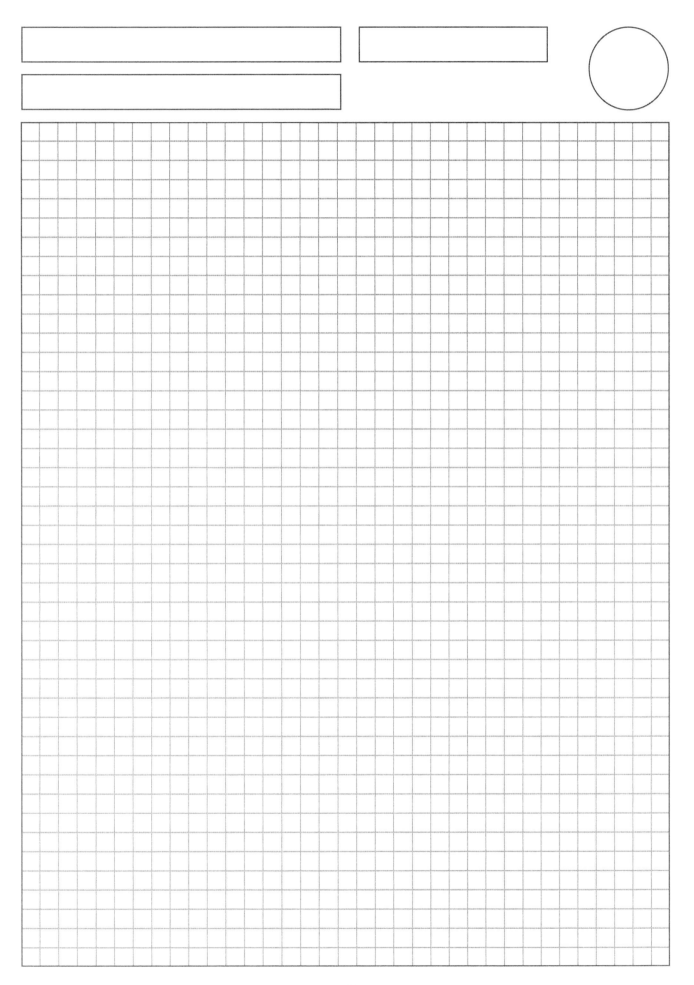

SECTOR 1
TACTICAL PLANS OF ACTION
(WHERE VULNERABILITIES CANNOT BE MITIGATED)

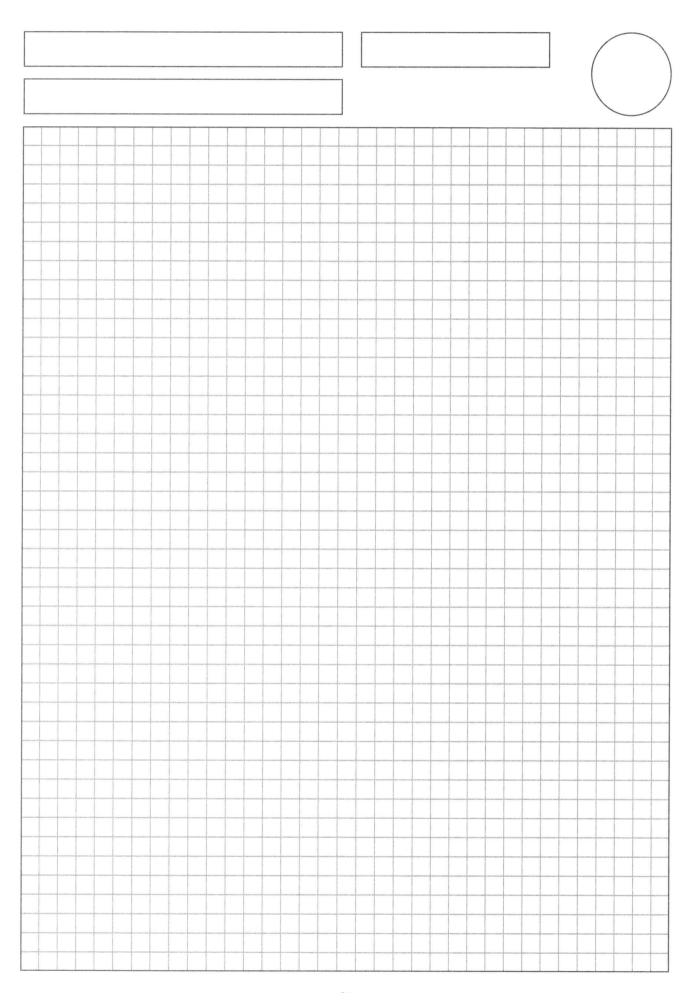

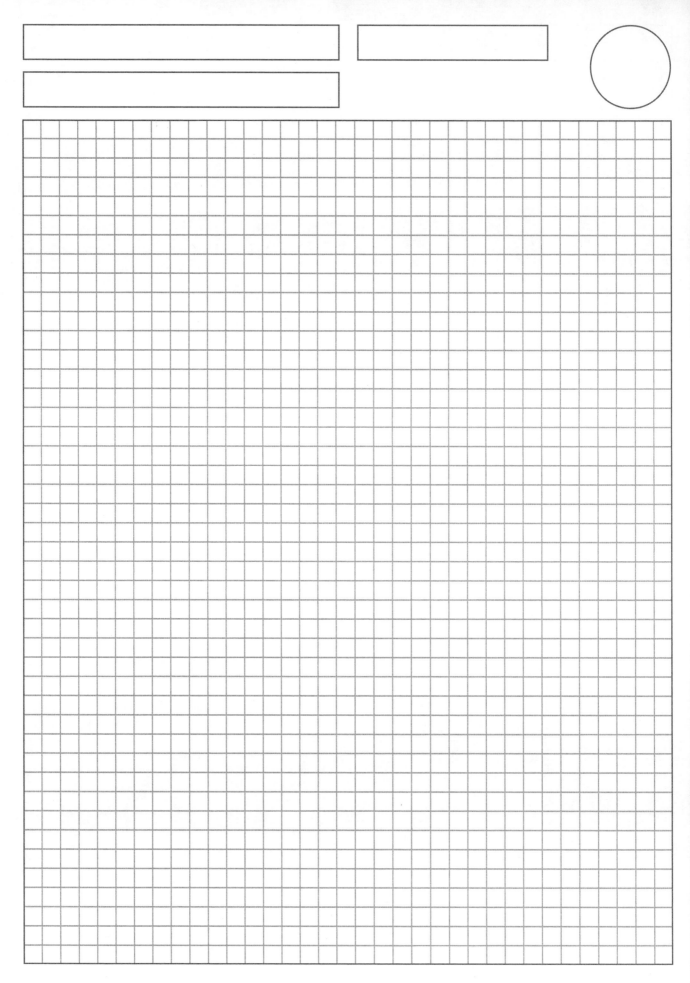

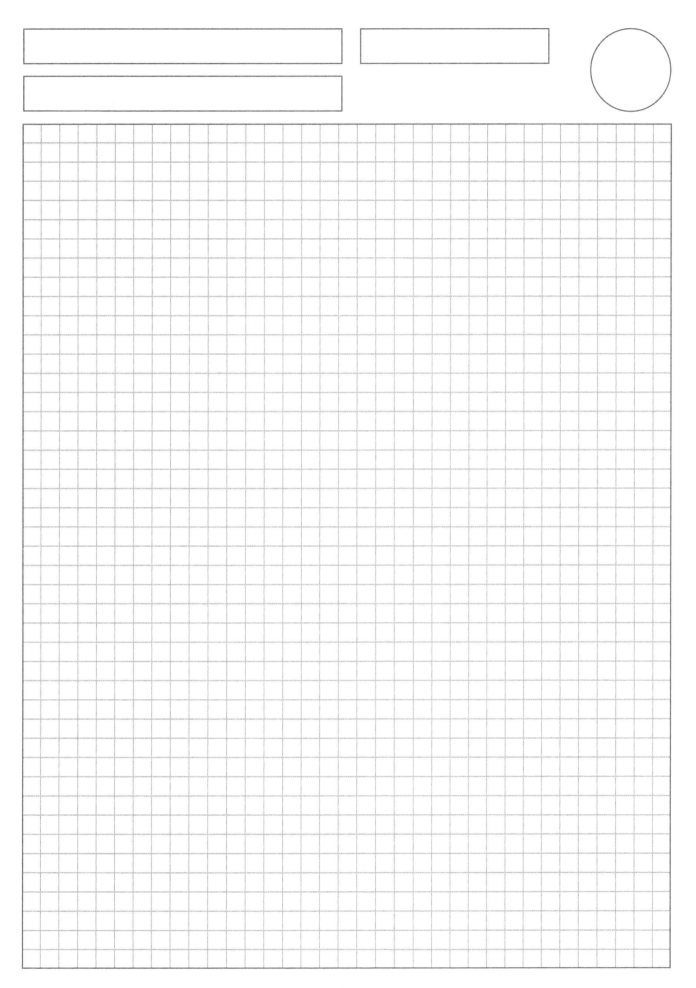

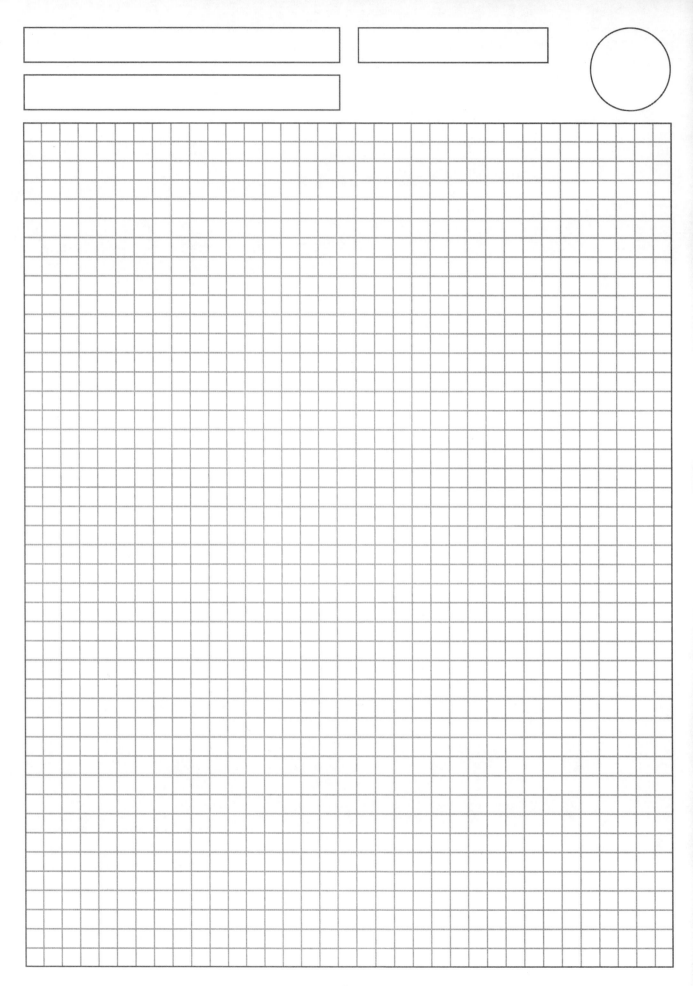

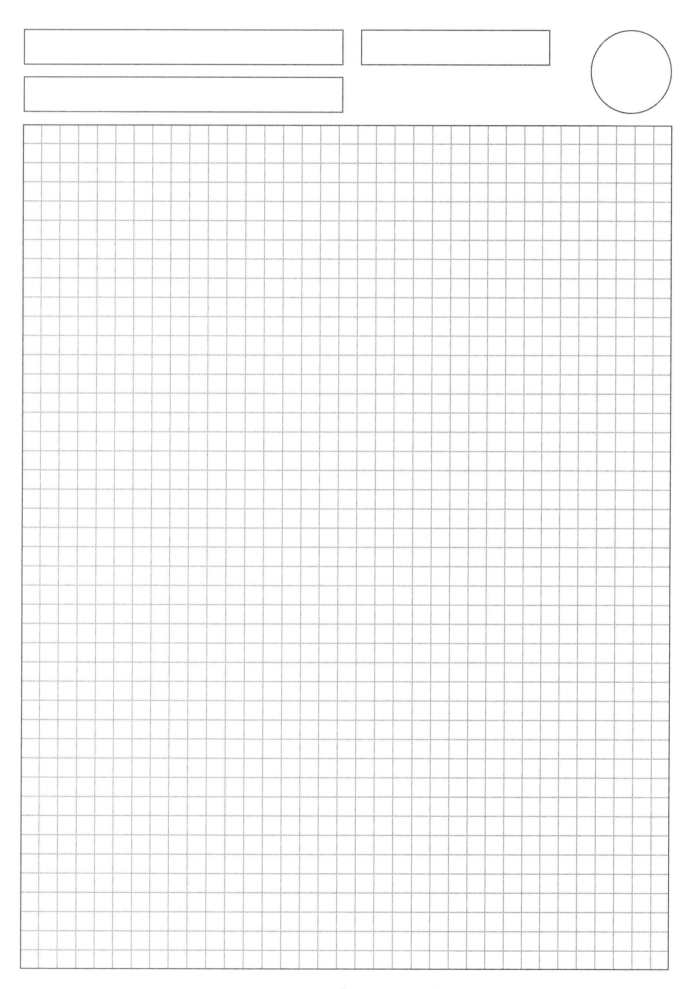

S2

SECTOR 2

SECTOR 2
FIRST RESPONDER OVERVIEW

THREAT ASSESSMENT SECTOR OVERVIEW

Sector:

Date:

Prepared by:

Situation:

Sector Overview:

Note: Make sure you print out map and directions to pertinent police precincts.

Police Departments:

PD Contact Information:

PD Response Times:

Crime Level:

Possible Threat Level:

Known Terror Threats:

Known Criminal Threats:

Note: Make sure you print out map and directions to all trauma centers. Always make the effort to proceed to a level 1 trauma center if the injury is life threatening.

Trauma Centers:

Trauma Center Level (I, II, III):

Response Times:

Weather Conditions:

Spring   Summer   Fall   Winter

Sector:

Date:

Prepared by:

RESPONSE RESOURCES

(Specific To This Sector)

Federal

- Department of Homeland Security (DHS)

  ____

  ____

- Federal Emergency Management Agency (FEMA)

  ____

  ____

- Federal Bureau of Investigation (FBI)

  ____

  ____

- Environmental Protection Agency (EPA)

  ____

  ____

- Health and Human Services (HHS)

  ____

  ____

State/Regional

- Emergency Management

  ____

  ____

- State Emergency Operations Center

  ____

  ____

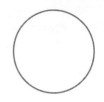

- State Police

_____

_____

- National Guard

_____

_____

- Joint Terrorism Task Forces (JTTF)

_____

_____

Note: Make sure you print out map and directions to pertinent police precincts. Always make the effort to proceed to a level 1 trauma center if the injury is life threatening.

Local First Responders

- Police

_____

_____

  - Special Weapons And Tactics (SWAT) Teams

  _____

  - Explosive Ordnance Disposal (EOD)

  _____

- Police

_____

_____

  - Special Weapons And Tactics (SWAT) Teams

  _____

  - Explosive Ordnance Disposal (EOD)

  _____

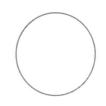

- Police

  _____

  _____

  - Special Weapons And Tactics (SWAT) Teams

    _____

  - Explosive Ordnance Disposal (EOD)

    _____

- Fire

  _____

  _____

  - Rescue / Emergency Medical Services

    _____

  - Hazardous Materials Response Teams

    _____

- Emergency Management

  _____

  _____

> *Note: Make sure you print out map and directions to all trauma centers. Always make the effort to proceed to a level 1 trauma center if the injury is life threatening.*

Hospitals

- Level I Trauma Center

  _____

  _____

- Level II Trauma Center

  _____

  _____

RESPONSE RESOURCES (continued)
(Specific To This Sector)

- Urgent Care

  _____

  _____

- Other Medical Center

  _____

  _____

- Other Medical Center

  _____

  _____

Known Threats

- Crime

  _____

  _____

  _____

  _____

  _____

  _____

- Terror

  _____

  _____

  _____

  _____

  _____

Note: If this sector is a special event or a vacation, take a screen shot of the weather report and attach here

SECTOR 2
VULNERABILITY MITIGATION

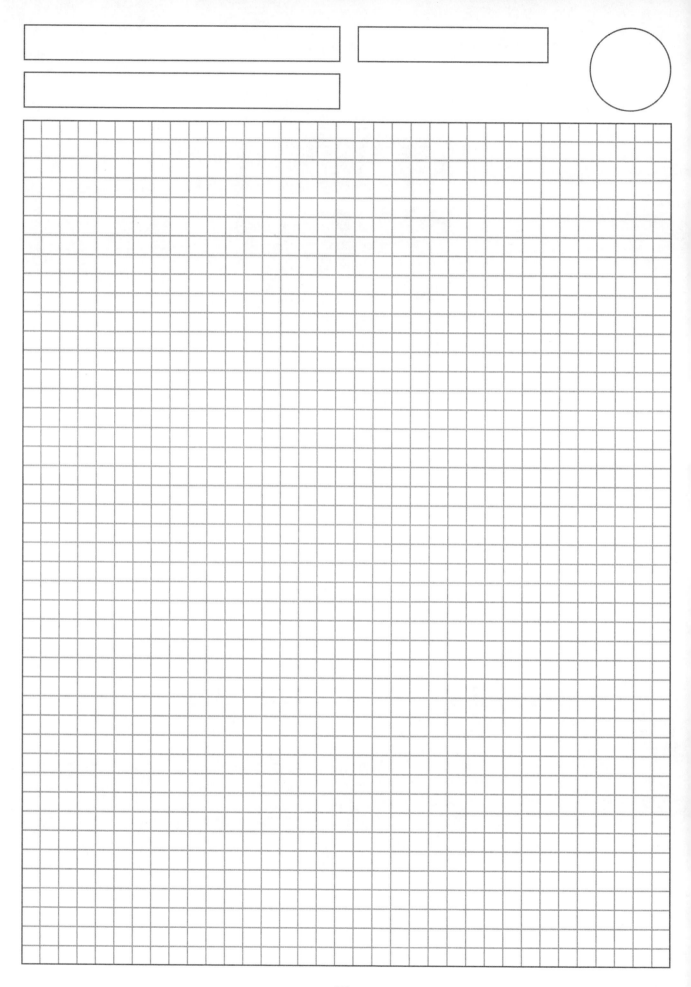

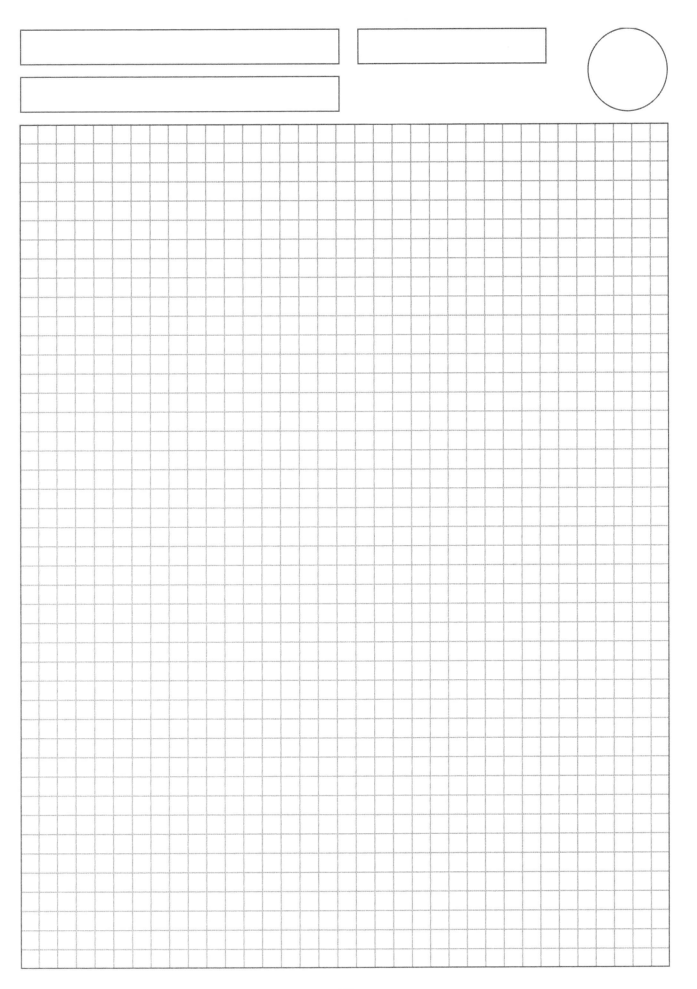

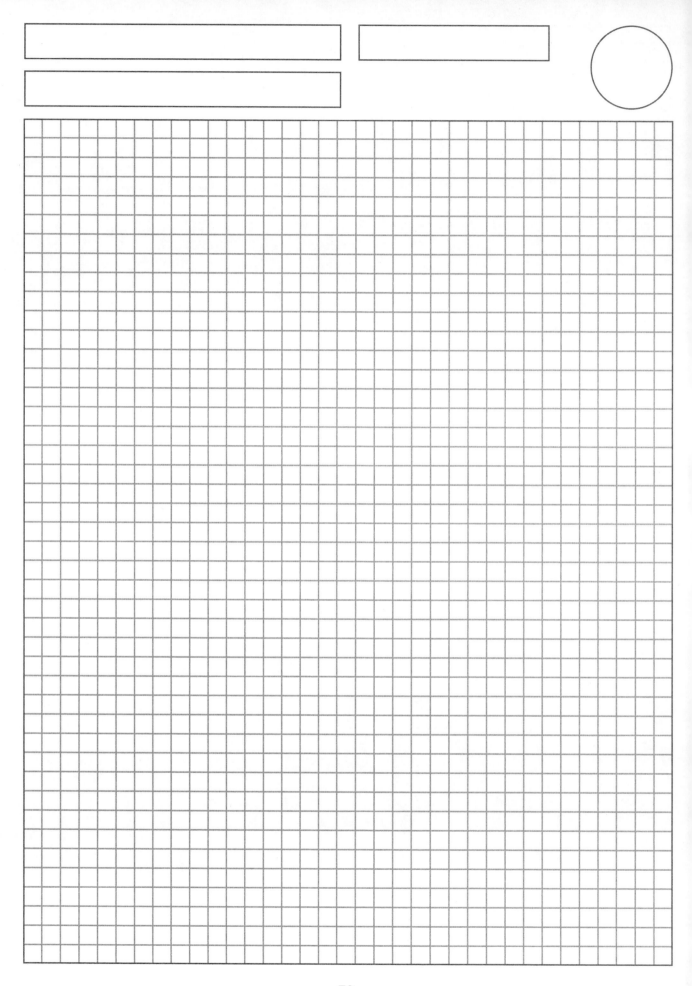

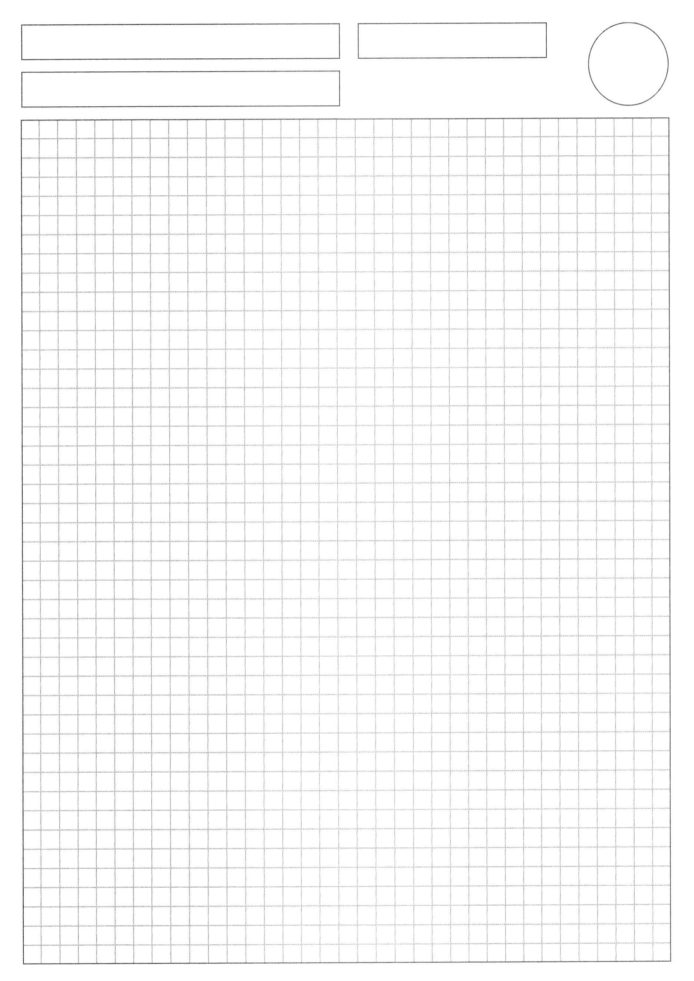

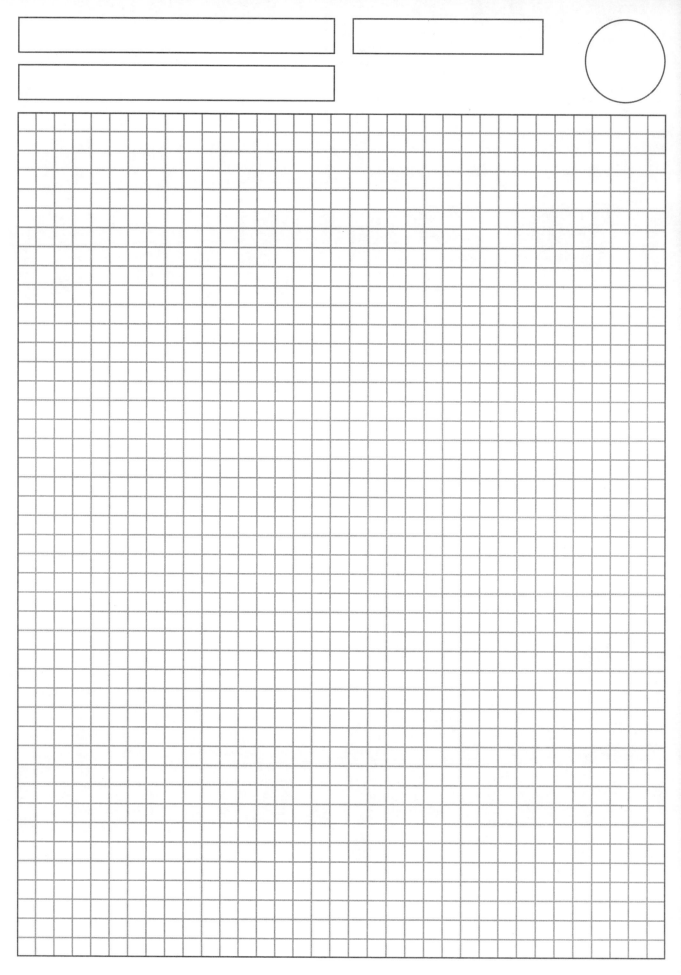

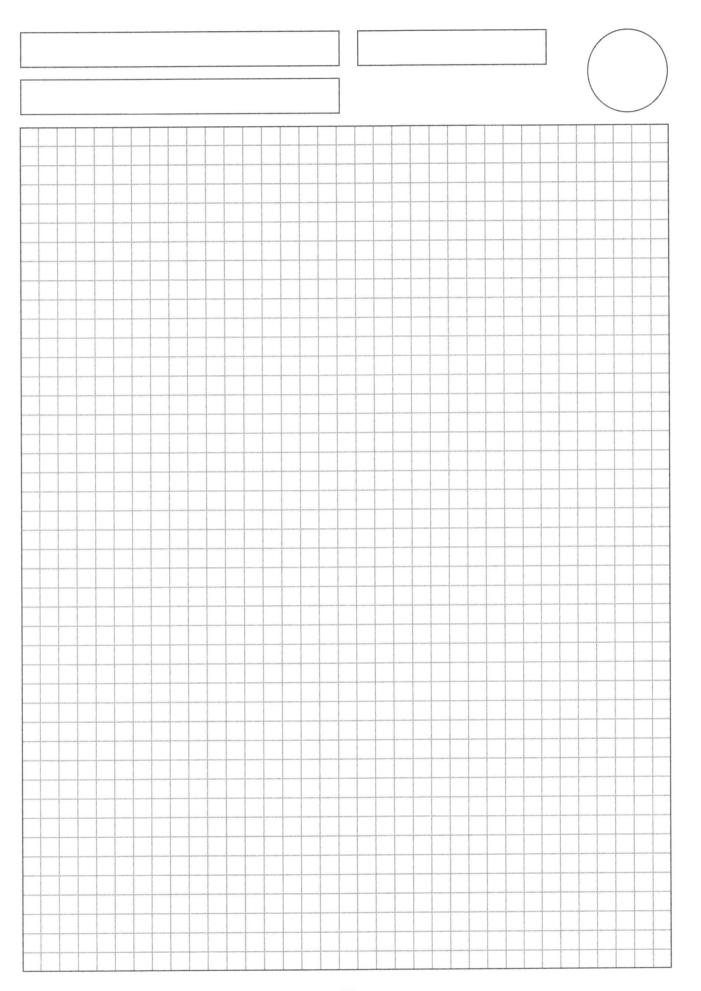

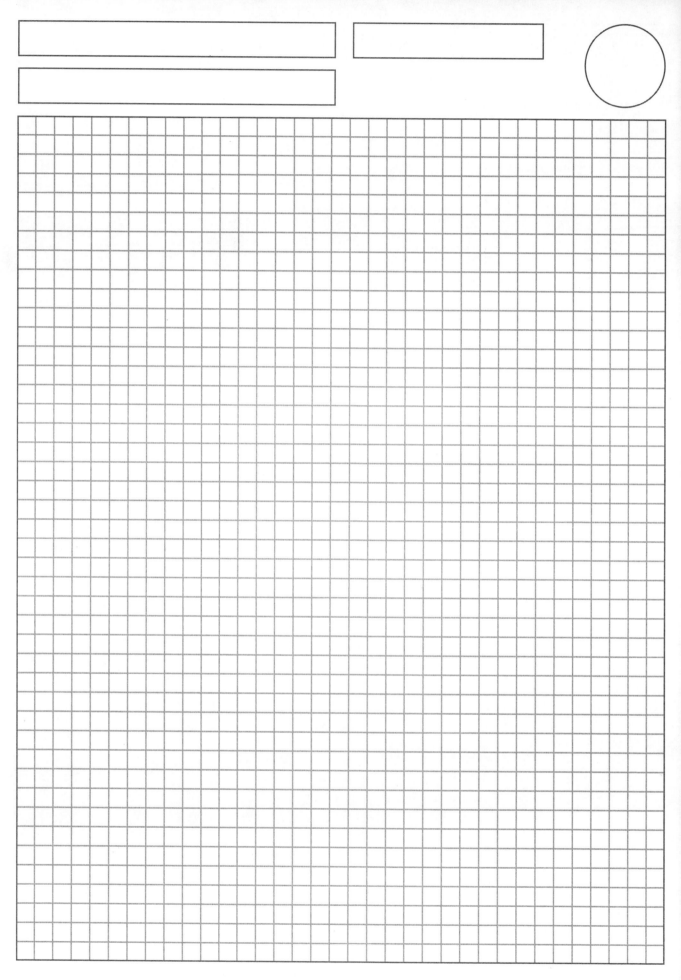

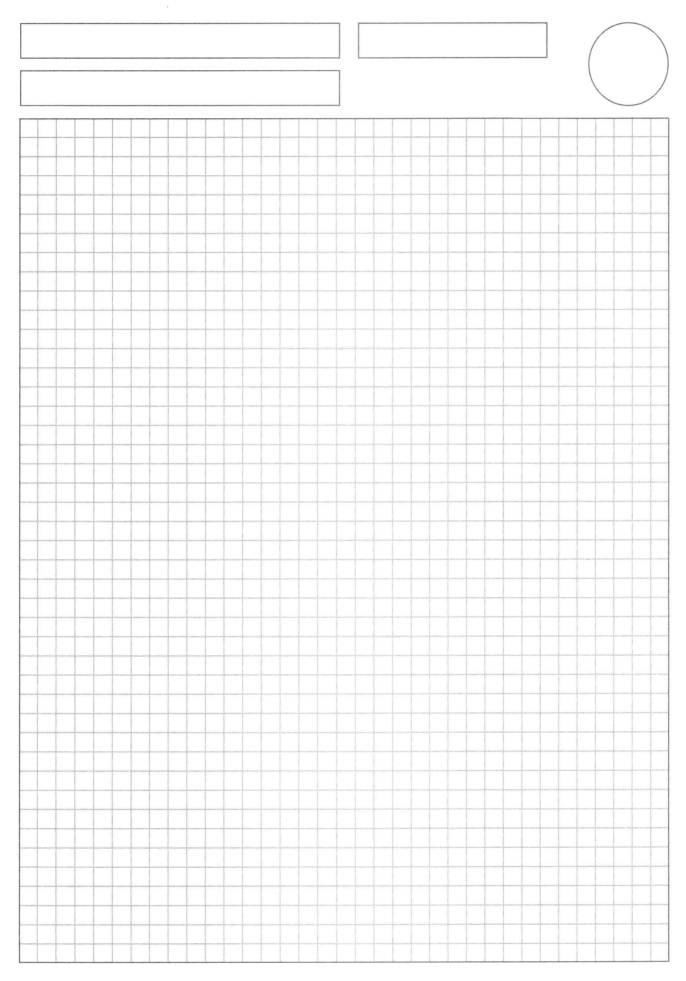

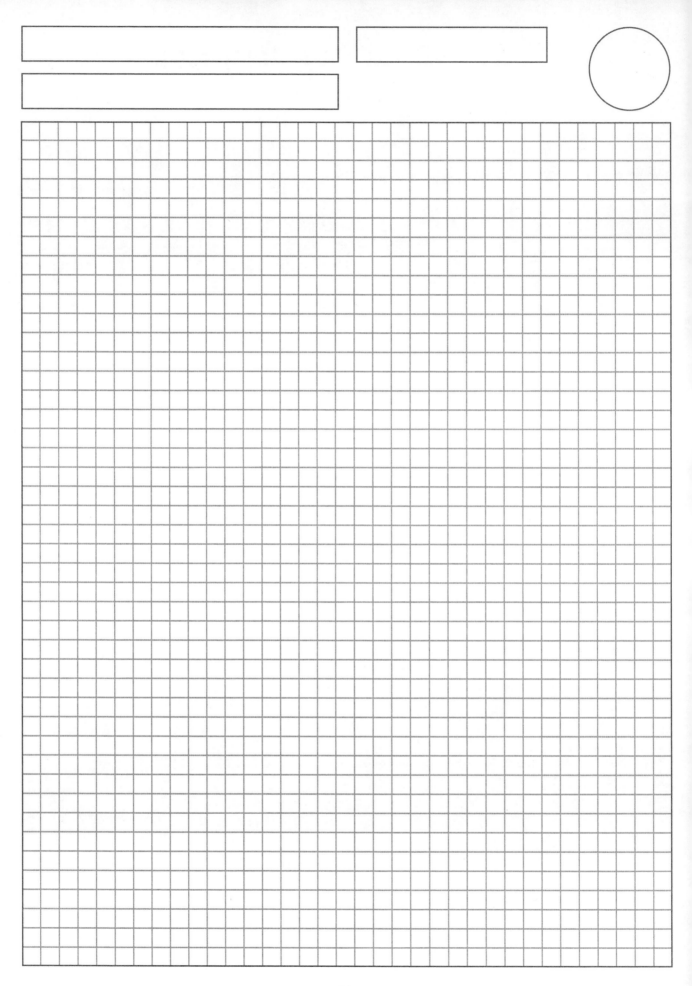

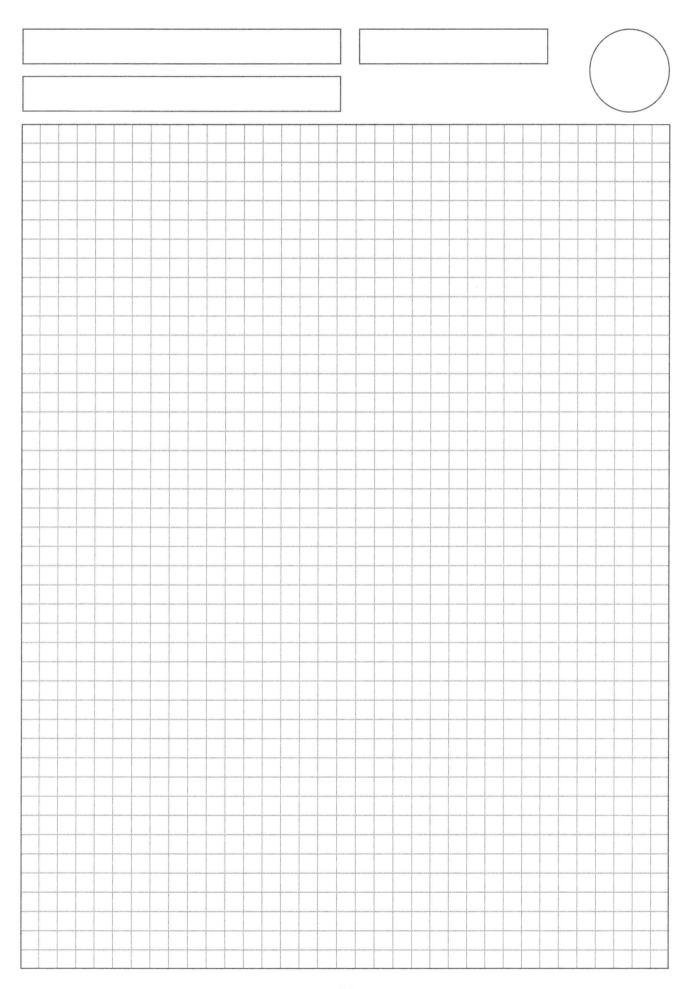

SECTOR 2
IMPLEMENTATION OF PHYSICAL
DEFENSE AND TECHNOLOGY

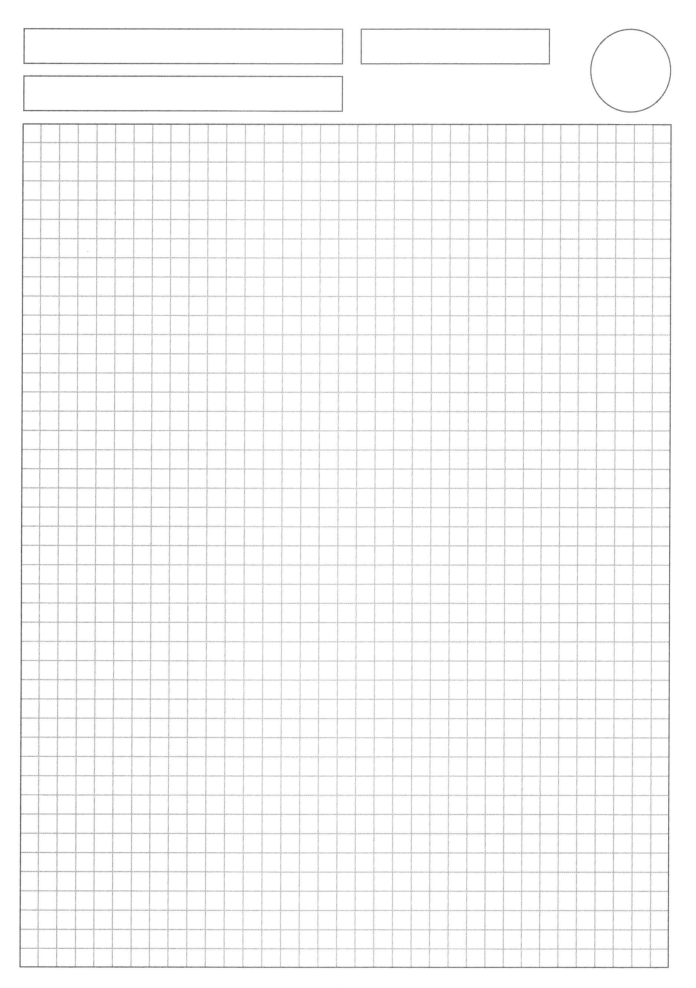

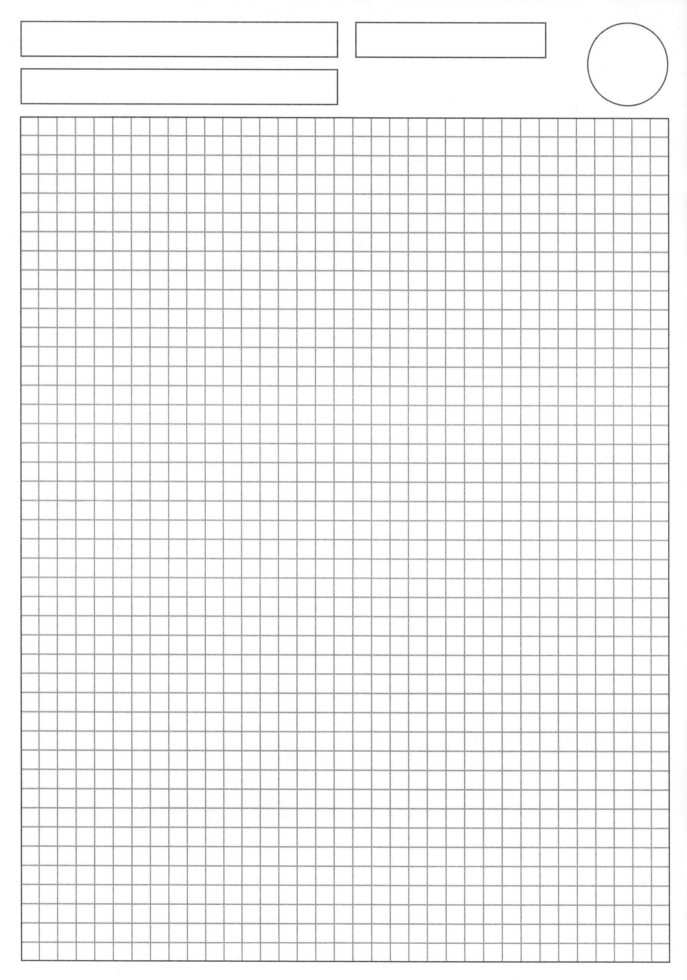

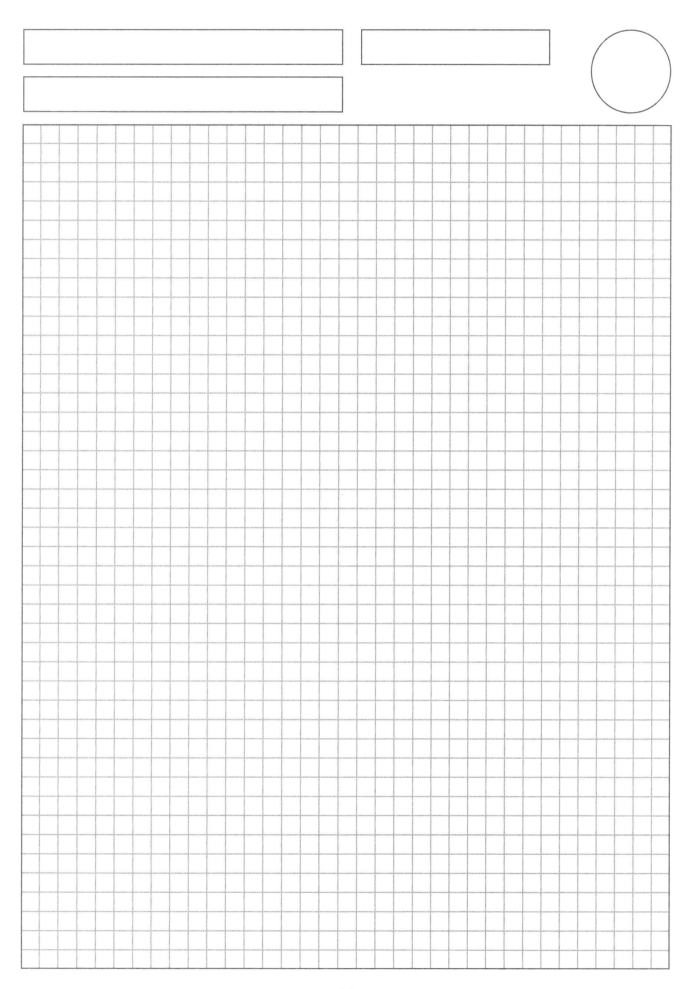

SECTOR 2
BEHAVIORS AND ATTACK
INDICATORS

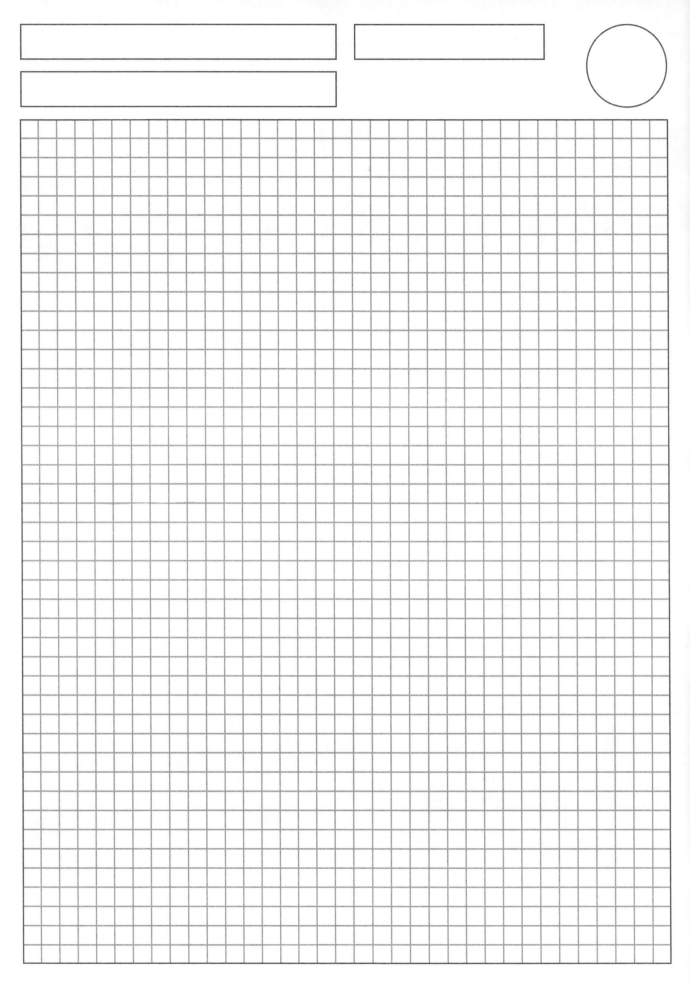

SECTOR 2
SHARED THREATS

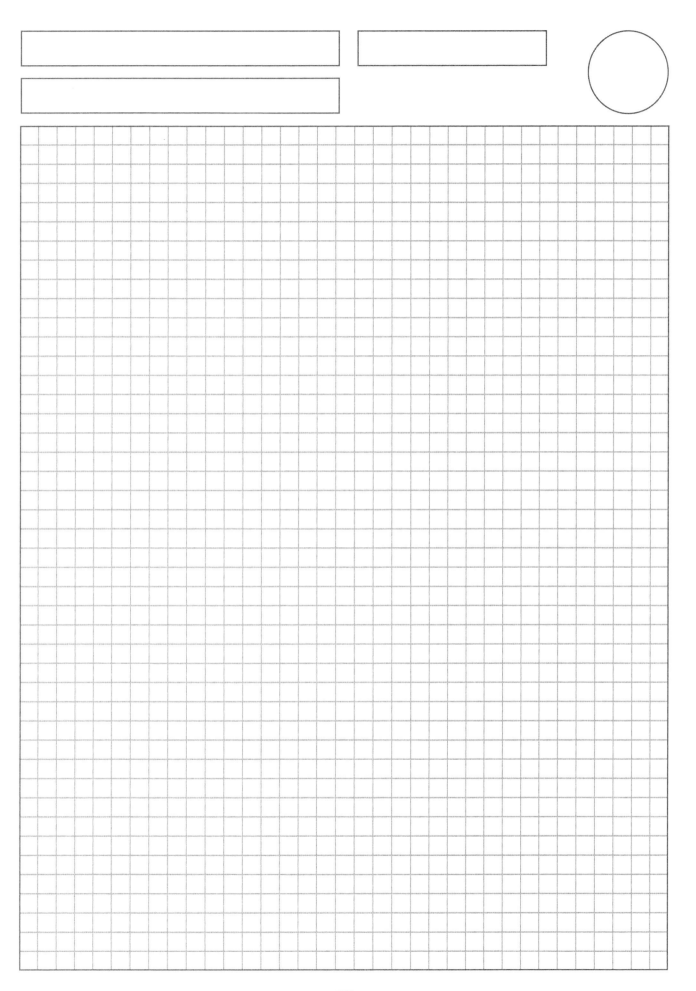

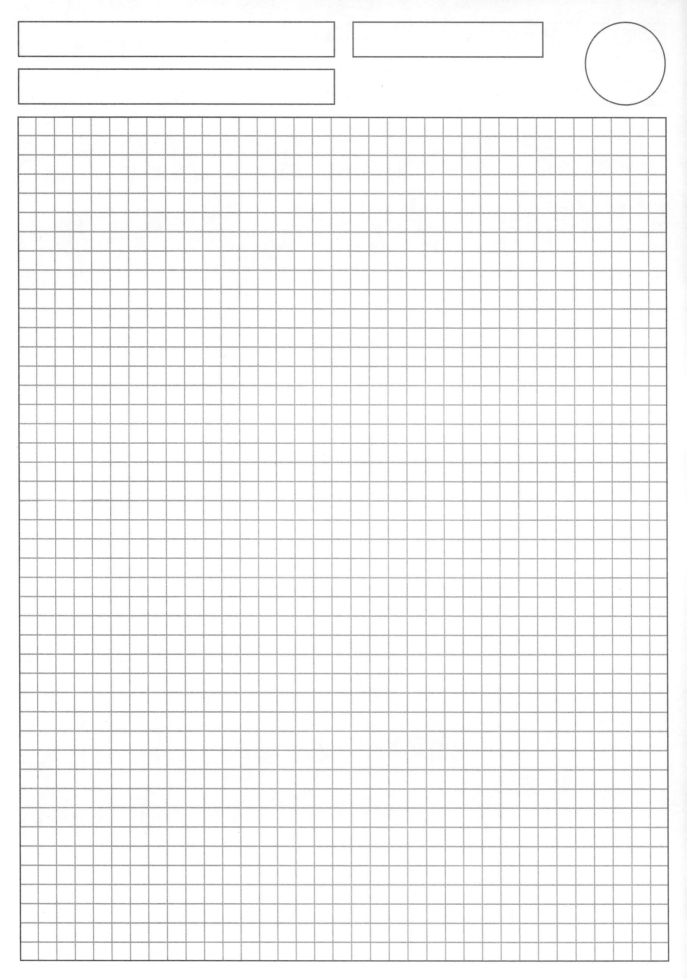

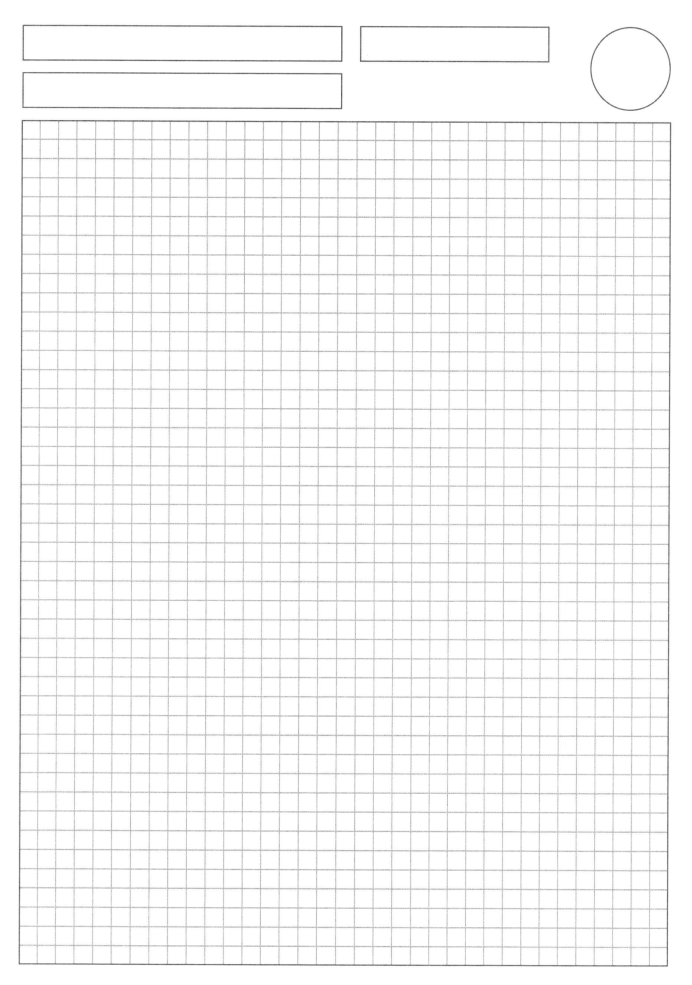

SECTOR 2
TACTICAL PLANS OF ACTION
(WHERE VULNERABILITIES CANNOT BE MITIGATED)

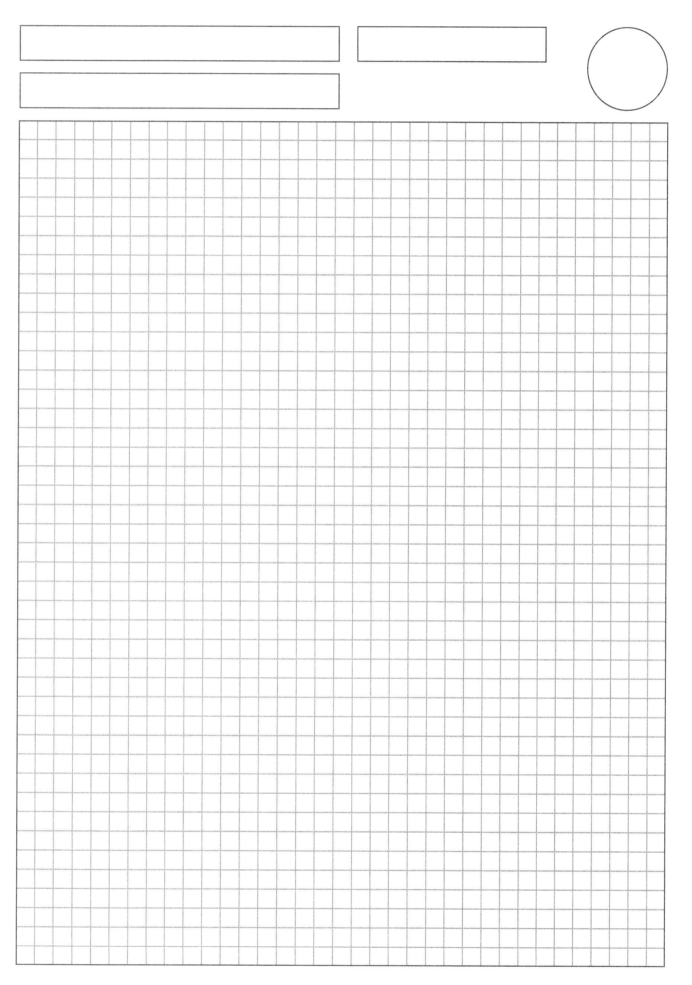

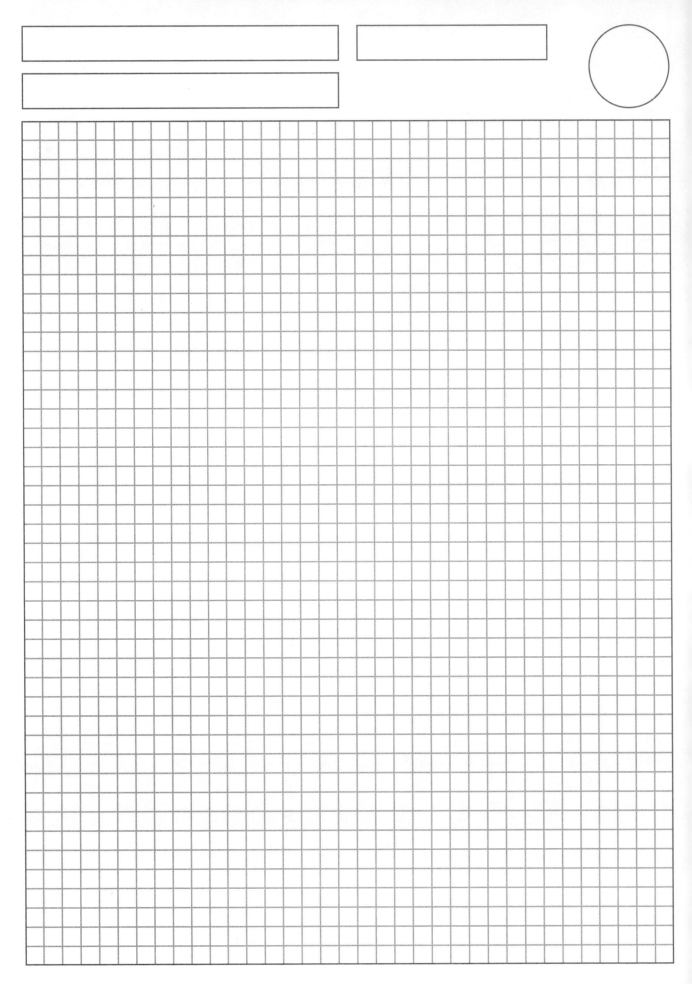

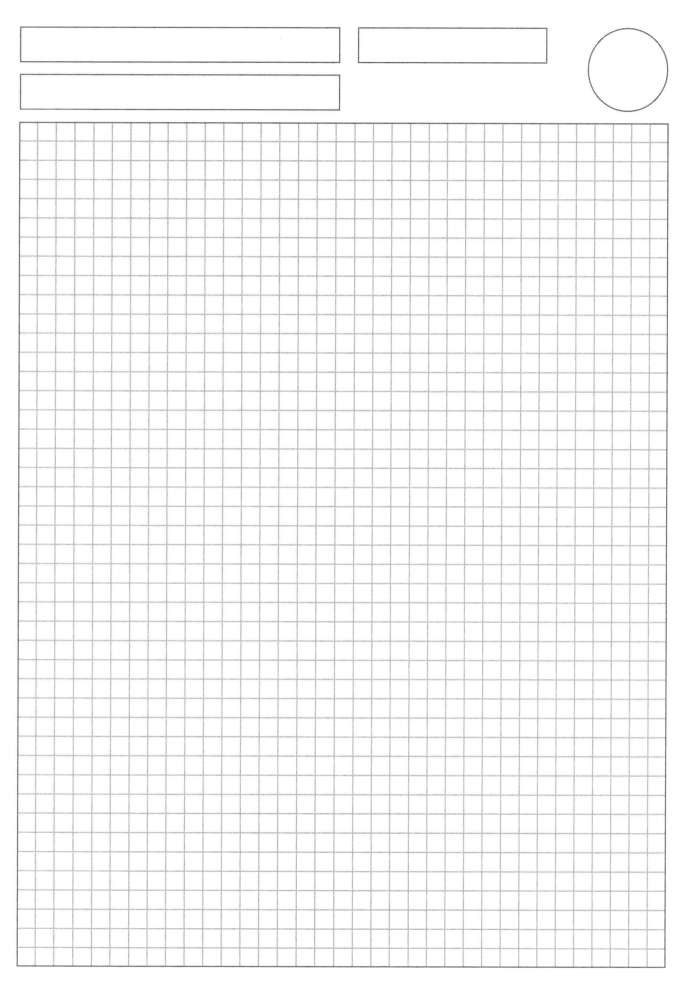

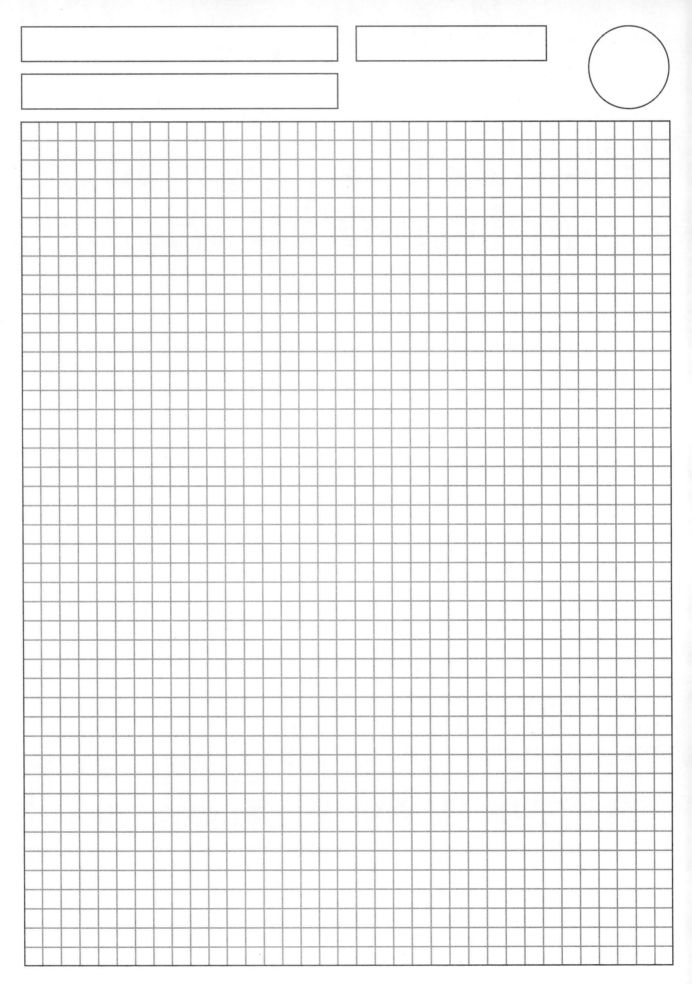

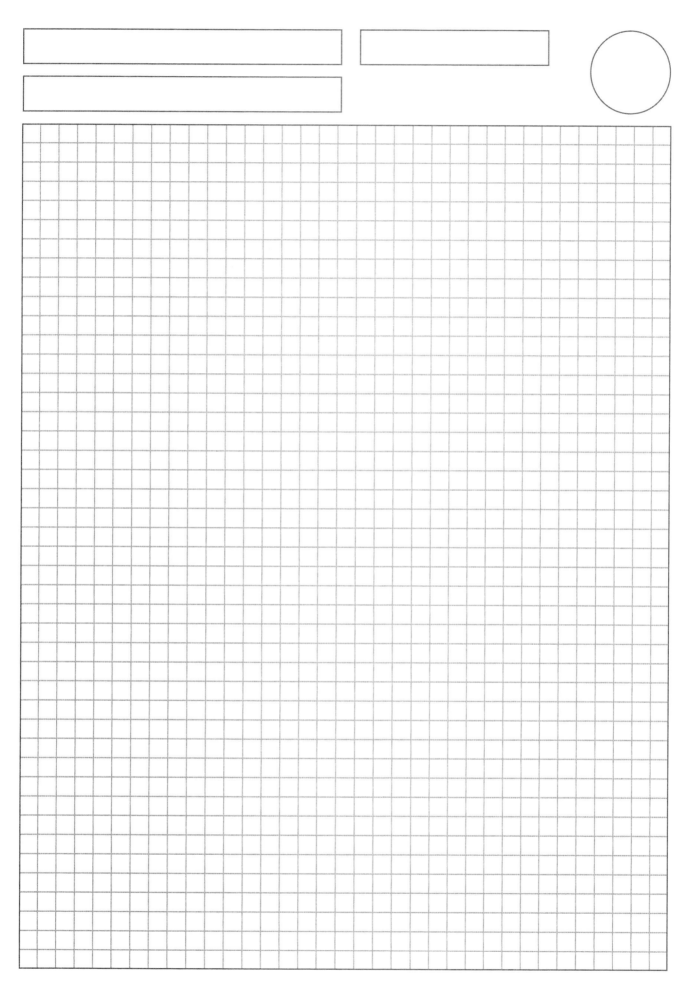

S3

SECTOR 3

SECTOR 3
FIRST RESPONDER OVERVIEW

THREAT ASSESSMENT SECTOR OVERVIEW

Sector:

Date:

Prepared by:

Situation:

Sector Overview:

Note: Make sure you print out map and directions to pertinent police precincts.

Police Departments:

PD Contact Information:

PD Response Times:

Crime Level:

Possible Threat Level:

Known Terror Threats:

Known Criminal Threats:

Note: Make sure you print out map and directions to all trauma centers. Always make the effort to proceed to a level 1 trauma center if the injury is life threatening.

Trauma Centers:

Trauma Center Level (I, II, III):

Response Times:

Weather Conditions:

| Spring | Summer | Fall | Winter |

Sector:

Date:

Prepared by:

RESPONSE RESOURCES

(Specific To This Sector)

Federal

- Department of Homeland Security (DHS)

  ____

  ____

- Federal Emergency Management Agency (FEMA)

  ____

  ____

- Federal Bureau of Investigation (FBI)

  ____

  ____

- Environmental Protection Agency (EPA)

  ____

  ____

- Health and Human Services (HHS)

  ____

  ____

State/Regional

- Emergency Management

  ____

  ____

- State Emergency Operations Center

  ____

  ____

RESPONSE RESOURCES (continued)
(Specific To This Sector)

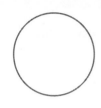

- State Police

  _____

  _____

- National Guard

  _____

  _____

- Joint Terrorism Task Forces (JTTF)

  _____

  _____

> *Note: Make sure you print out map and directions to pertinent police precincts. Always make the effort to proceed to a level 1 trauma center if the injury is life threatening.*

Local First Responders

- Police

  _____

  _____

  - Special Weapons And Tactics (SWAT) Teams

    _____

  - Explosive Ordnance Disposal (EOD)

    _____

- Police

  _____

  _____

  - Special Weapons And Tactics (SWAT) Teams

    _____

  - Explosive Ordnance Disposal (EOD)

    _____

RESPONSE RESOURCES (continued)
(Specific To This Sector)

- Police

  _____

  _____

  - Special Weapons And Tactics (SWAT) Teams

    _____

  - Explosive Ordnance Disposal (EOD)

    _____

- Fire

  _____

  _____

  - Rescue / Emergency Medical Services

    _____

  - Hazardous Materials Response Teams

    _____

- Emergency Management

  _____

  _____

Note: Make sure you print out map and directions to all trauma centers. Always make the effort to proceed to a level 1 trauma center if the injury is life threatening.

Hospitals

- Level I Trauma Center

  _____

  _____

- Level II Trauma Center

  _____

  _____

RESPONSE RESOURCES (continued)
(Specific To This Sector)

- Urgent Care

  _____

  _____

- Other Medical Center

  _____

  _____

- Other Medical Center

  _____

  _____

Known Threats

- Crime

  _____

  _____

  _____

  _____

  _____

  _____

- Terror

  _____

  _____

  _____

  _____

  _____

  _____

Note: If this sector is a special event or a vacation, take a screen shot of the weather report and attach here

SECTOR 3
VULNERABILITY MITIGATION

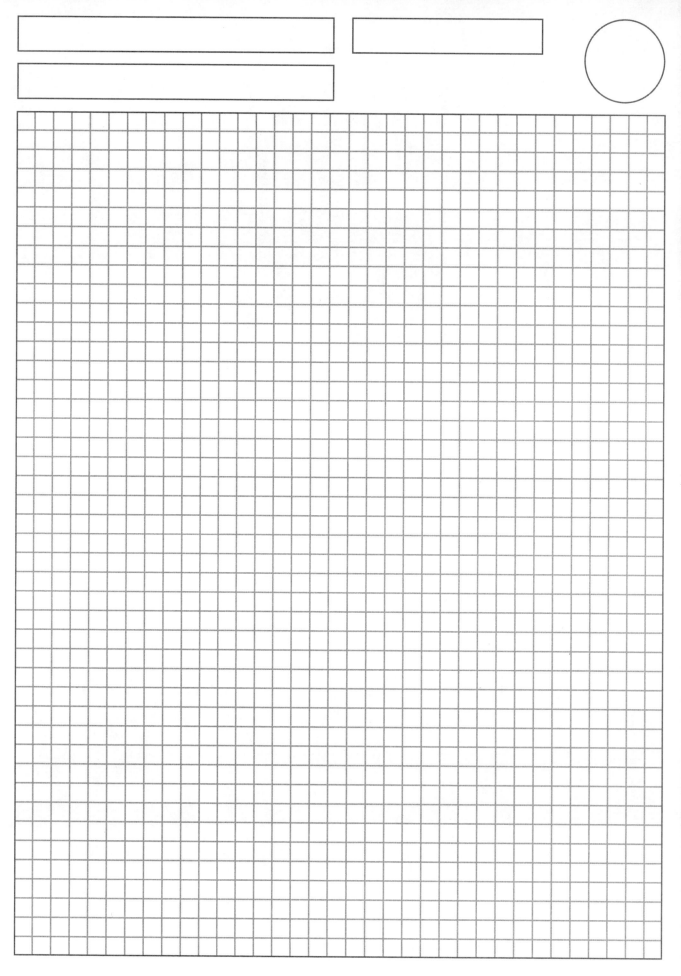

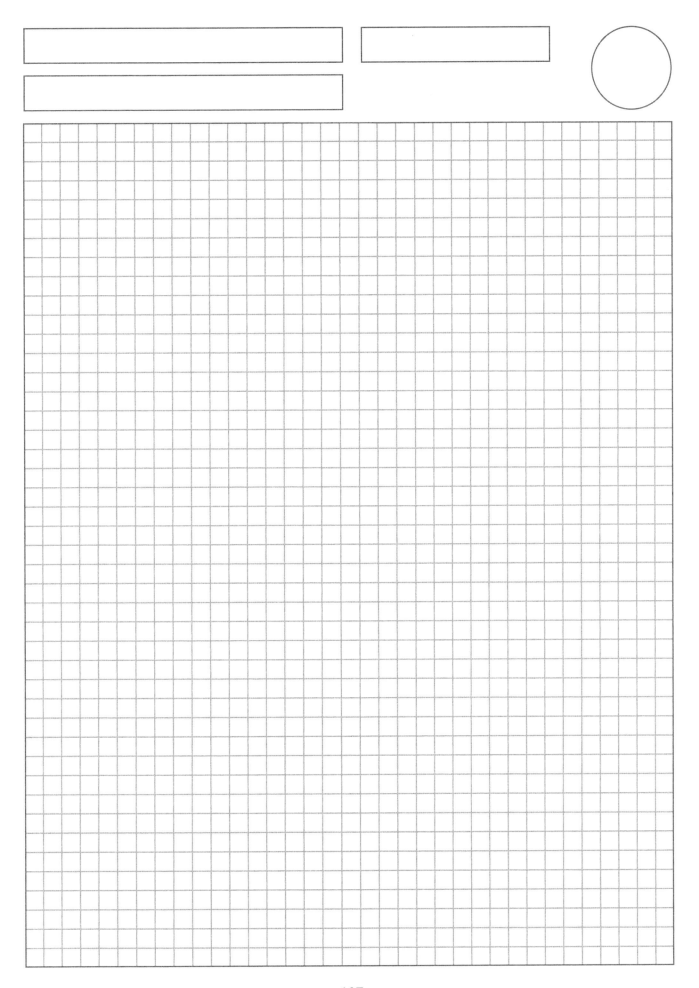

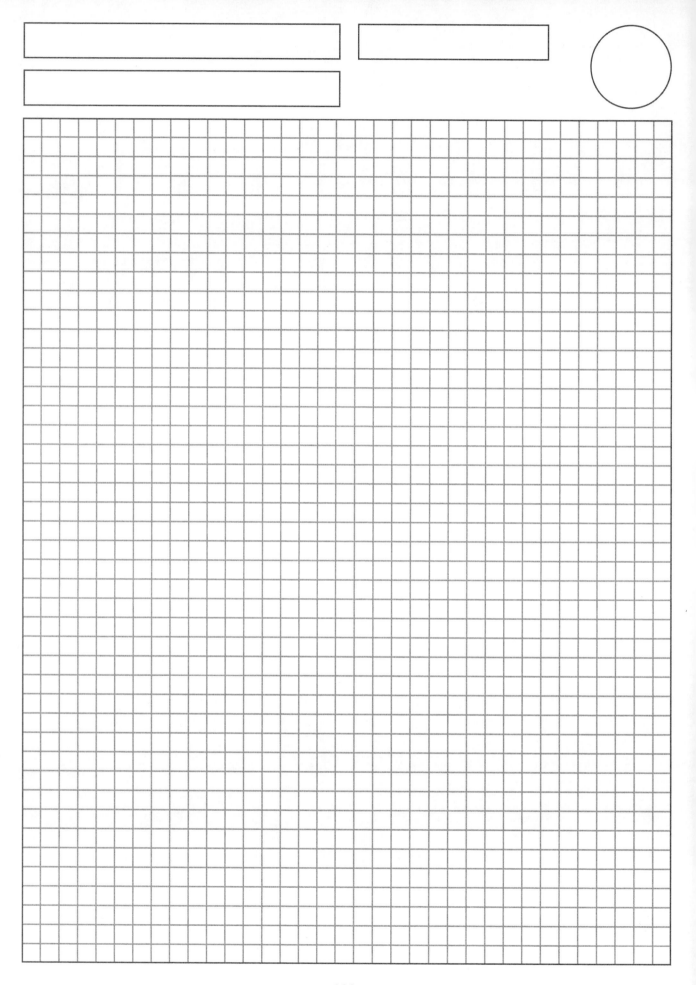

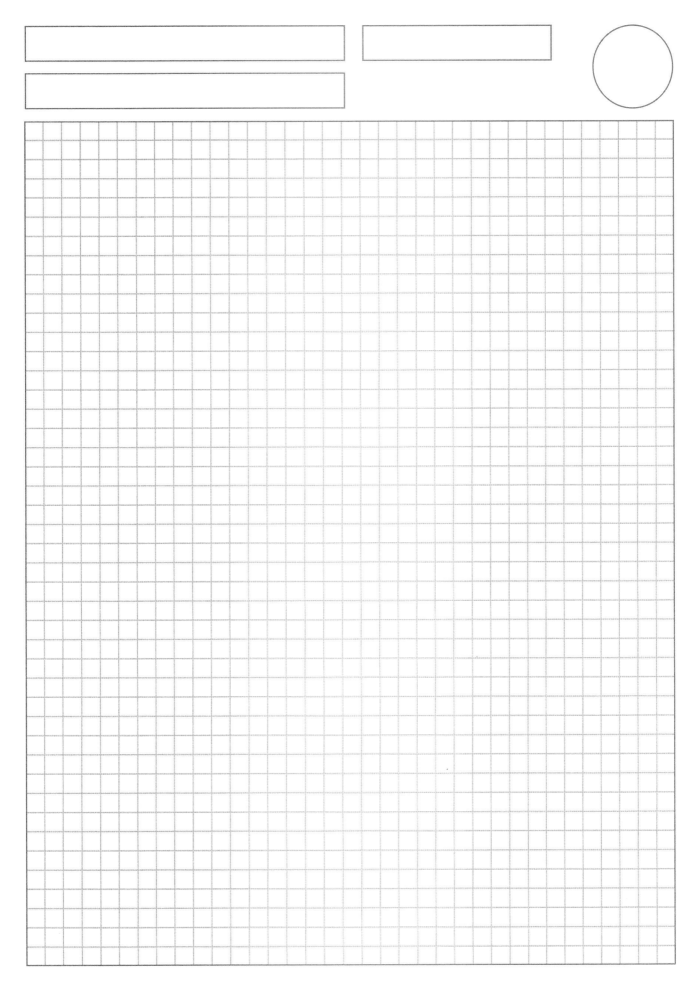

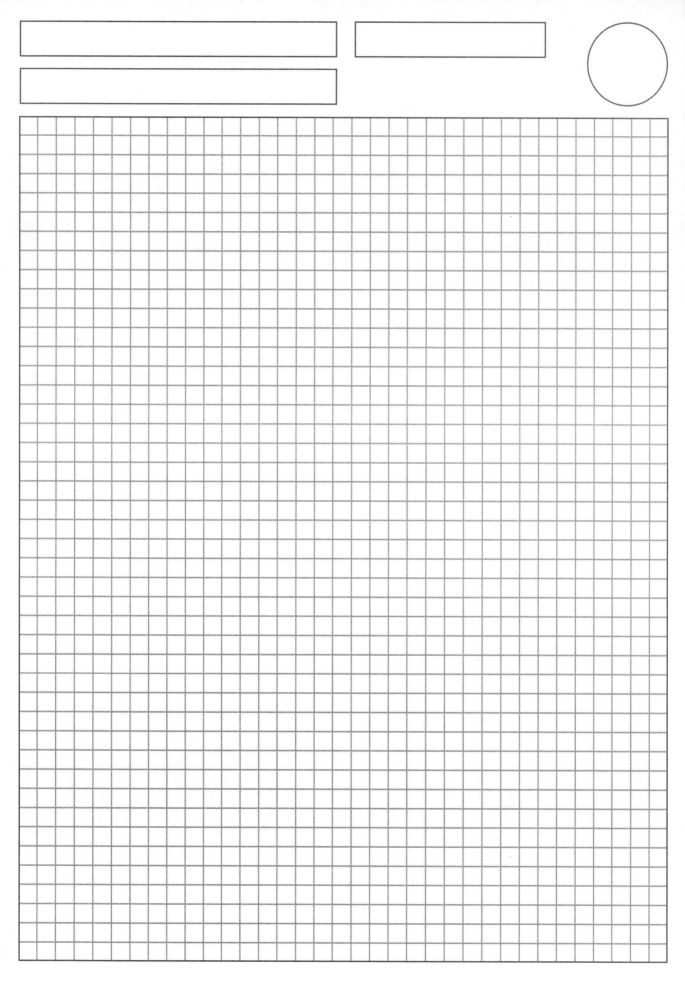

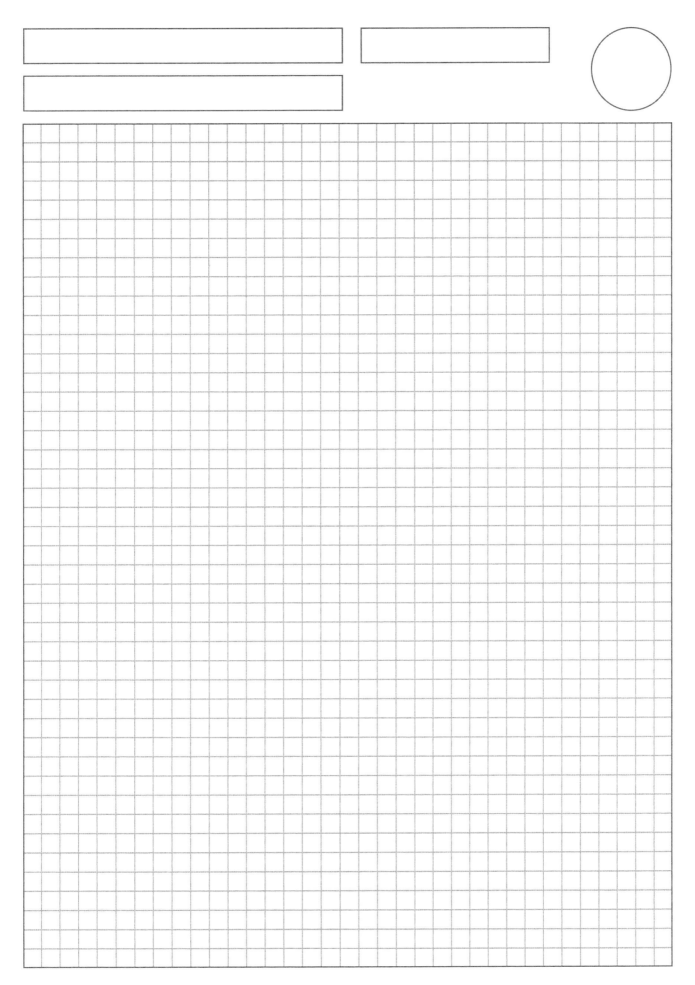

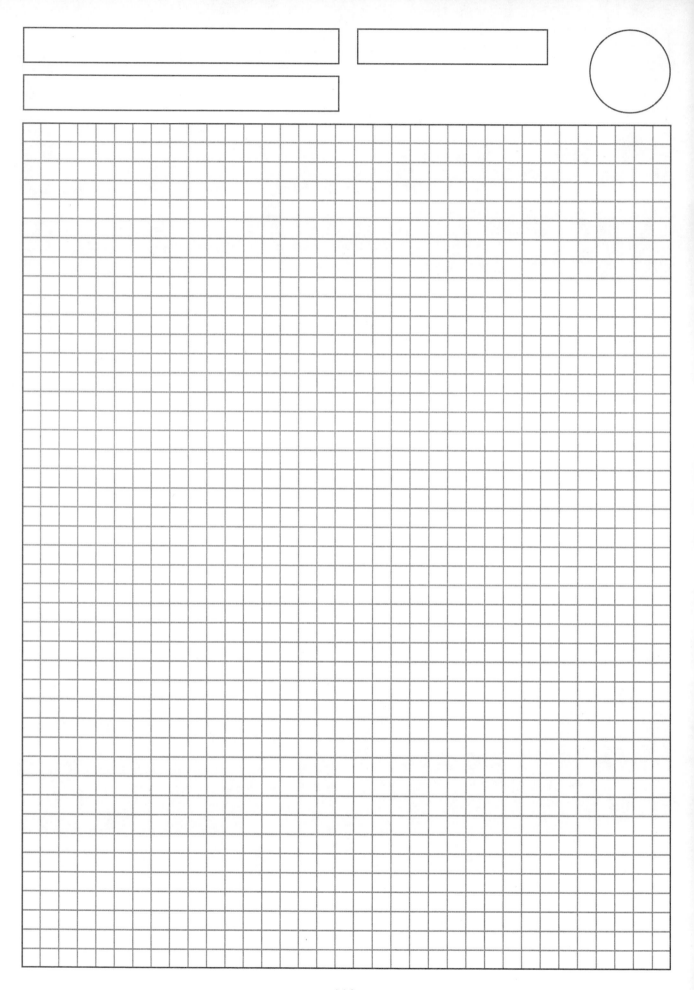

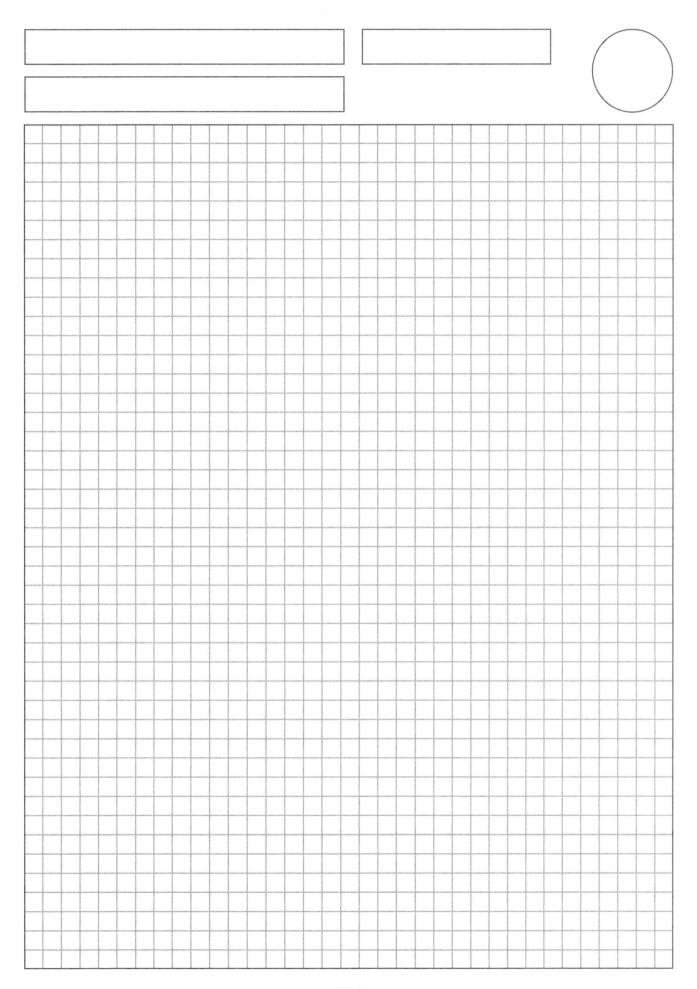

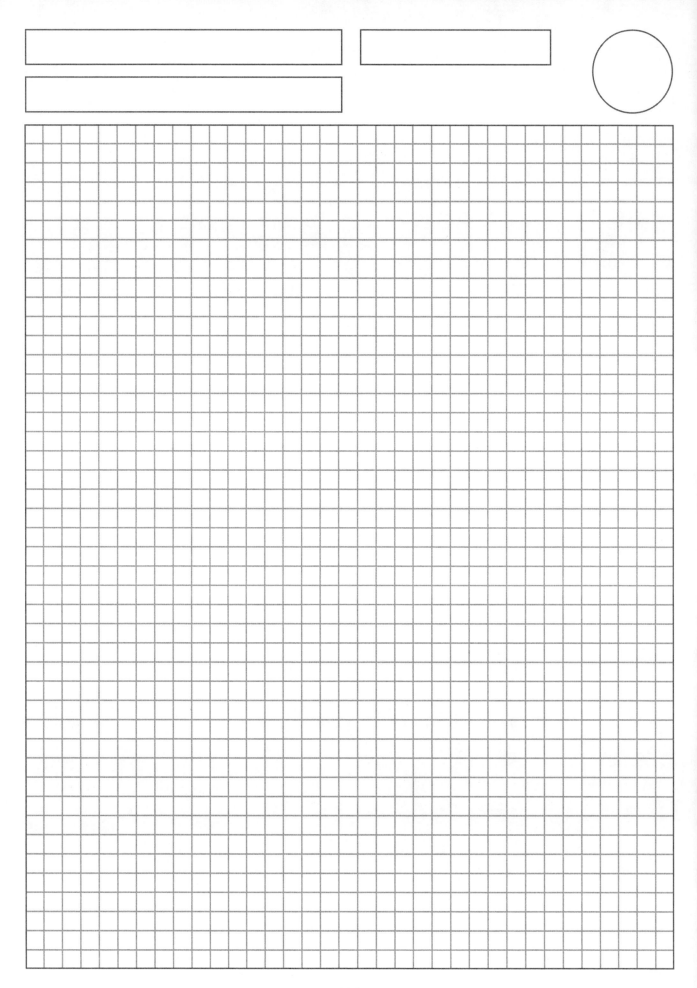

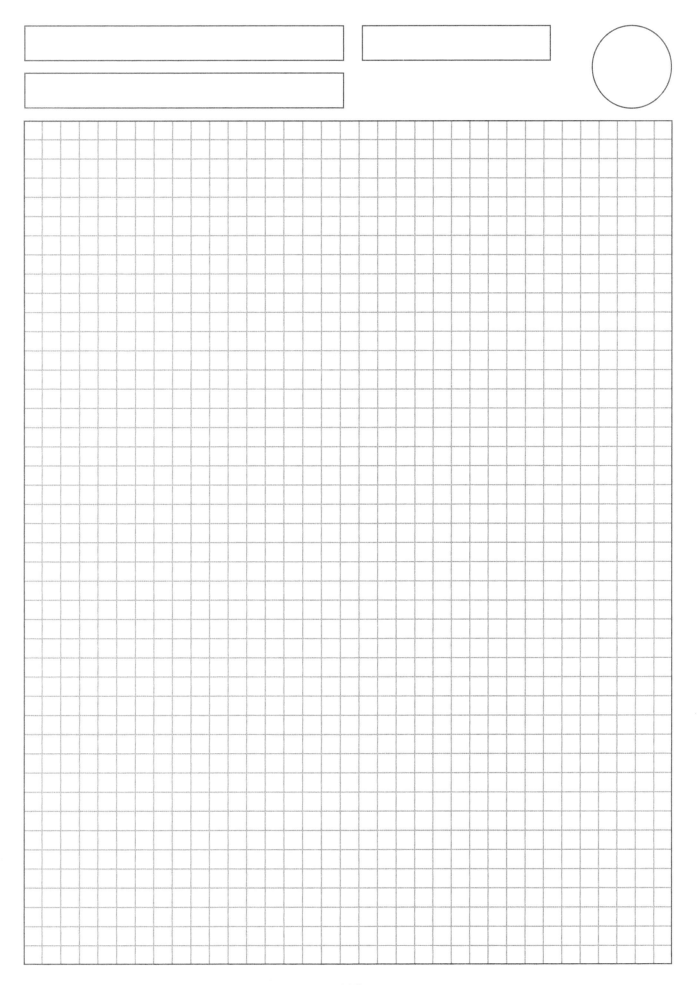

SECTOR 3
IMPLEMENTATION OF PHYSICAL
DEFENSE AND TECHNOLOGY

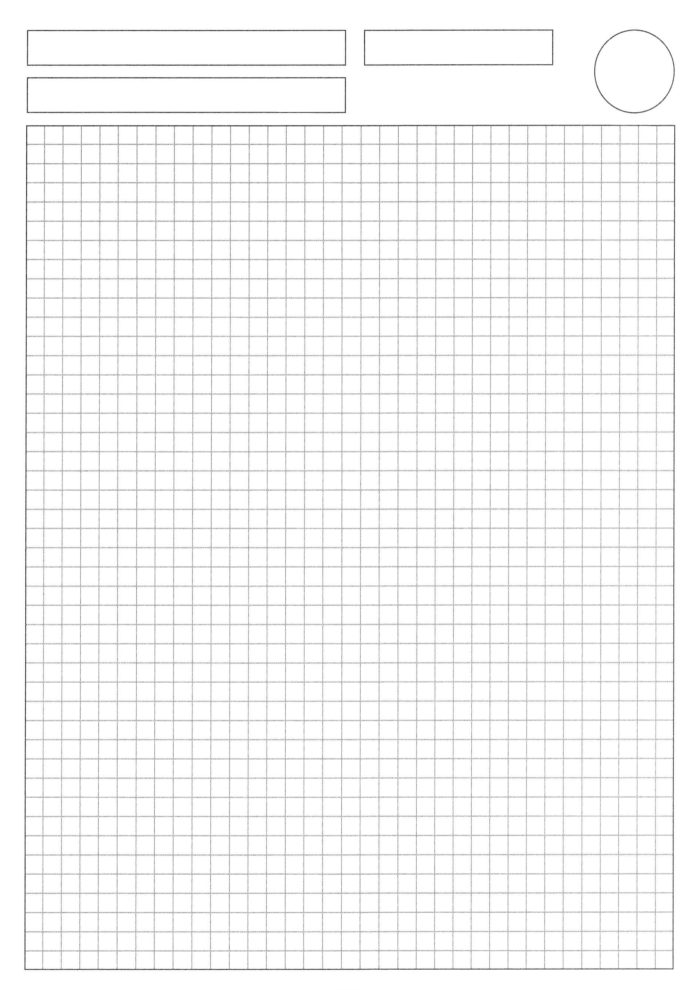

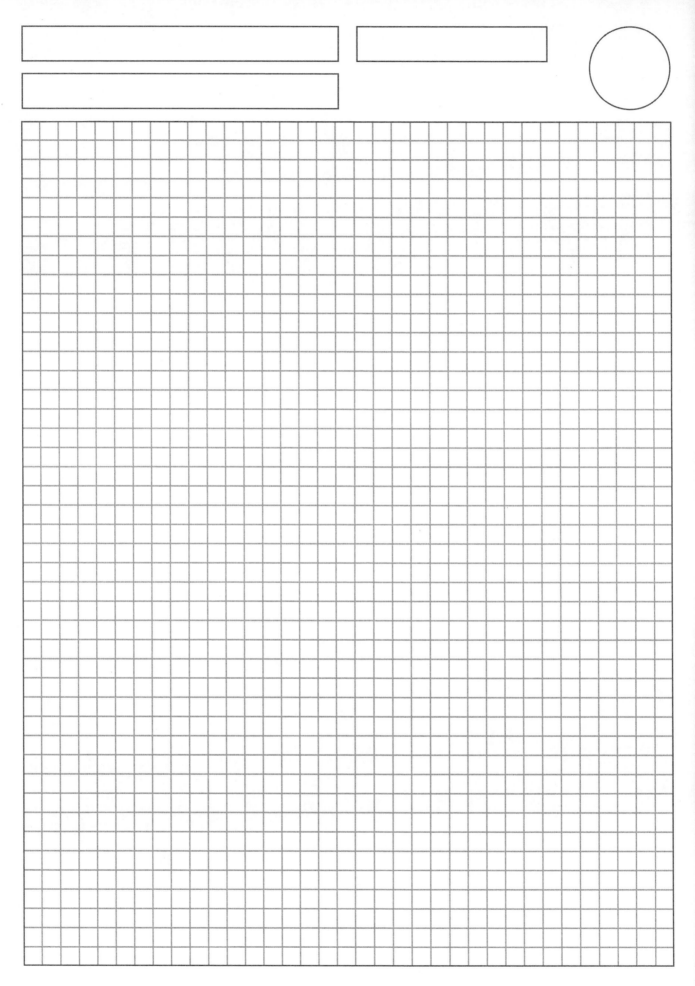

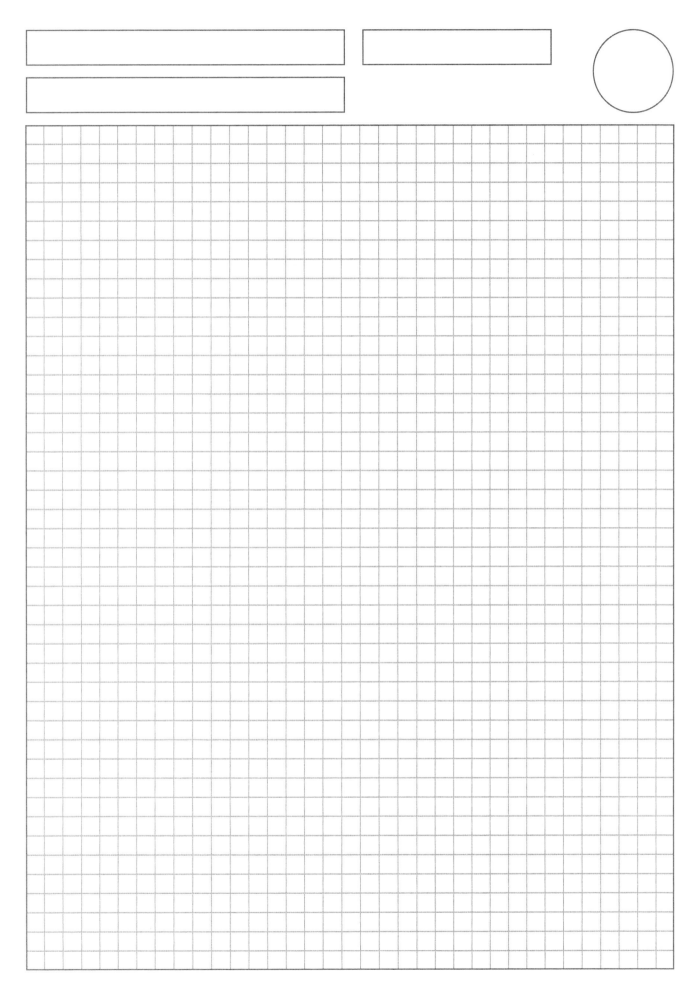

SECTOR 3
BEHAVIORS AND ATTACK
INDICATORS

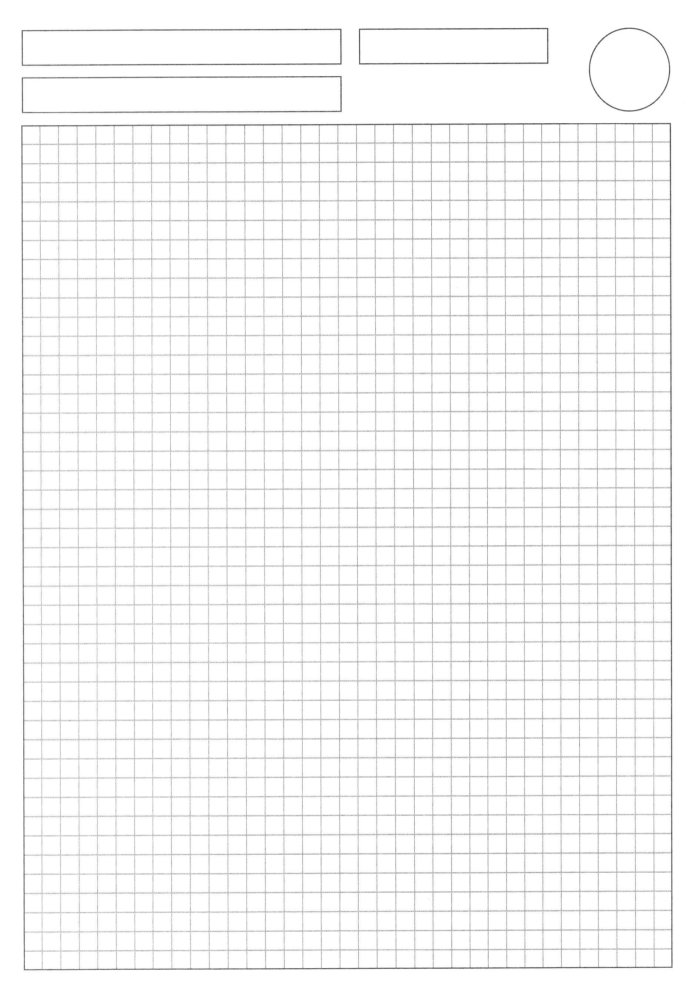

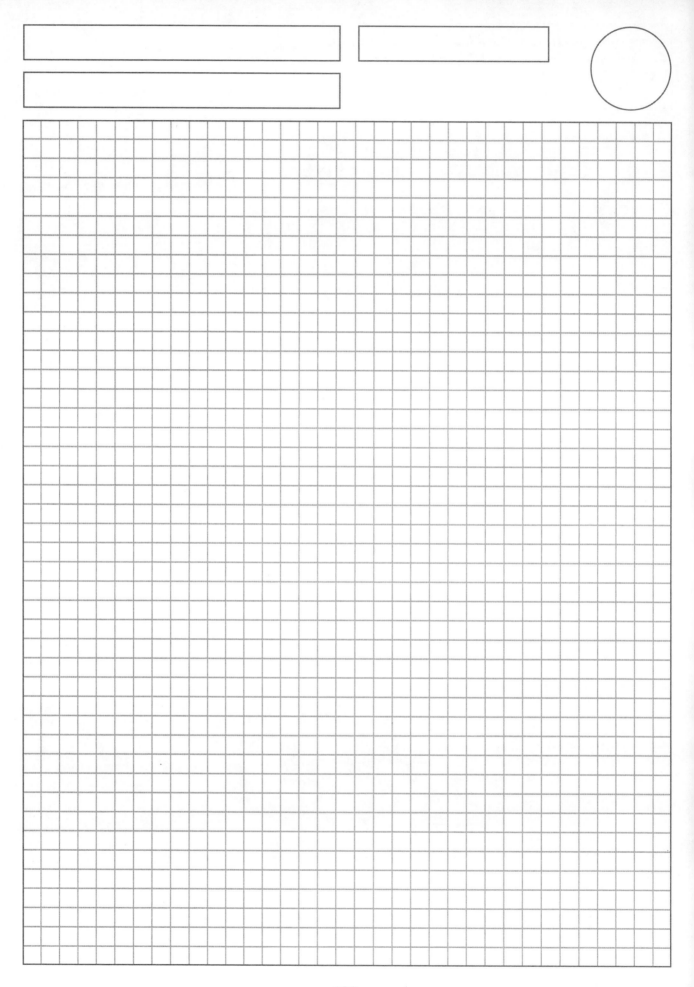

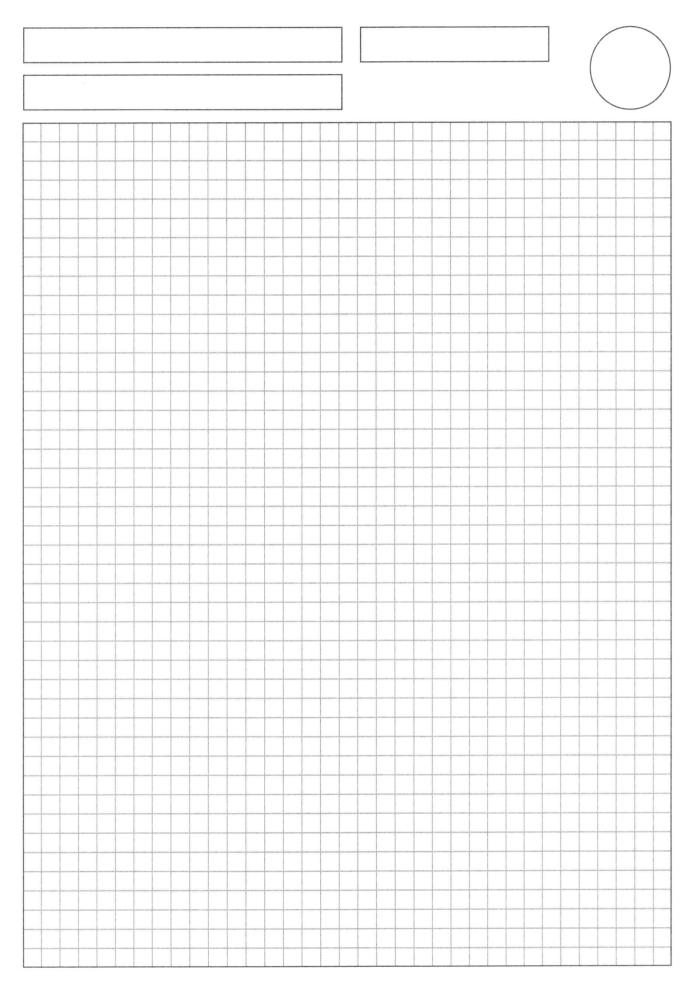

SECTOR 3
SHARED THREATS

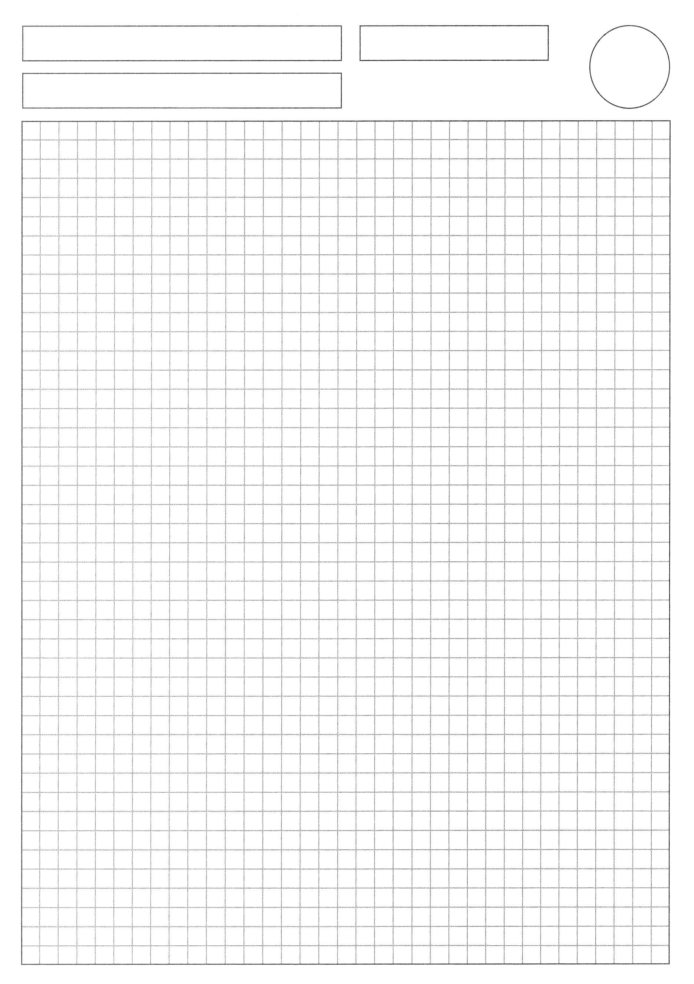

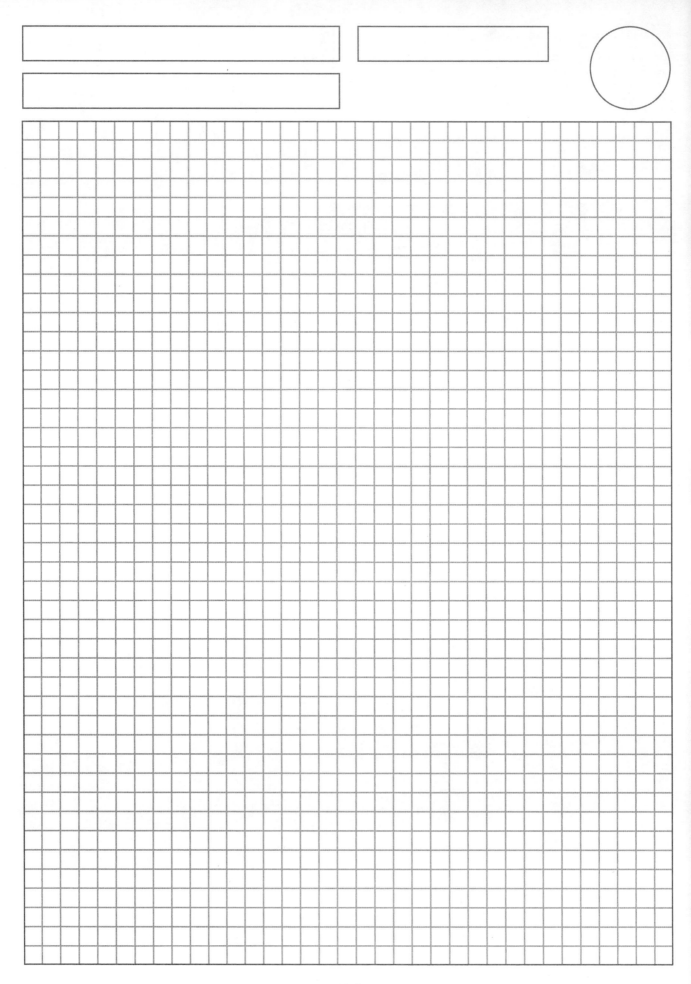

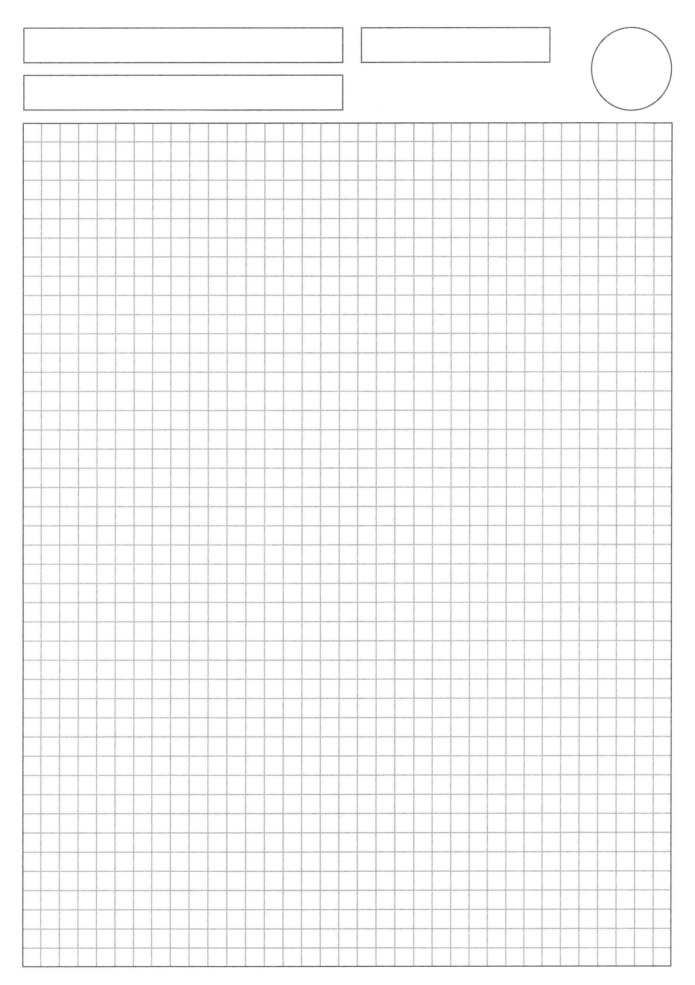

SECTOR 3

TACTICAL PLANS OF ACTION
(WHERE VULNERABILITIES CANNOT BE MITIGATED)

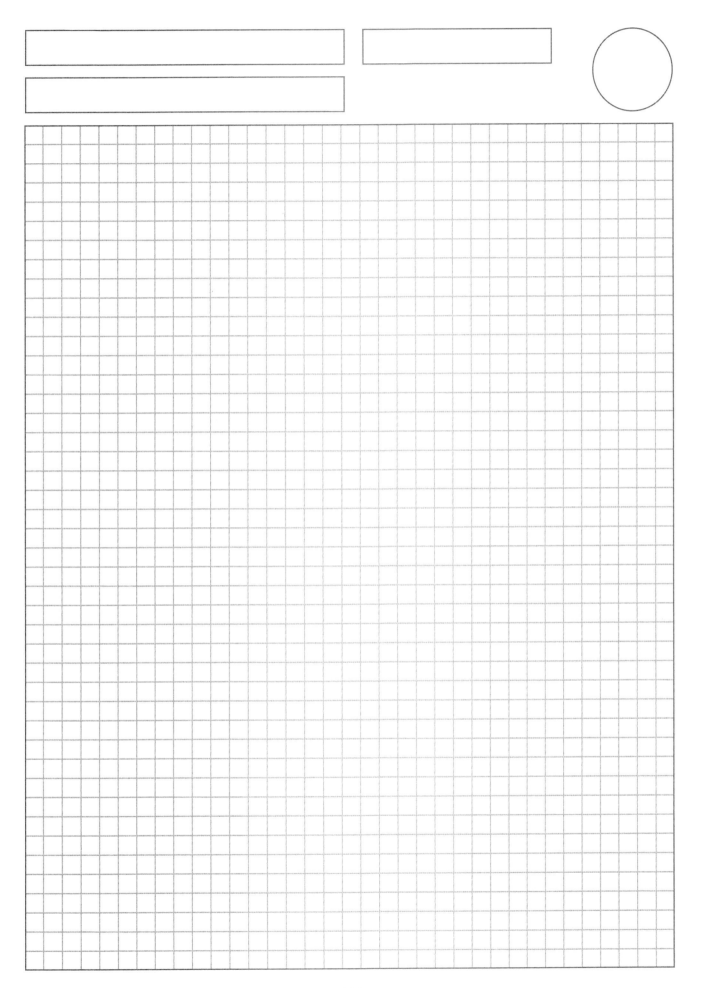

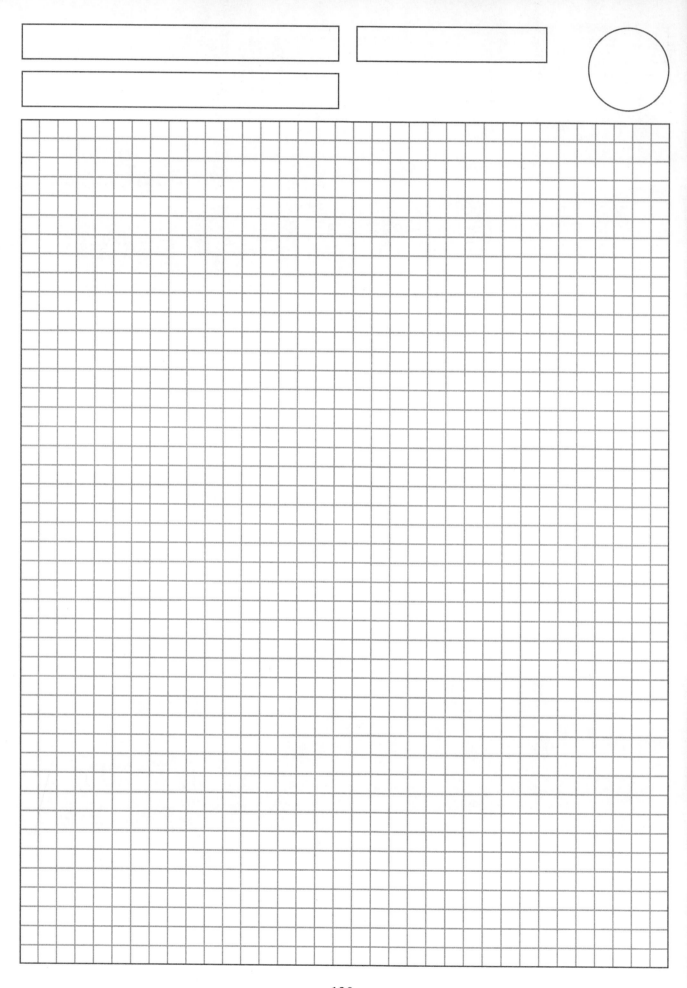

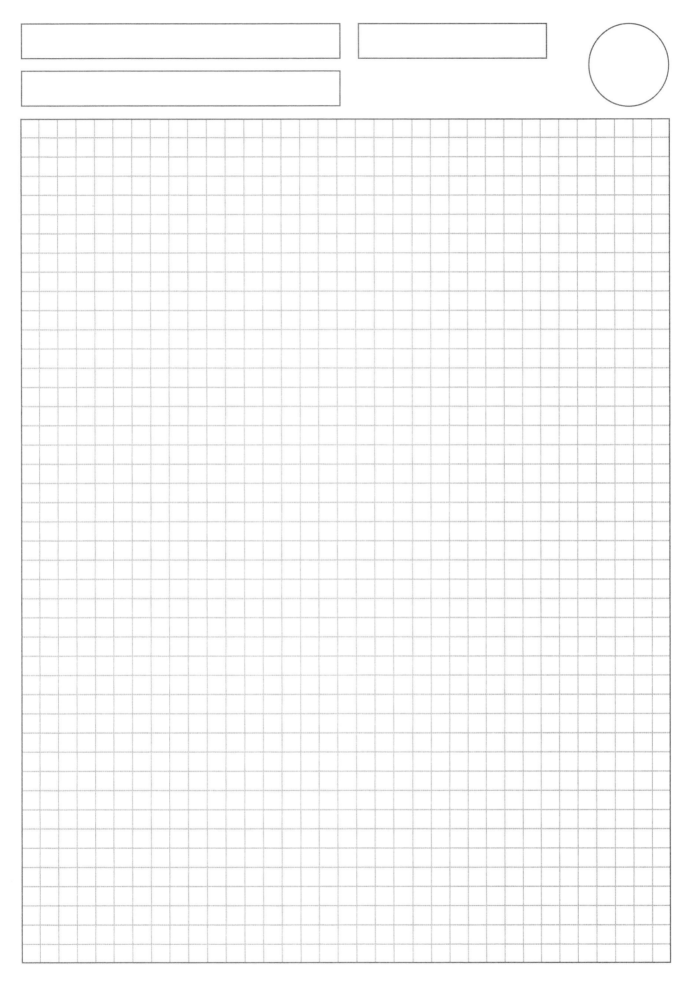

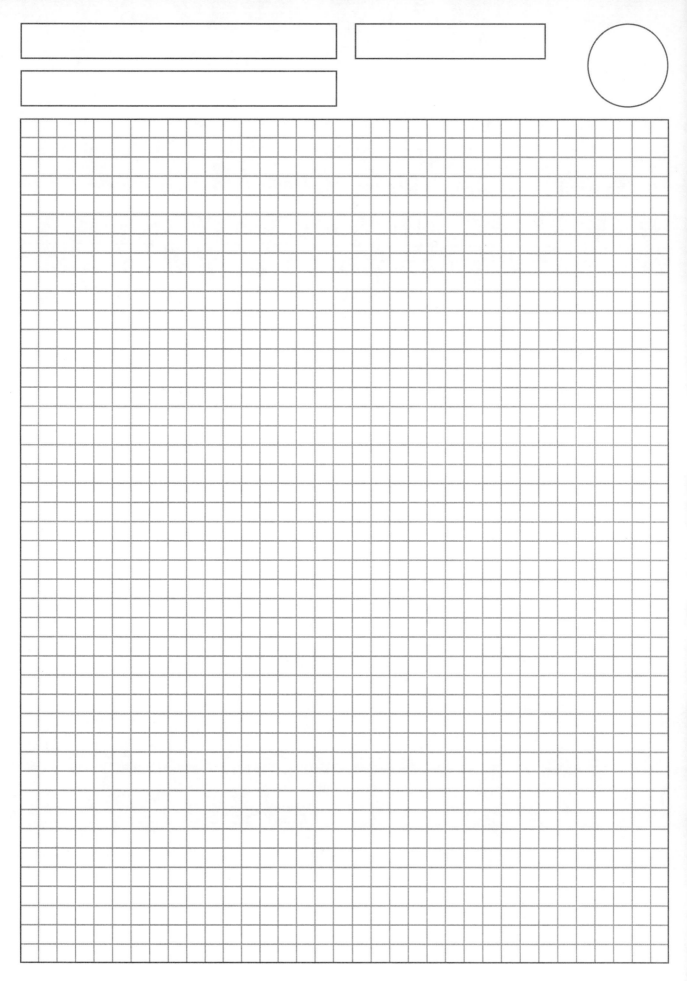

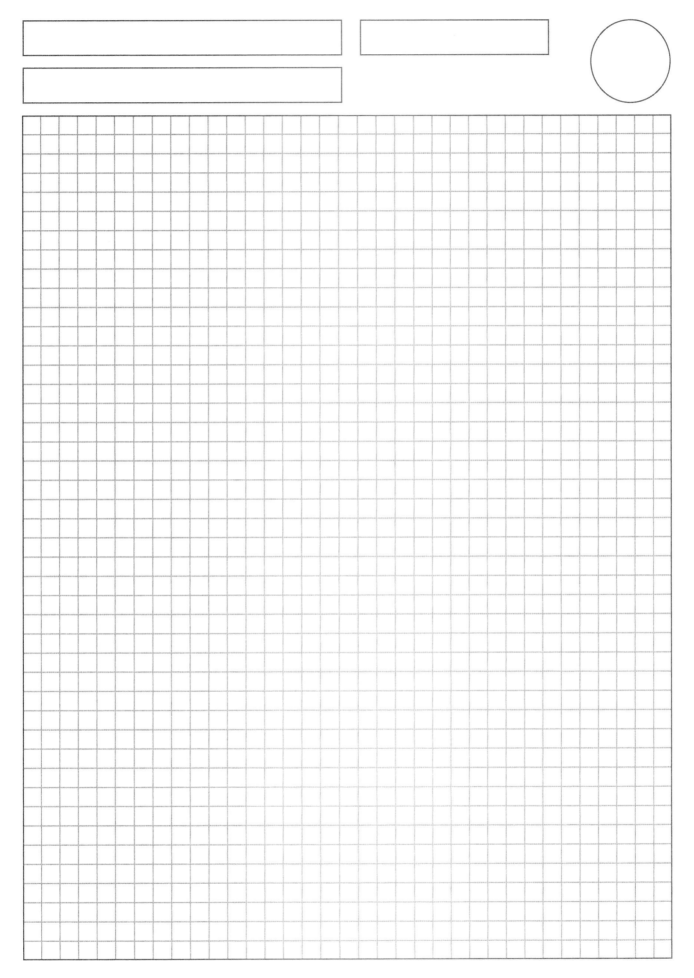

S4

SECTOR 4

SECTOR 4
FIRST RESPONDER OVERVIEW

THREAT ASSESSMENT SECTOR OVERVIEW

Sector:

Date:

Prepared by:

Situation:

Sector Overview:

Note: Make sure you print out map and directions to pertinent police precincts.

Police Departments:

PD Contact Information:

PD Response Times:

Crime Level:

Possible Threat Level:

Known Terror Threats:

Known Criminal Threats:

Note: Make sure you print out map and directions to all trauma centers. Always make the effort to proceed to a level 1 trauma center if the injury is life threatening.

Trauma Centers:

Trauma Center Level (I, II, III):

Response Times:

Weather Conditions:

Spring   Summer   Fall   Winter

RESPONSE RESOURCES
(Specific To This Sector)

Federal

- Department of Homeland Security (DHS)

  _____

  _____

- Federal Emergency Management Agency (FEMA)

  _____

  _____

- Federal Bureau of Investigation (FBI)

  _____

  _____

- Environmental Protection Agency (EPA)

  _____

  _____

- Health and Human Services (HHS)

  _____

  _____

State/Regional

- Emergency Management

  _____

  _____

- State Emergency Operations Center

  _____

  _____

RESPONSE RESOURCES (continued)
(Specific To This Sector)

- State Police

  _____

  _____

- National Guard

  _____

  _____

- Joint Terrorism Task Forces (JTTF)

  _____

  _____

> Note: Make sure you print out map and directions to pertinent police precincts. Always make the effort to proceed to a level 1 trauma center if the injury is life threatening.

Local First Responders

- Police

  _____

  _____

  - Special Weapons And Tactics (SWAT) Teams

    _____

  - Explosive Ordnance Disposal (EOD)

    _____

- Police

  _____

  _____

  - Special Weapons And Tactics (SWAT) Teams

    _____

  - Explosive Ordnance Disposal (EOD)

    _____

- Police

  _____

  _____

  - Special Weapons And Tactics (SWAT) Teams

    _____

  - Explosive Ordnance Disposal (EOD)

    _____

- Fire

  _____

  _____

  - Rescue / Emergency Medical Services

    _____

  - Hazardous Materials Response Teams

    _____

- Emergency Management

  _____

  _____

Note: Make sure you print out map and directions to all trauma centers. Always make the effort to proceed to a level 1 trauma center if the injury is life threatening.

Hospitals

- Level I Trauma Center

  _____

  _____

- Level II Trauma Center

  _____

  _____

RESPONSE RESOURCES (continued)
(Specific To This Sector)

- Urgent Care

  _____

  _____

- Other Medical Center

  _____

  _____

- Other Medical Center

  _____

  _____

Known Threats

- Crime

  _____

  _____

  _____

  _____

  _____

  _____

- Terror

  _____

  _____

  _____

  _____

  _____

  _____

_Note: If this sector is a special event or a vacation, take a screen shot
of the weather report and attach here_

SECTOR 4
VULNERABILITY MITIGATION

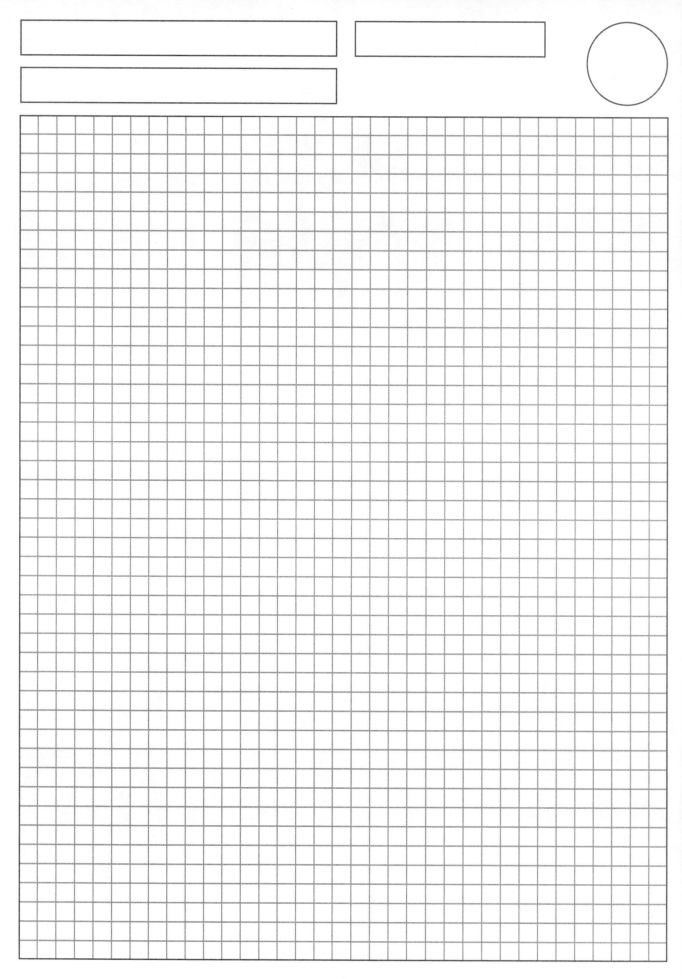

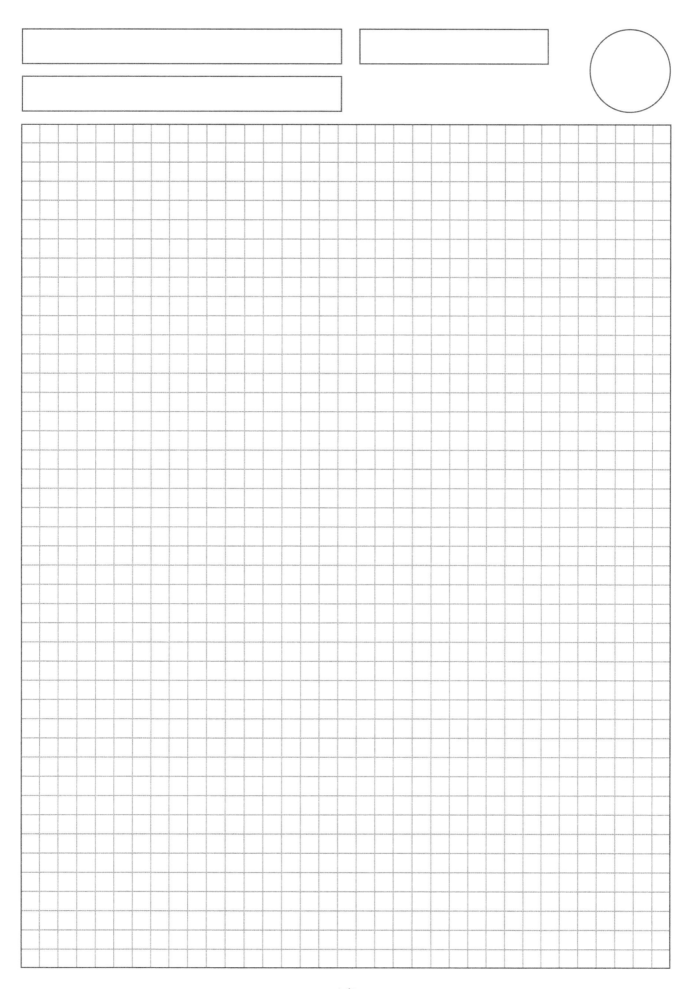

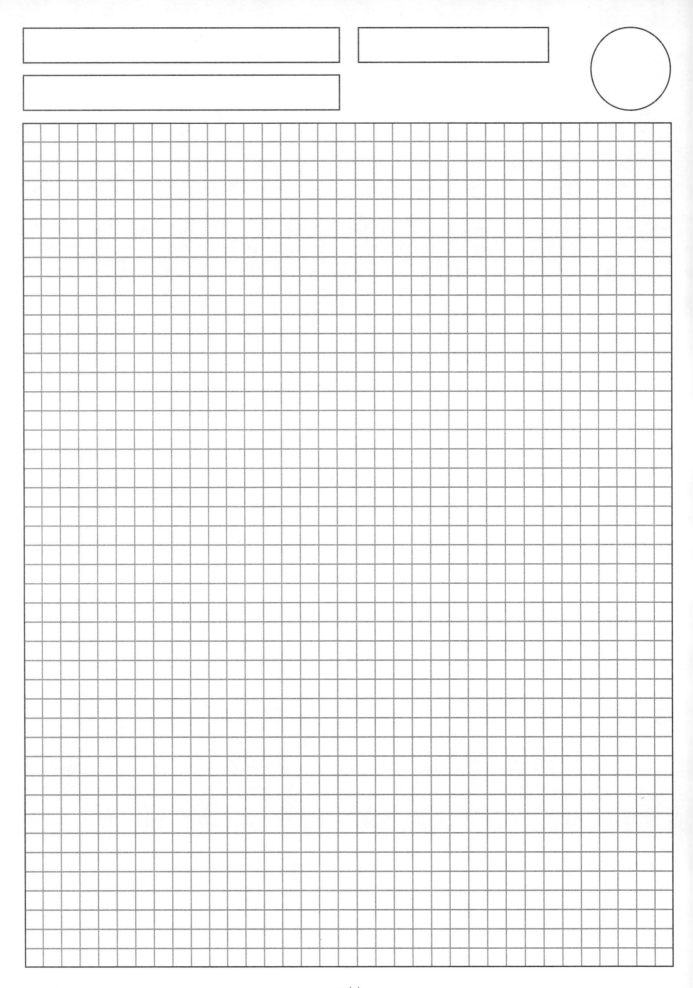

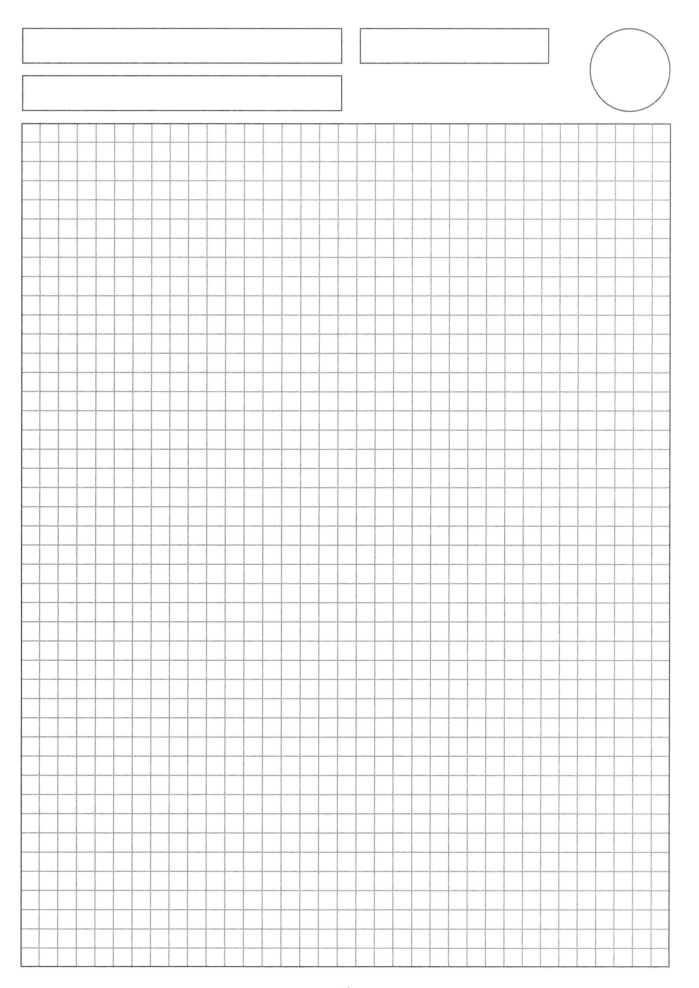

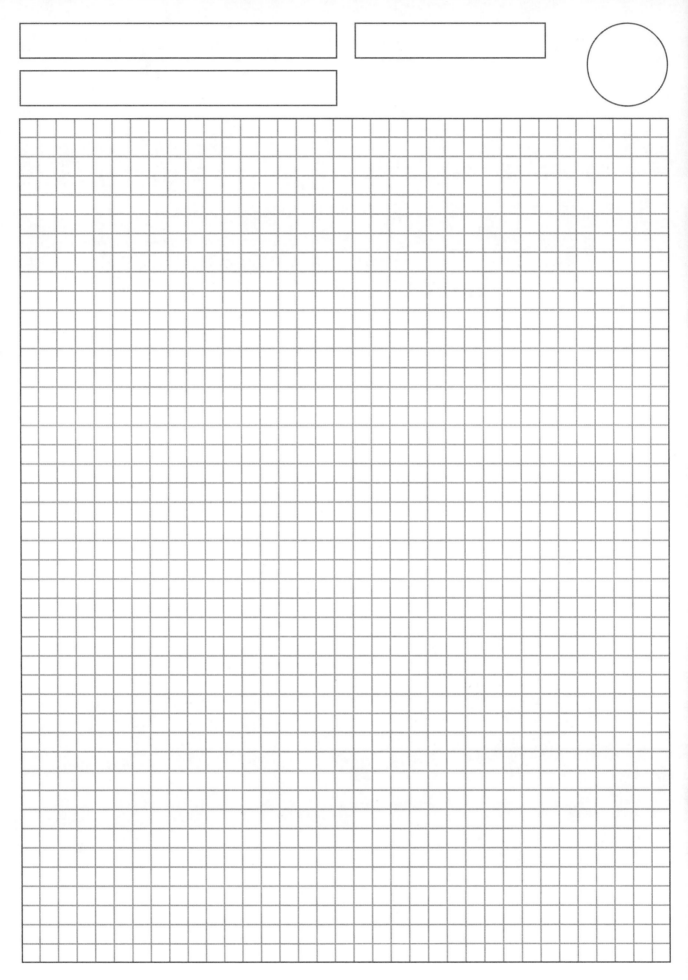

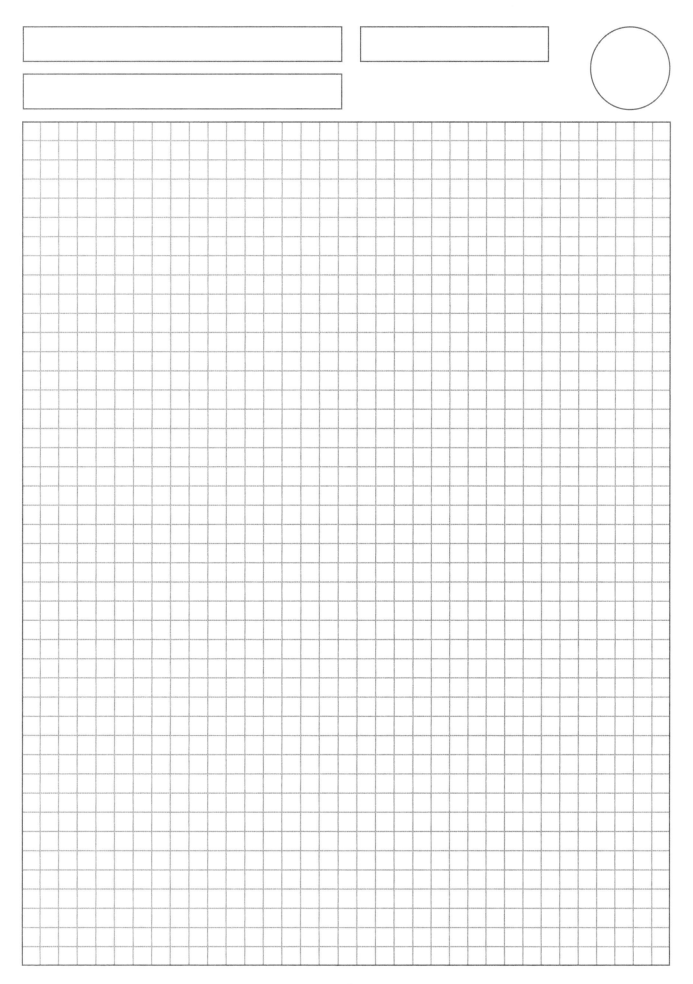

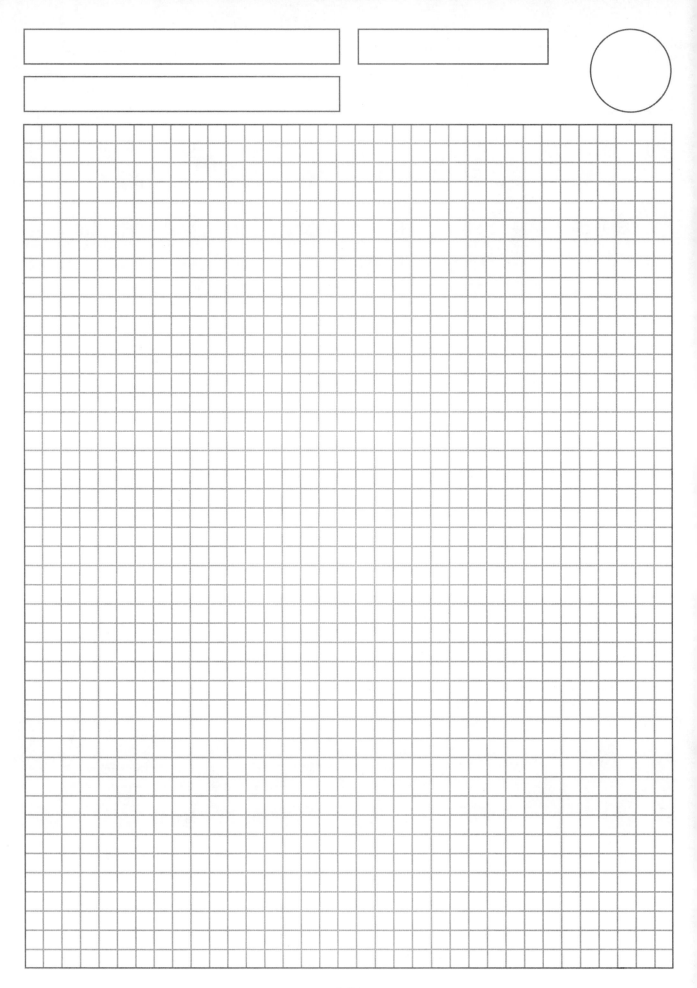

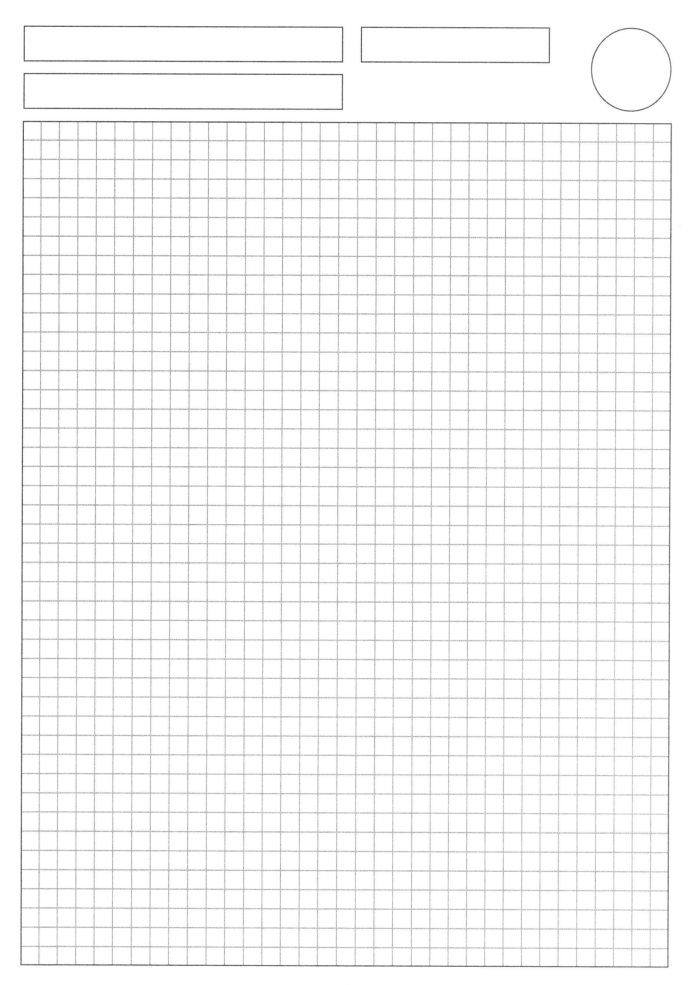

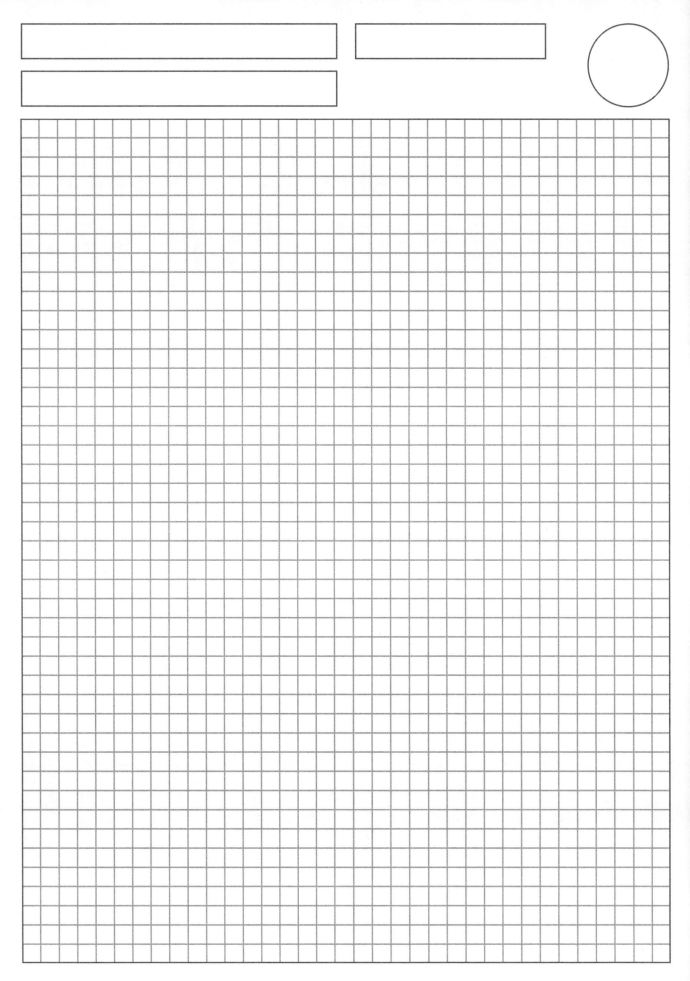

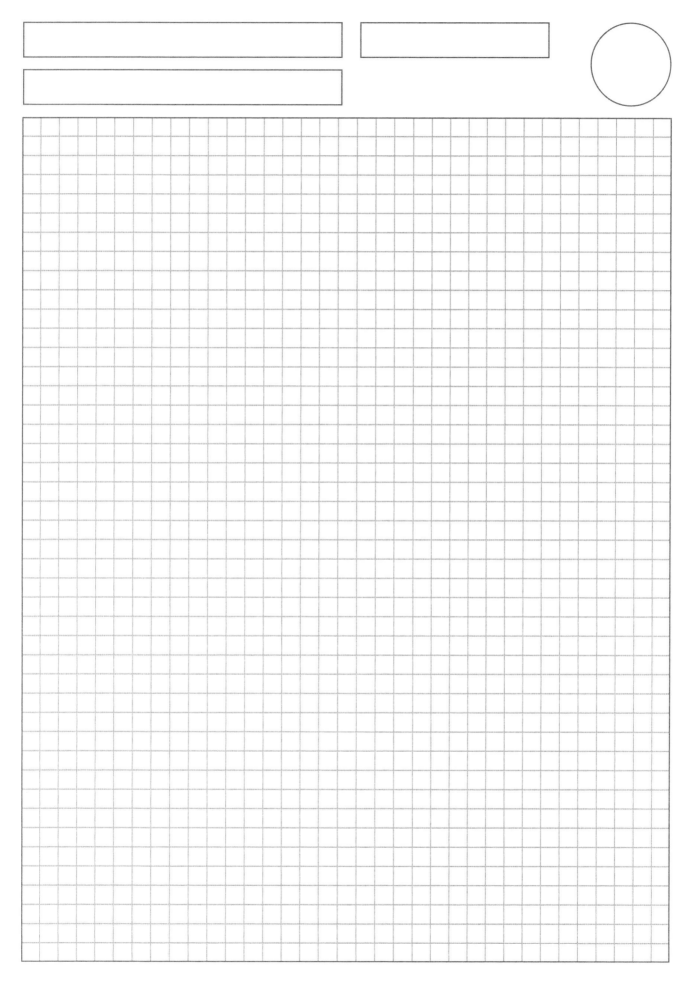

SECTOR 4
IMPLEMENTATION OF PHYSICAL
DEFENSE AND TECHNOLOGY

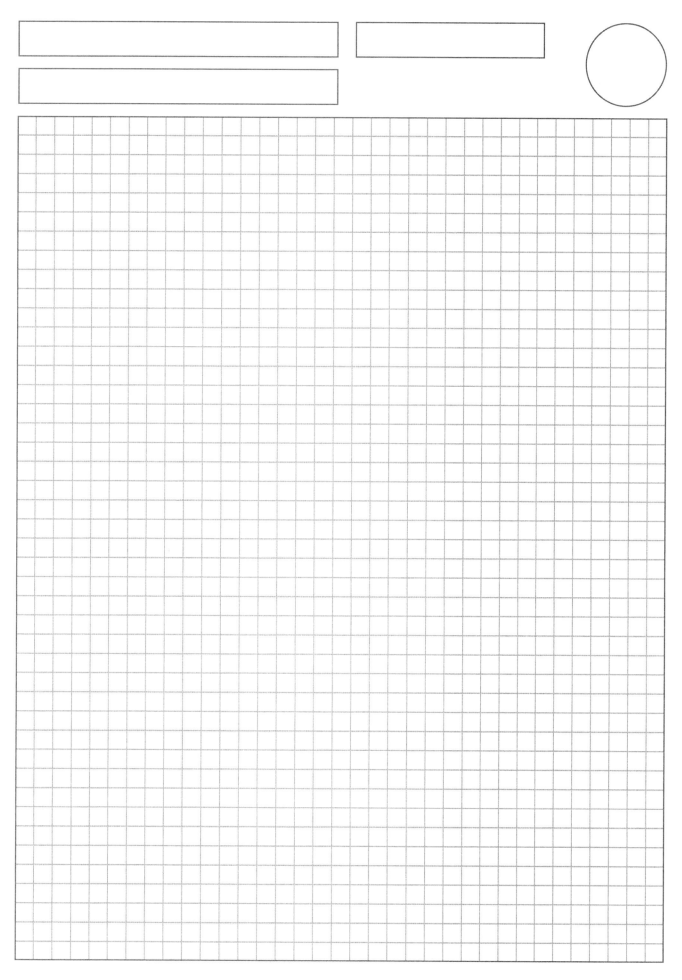

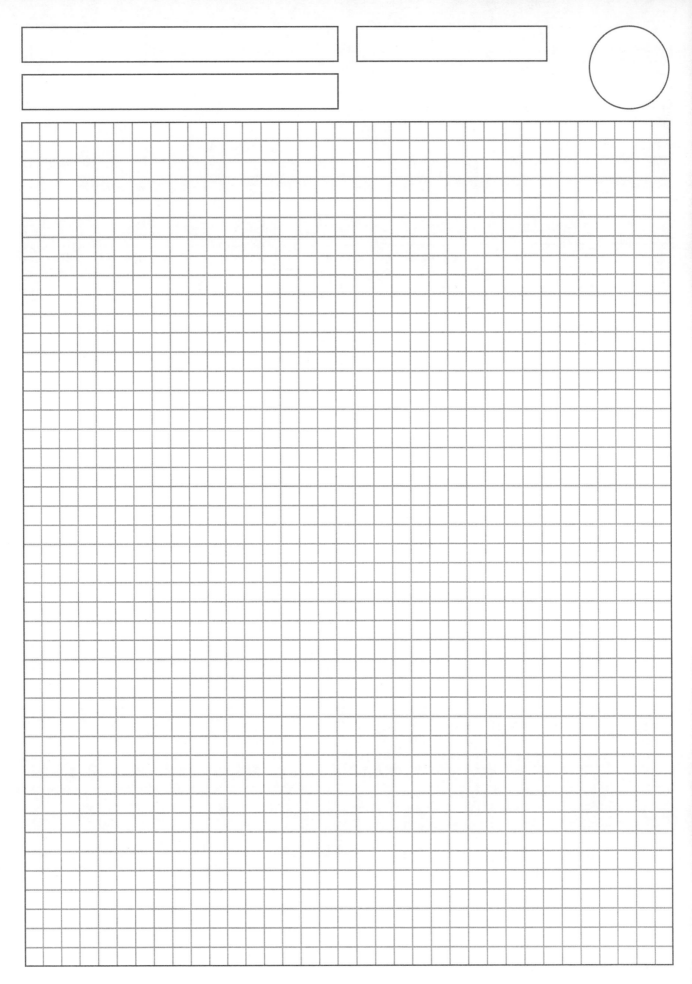

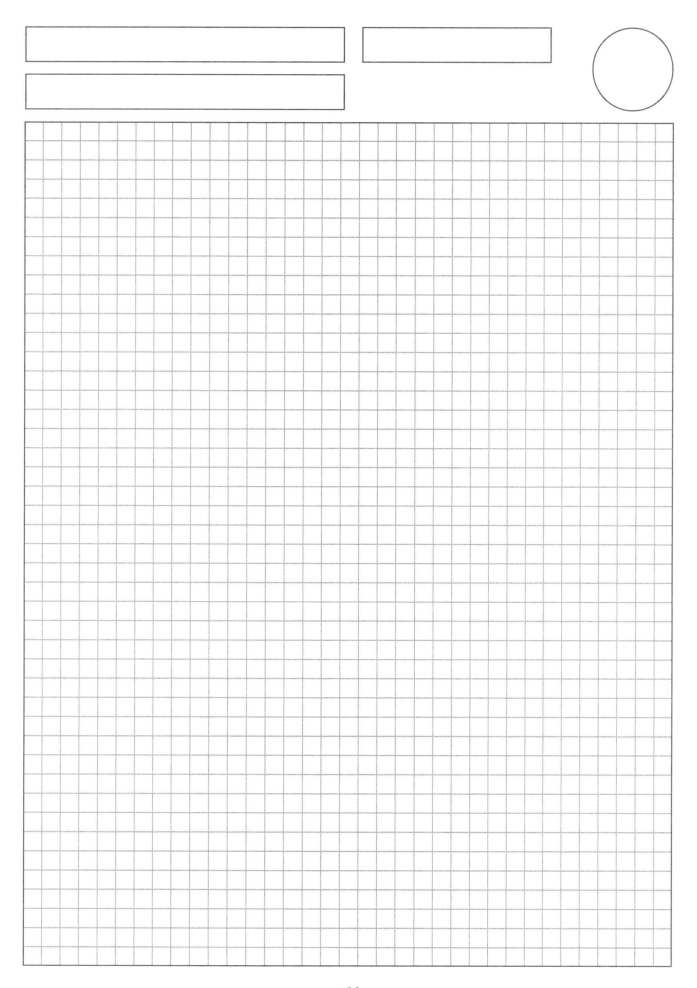

SECTOR 4
BEHAVIORS AND ATTACK
INDICATORS

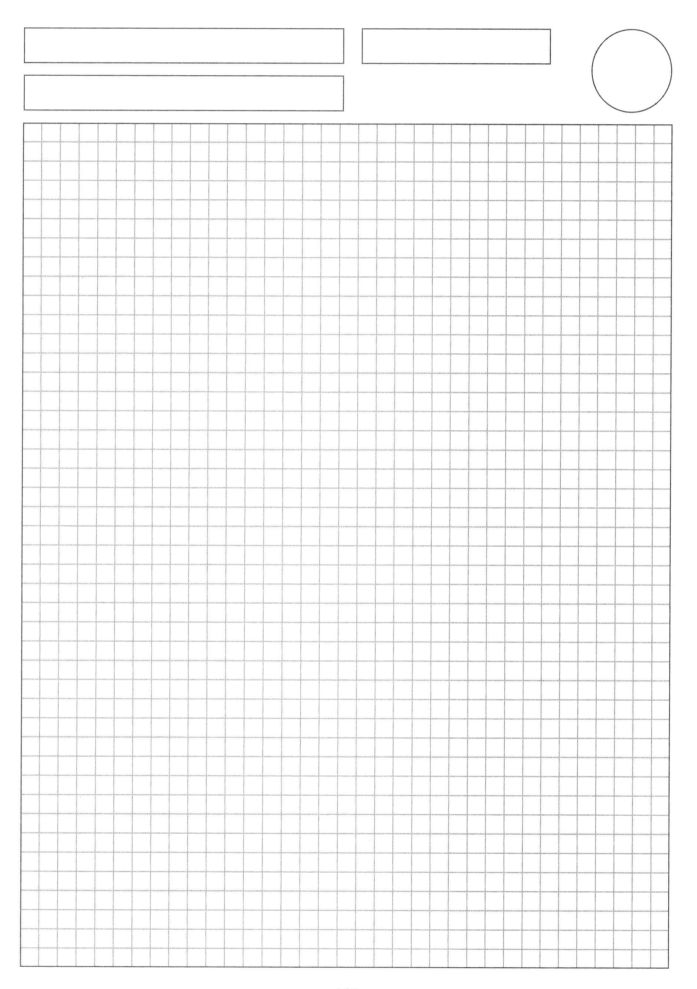

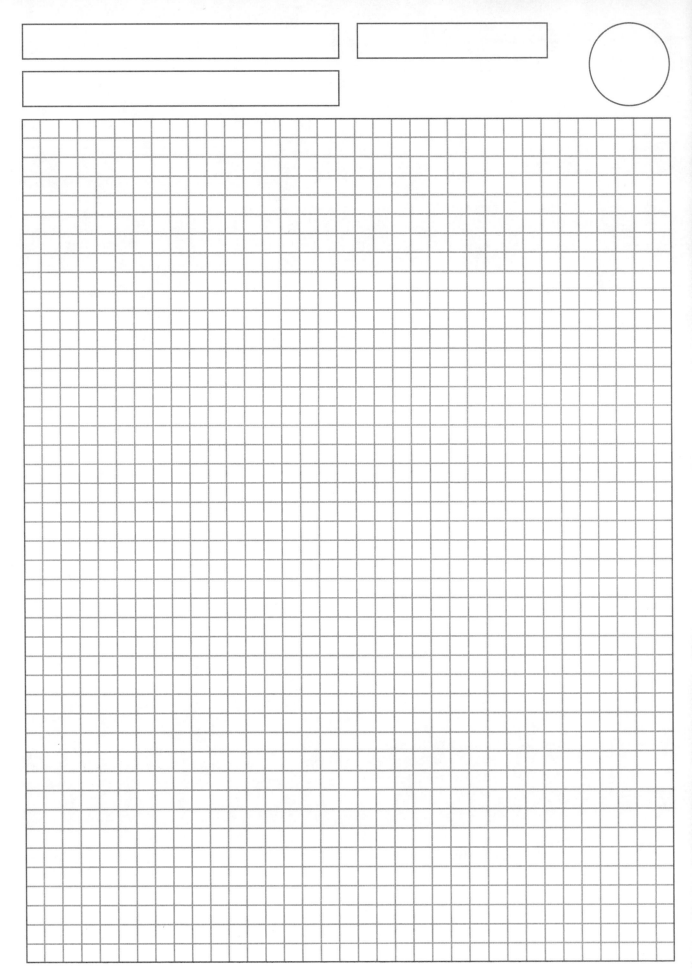

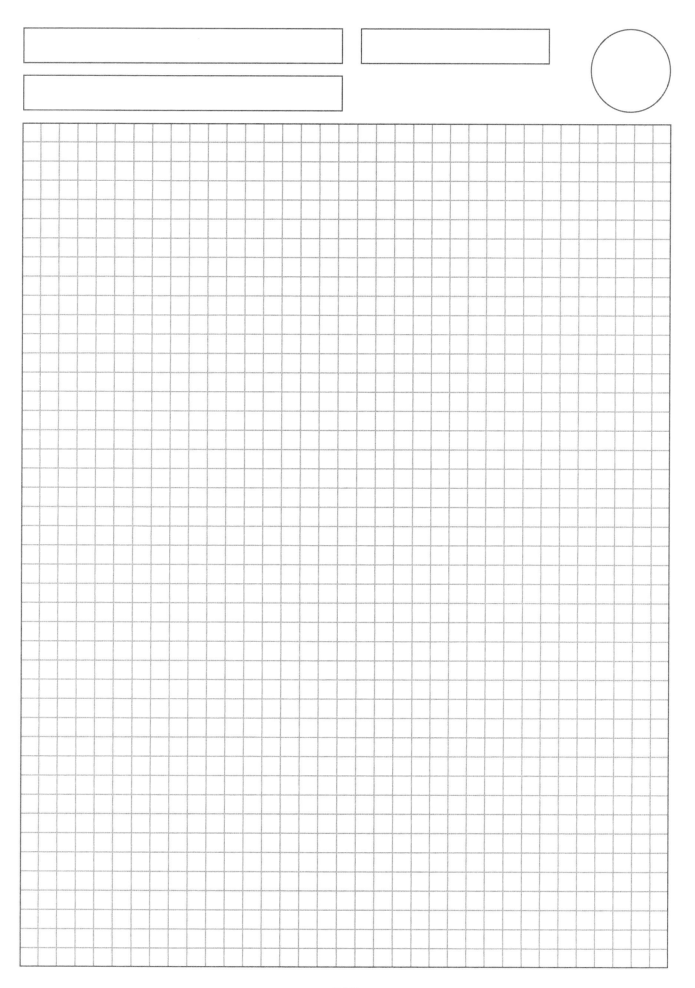

SECTOR 4
SHARED THREATS

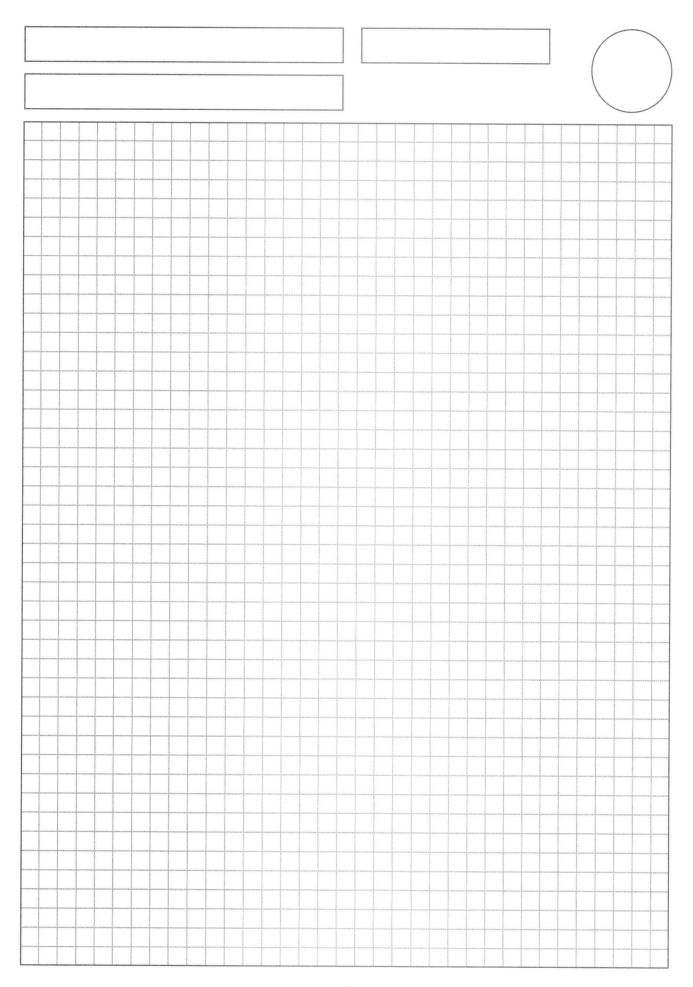

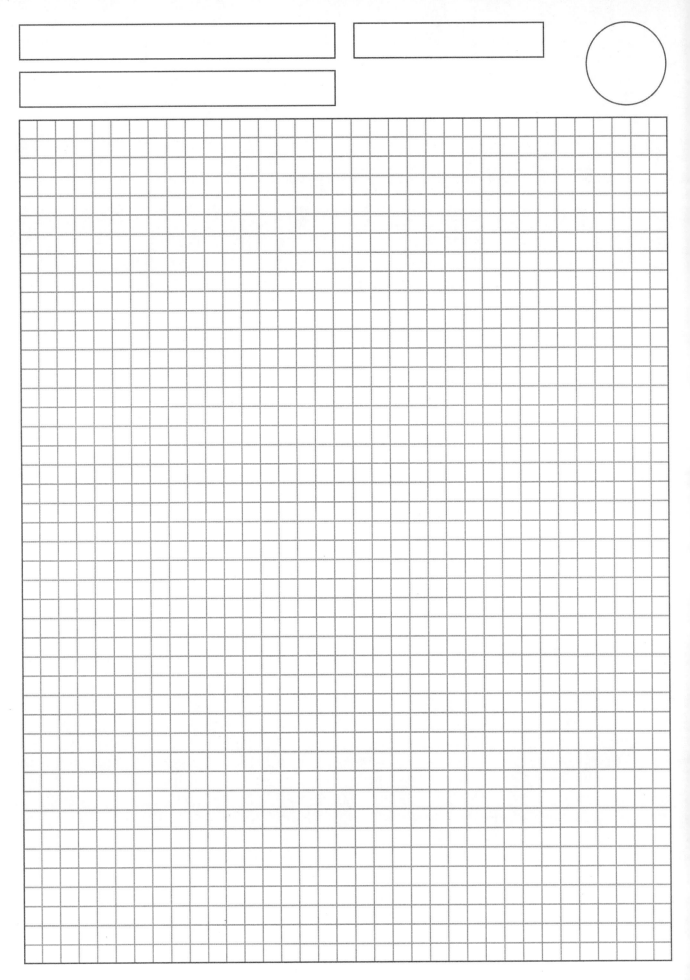

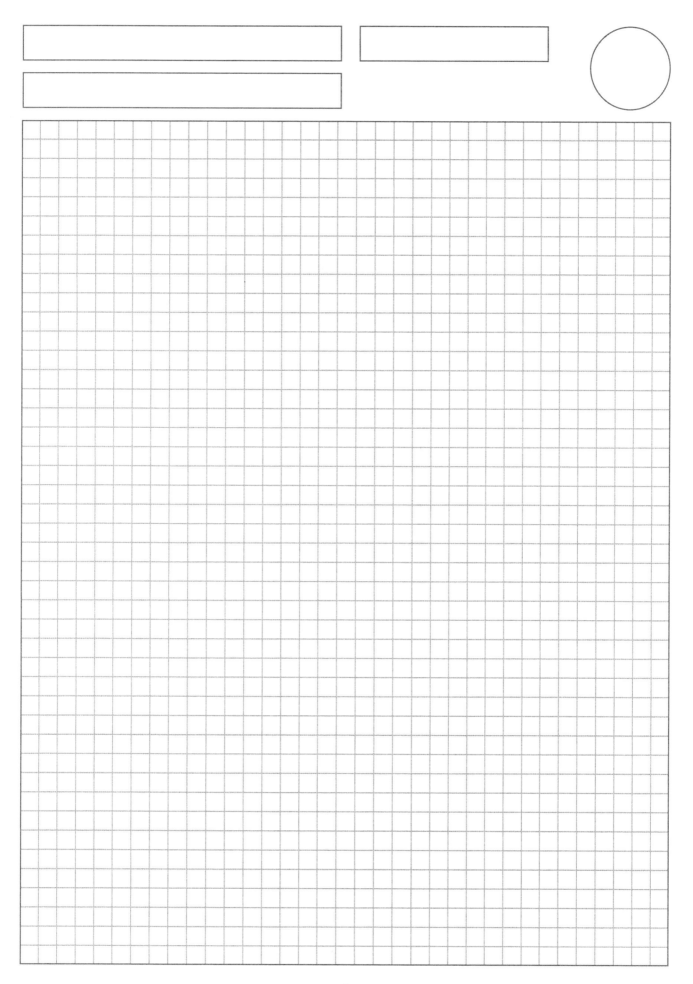

SECTOR 4
TACTICAL PLANS OF ACTION
(WHERE VULNERABILITIES CANNOT BE MITIGATED)

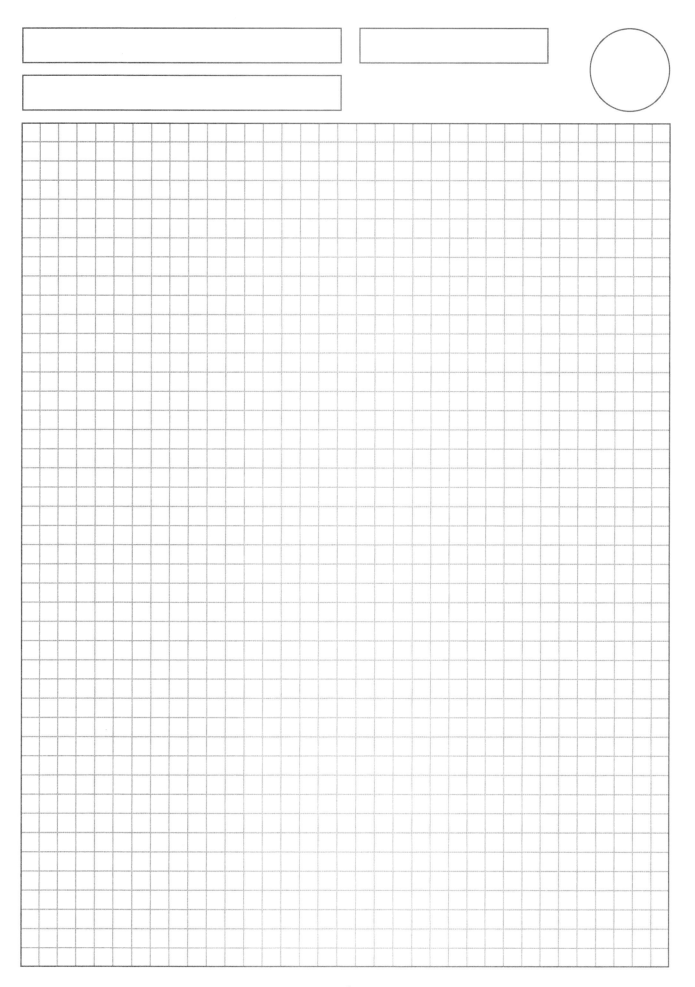

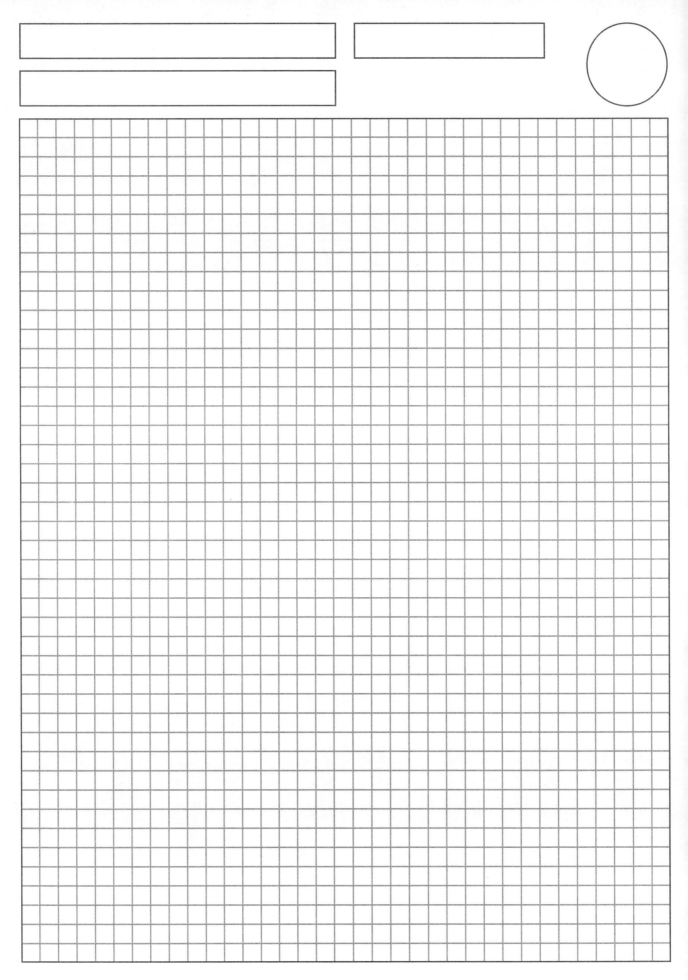

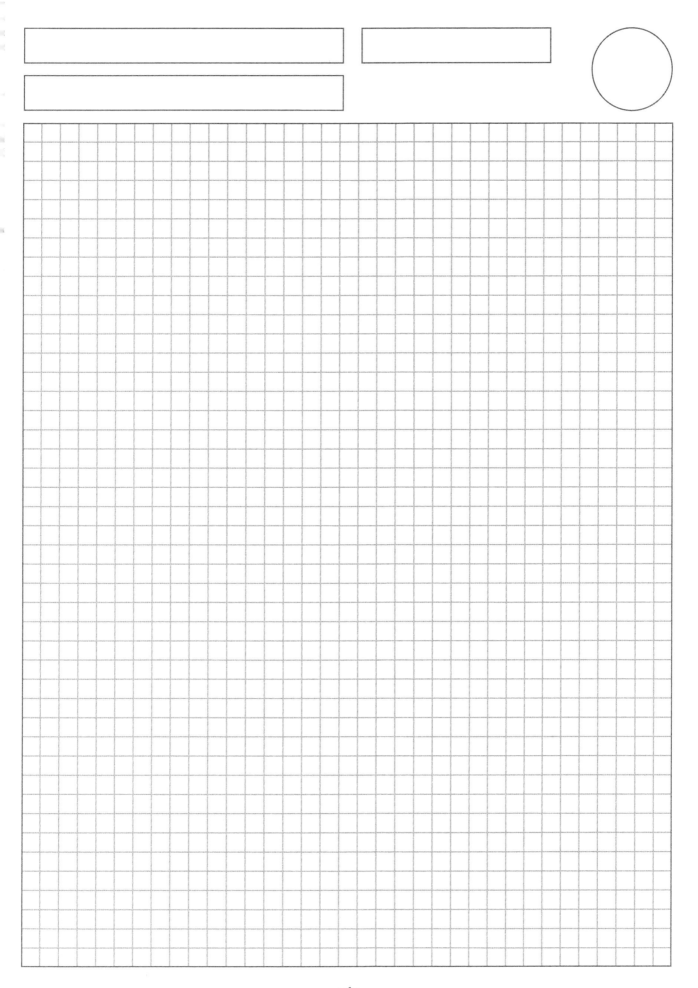

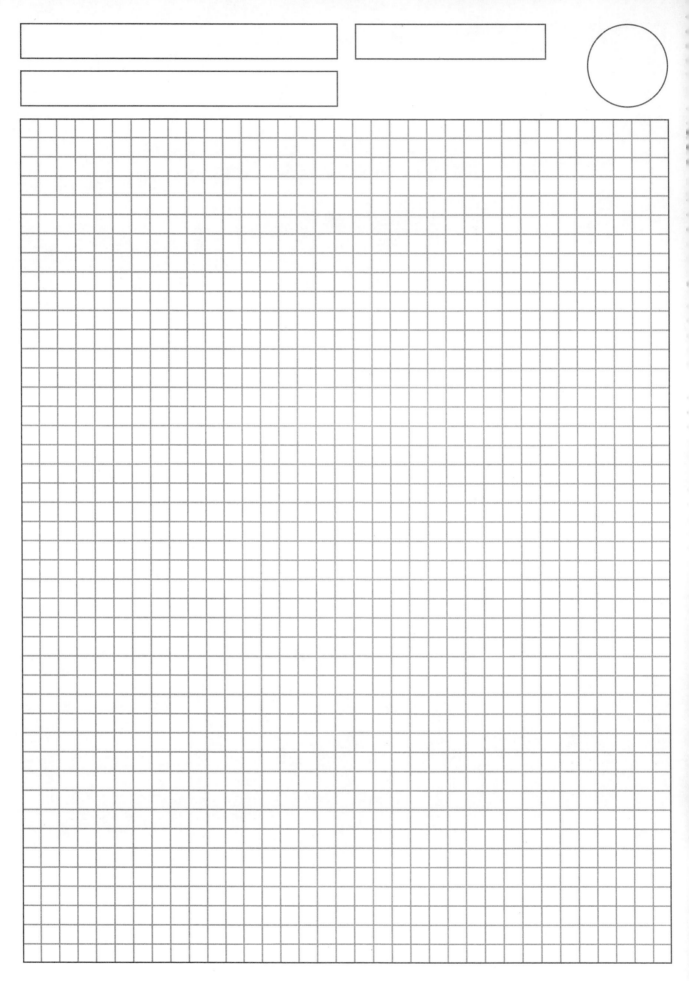

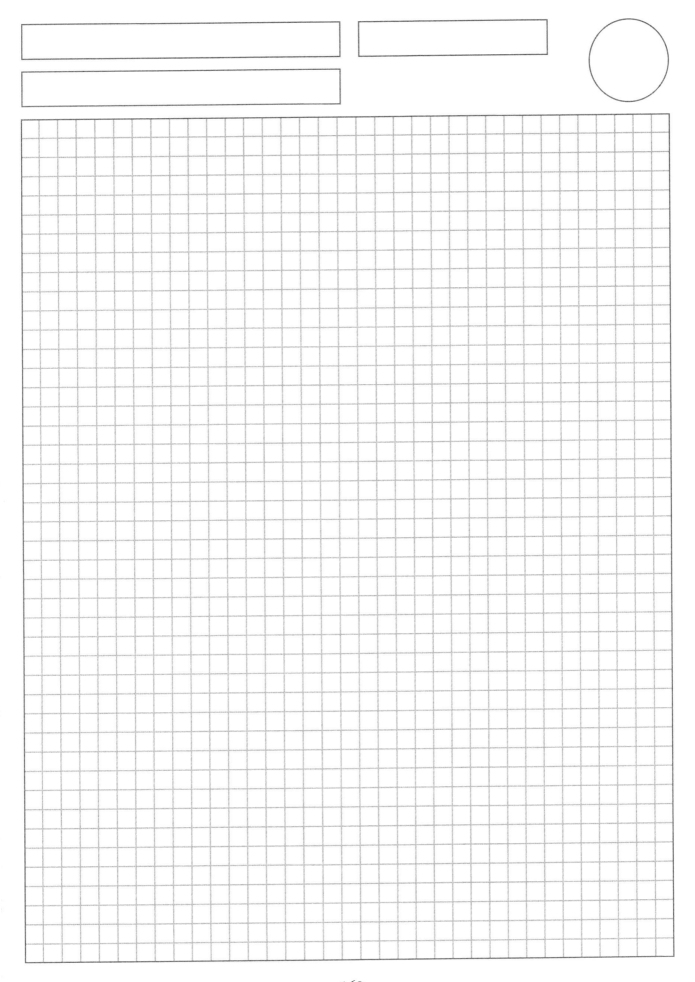

S5

SECTOR 5

SECTOR 5
FIRST RESPONDER OVERVIEW

THREAT ASSESSMENT SECTOR OVERVIEW

Sector:

Date:

Prepared by:

Situation:

Sector Overview:

Note: Make sure you print out map and directions to pertinent police precincts.

Police Departments:

PD Contact Information:

PD Response Times:

Crime Level:

Possible Threat Level:

Known Terror Threats:

Known Criminal Threats:

Note: Make sure you print out map and directions to all trauma centers. Always make the effort to proceed to a level 1 trauma center if the injury is life threatening.

Trauma Centers:

Trauma Center Level (I, II, III):

Response Times:

Weather Conditions:

Spring   Summer   Fall   Winter

RESPONSE RESOURCES
(Specific To This Sector)

Federal

- Department of Homeland Security (DHS)

  _____

  _____

- Federal Emergency Management Agency (FEMA)

  _____

  _____

- Federal Bureau of Investigation (FBI)

  _____

  _____

- Environmental Protection Agency (EPA)

  _____

  _____

- Health and Human Services (HHS)

  _____

  _____

State/Regional

- Emergency Management

  _____

  _____

- State Emergency Operations Center

  _____

  _____

- State Police

  _____

  _____

- National Guard

  _____

  _____

- Joint Terrorism Task Forces (JTTF)

  _____

  _____

> *Note: Make sure you print out map and directions to pertinent police precincts. Always make the effort to proceed to a level 1 trauma center if the injury is life threatening.*

Local First Responders

- Police

  _____

  _____

  - Special Weapons And Tactics (SWAT) Teams

    _____

  - Explosive Ordnance Disposal (EOD)

    _____

- Police

  _____

  _____

  - Special Weapons And Tactics (SWAT) Teams

    _____

  - Explosive Ordnance Disposal (EOD)

    _____

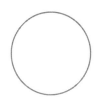

- Police

  _____

  _____

  - Special Weapons And Tactics (SWAT) Teams

    _____

  - Explosive Ordnance Disposal (EOD)

    _____

- Fire

  _____

  _____

  - Rescue / Emergency Medical Services

    _____

  - Hazardous Materials Response Teams

    _____

- Emergency Management

  _____

  _____

Note: Make sure you print out map and directions to all trauma centers. Always make the effort to proceed to a level 1 trauma center if the injury is life threatening.

Hospitals

- Level I Trauma Center

  _____

  _____

- Level II Trauma Center

  _____

  _____

RESPONSE RESOURCES (continued)
(Specific To This Sector)

- Urgent Care

  _____

  _____

- Other Medical Center

  _____

  _____

- Other Medical Center

  _____

  _____

Known Threats

- Crime

  _____

  _____

  _____

  _____

  _____

  _____

- Terror

  _____

  _____

  _____

  _____

  _____

  _____

Note: If this sector is a special event or a vacation, take a screen shot
of the weather report and attach here

SECTOR 5
VULNERABILITY MITIGATION

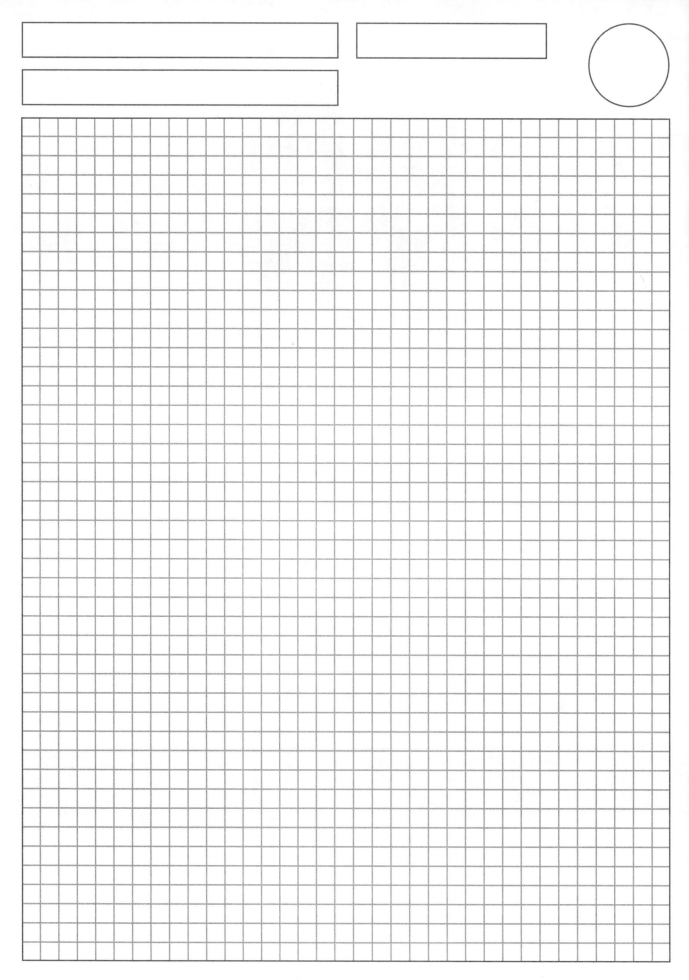

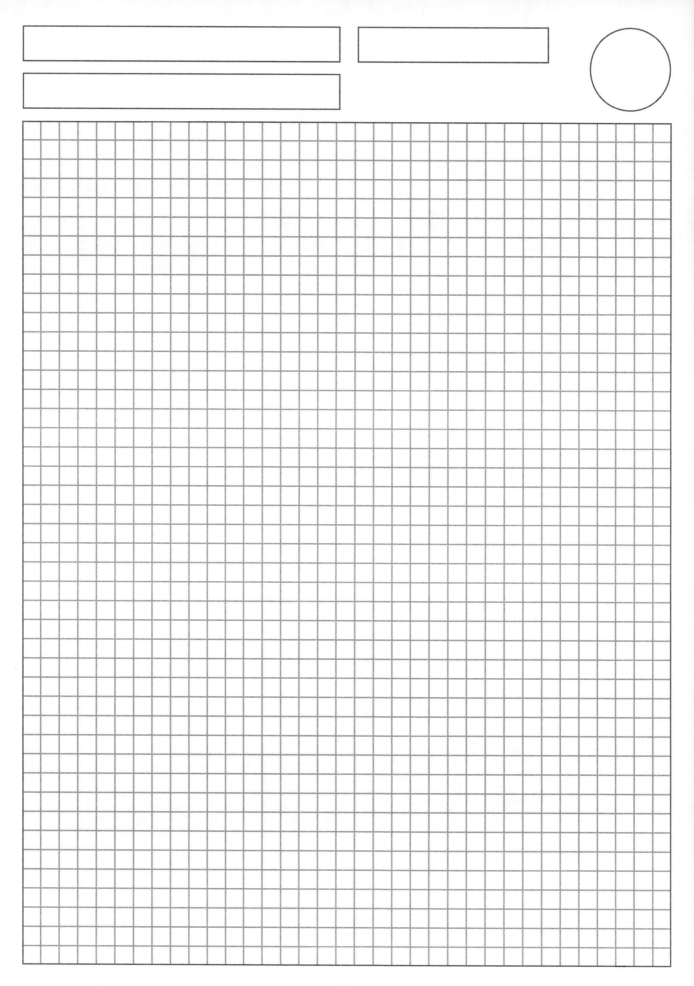

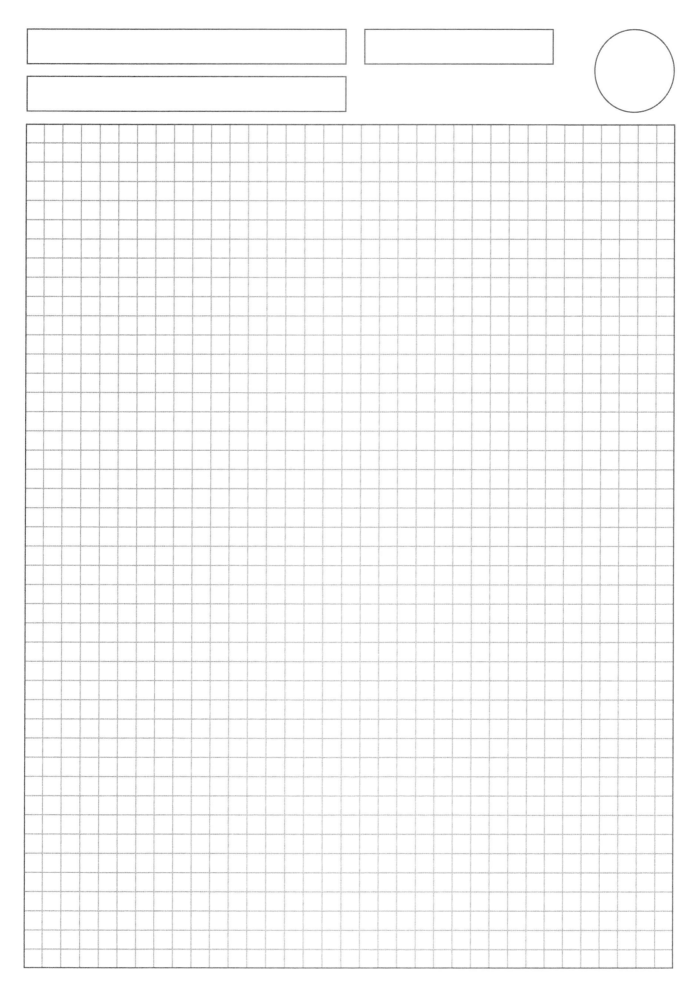

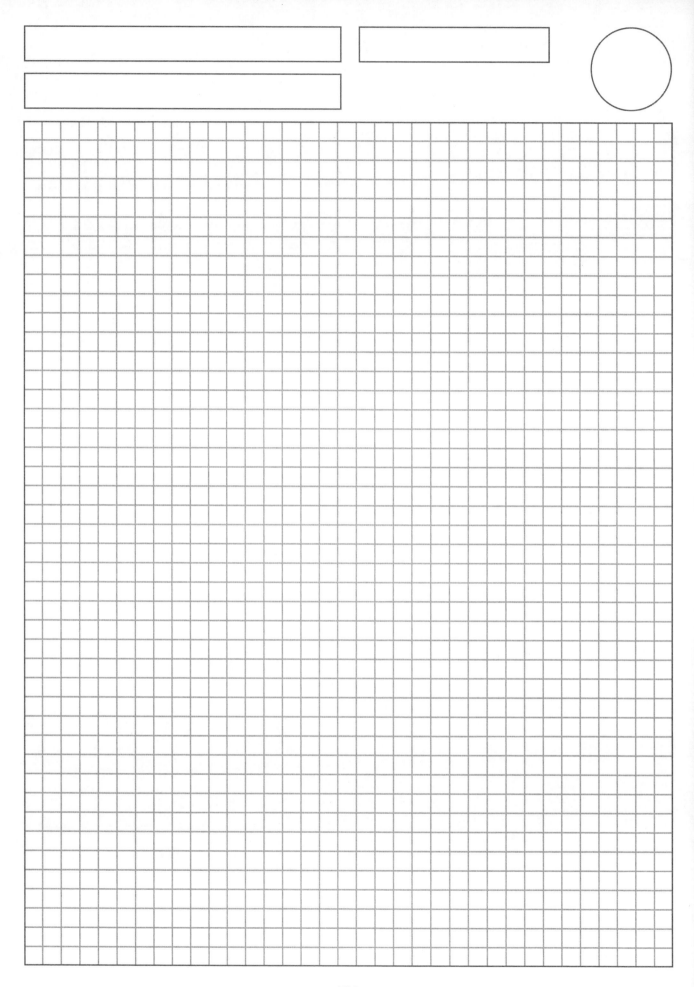

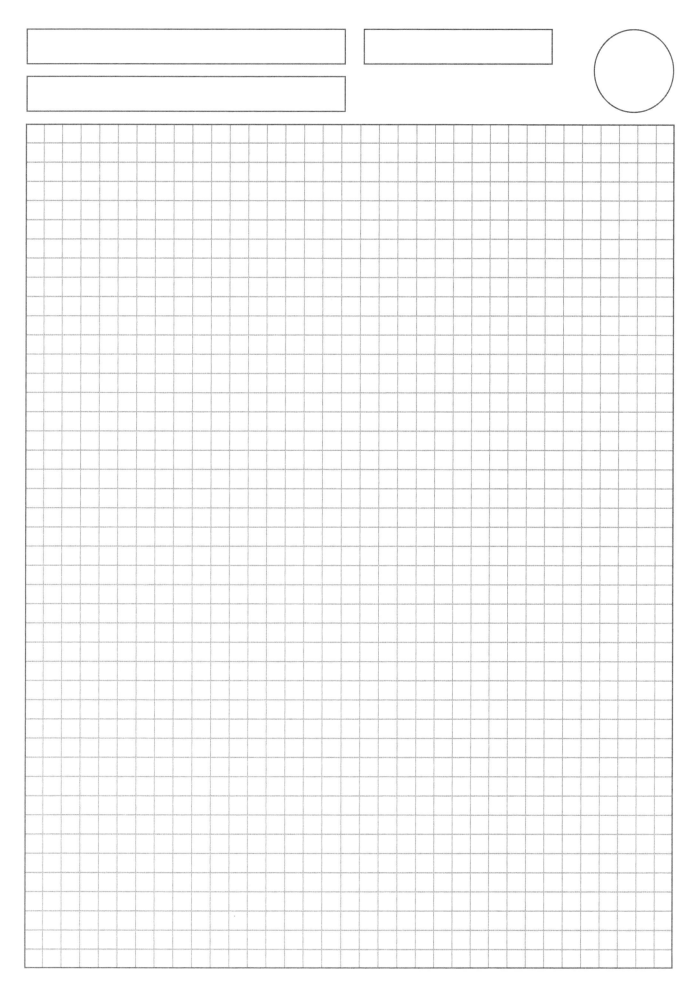

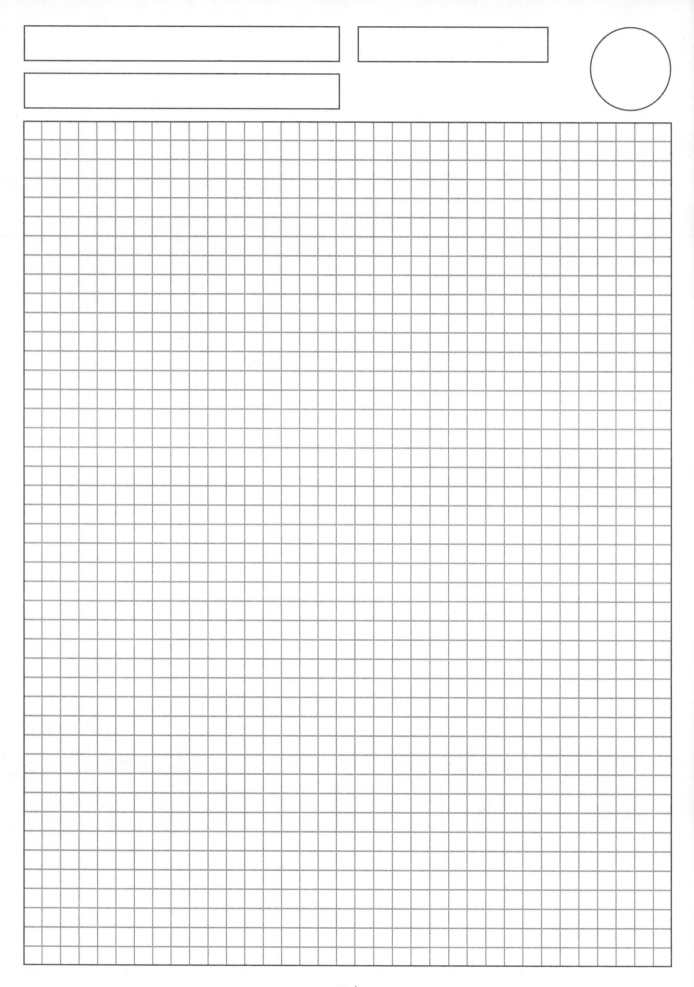

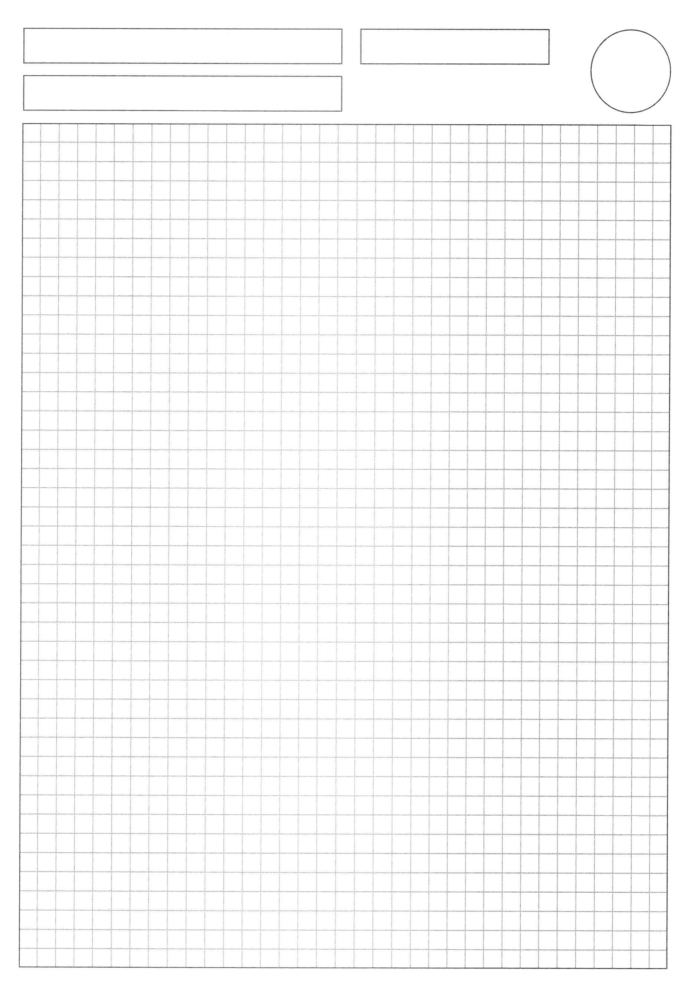

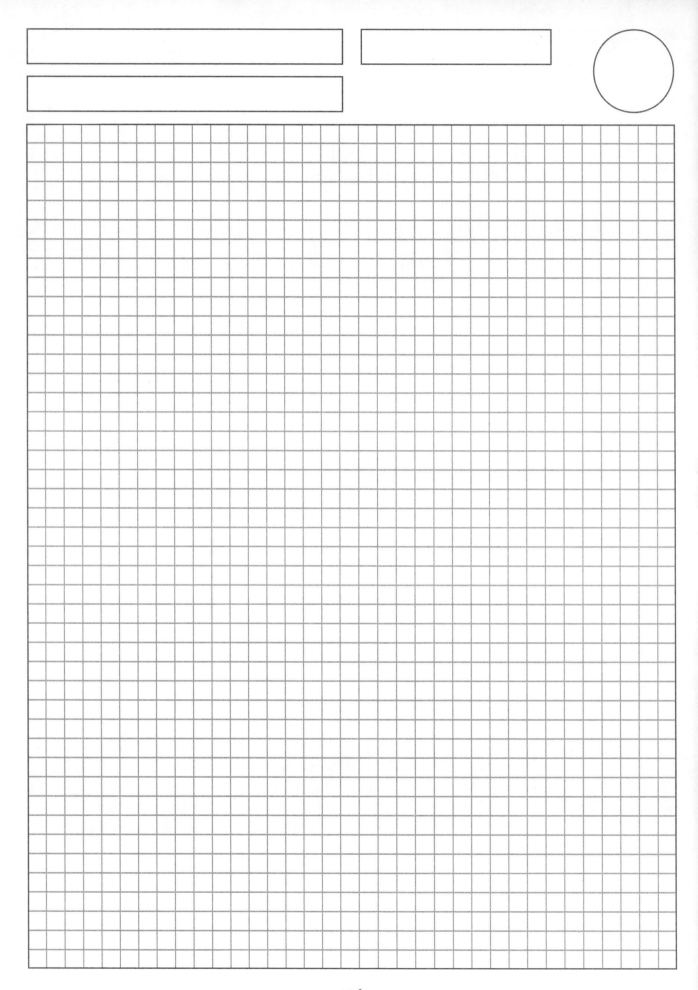

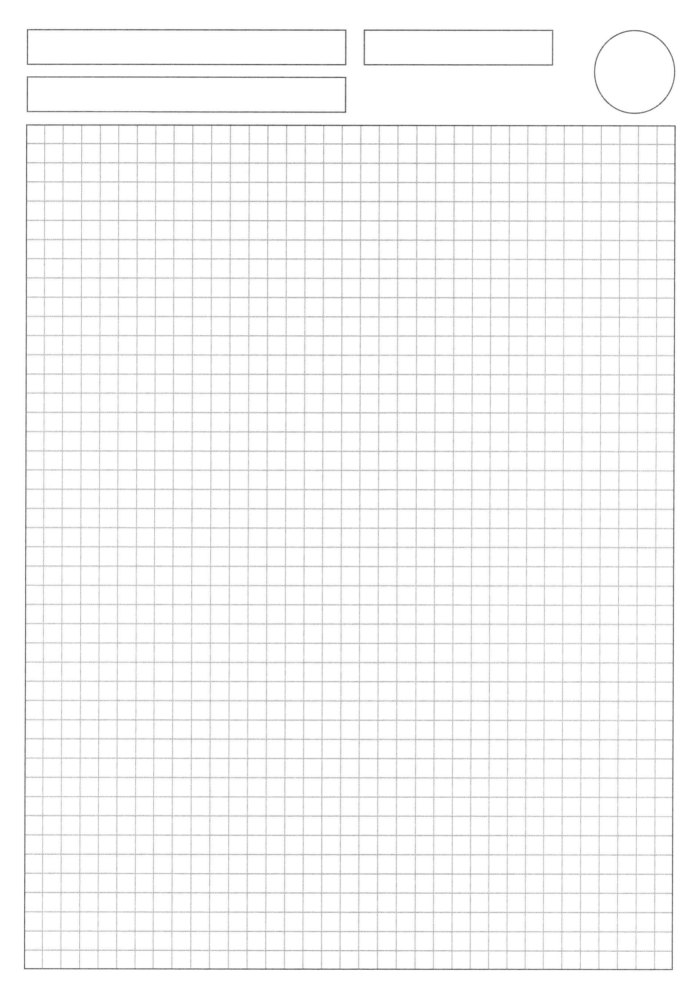

SECTOR 5

IMPLEMENTATION OF PHYSICAL

DEFENSE AND TECHNOLOGY

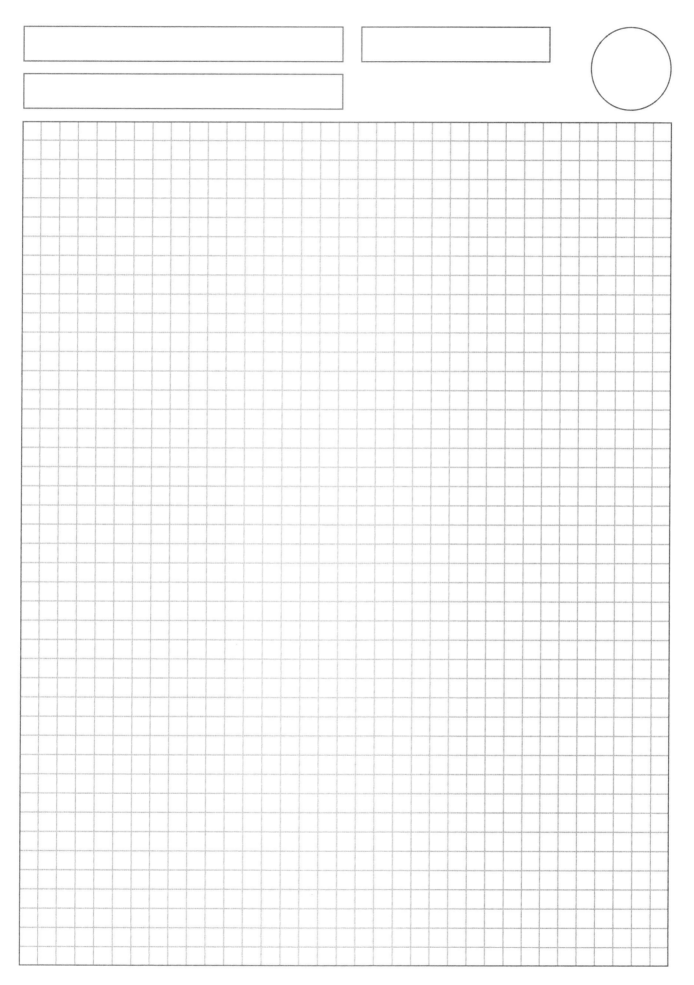

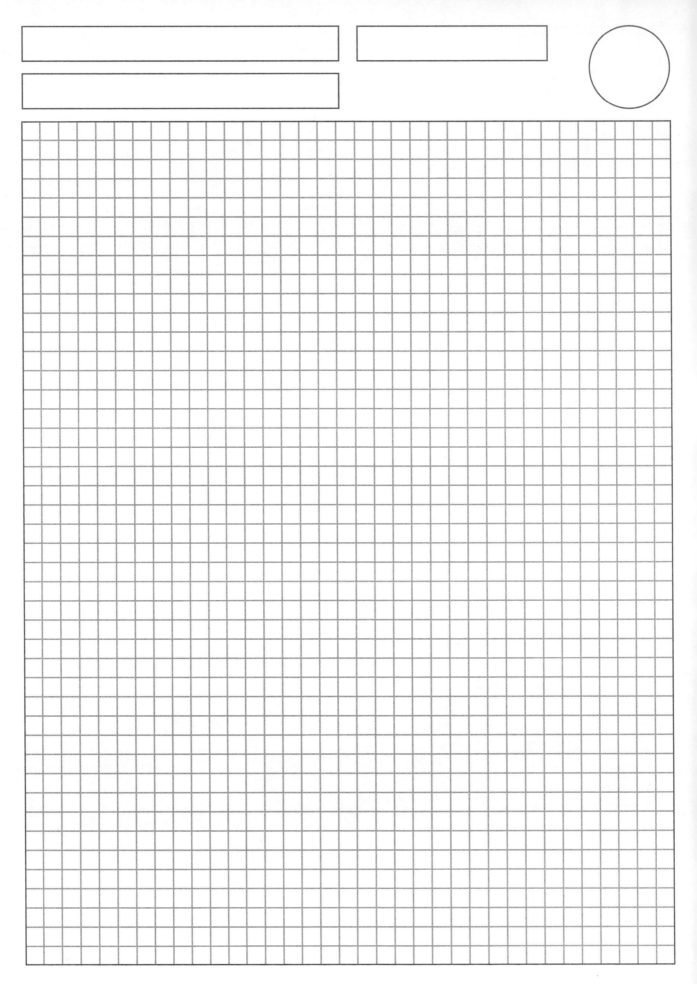

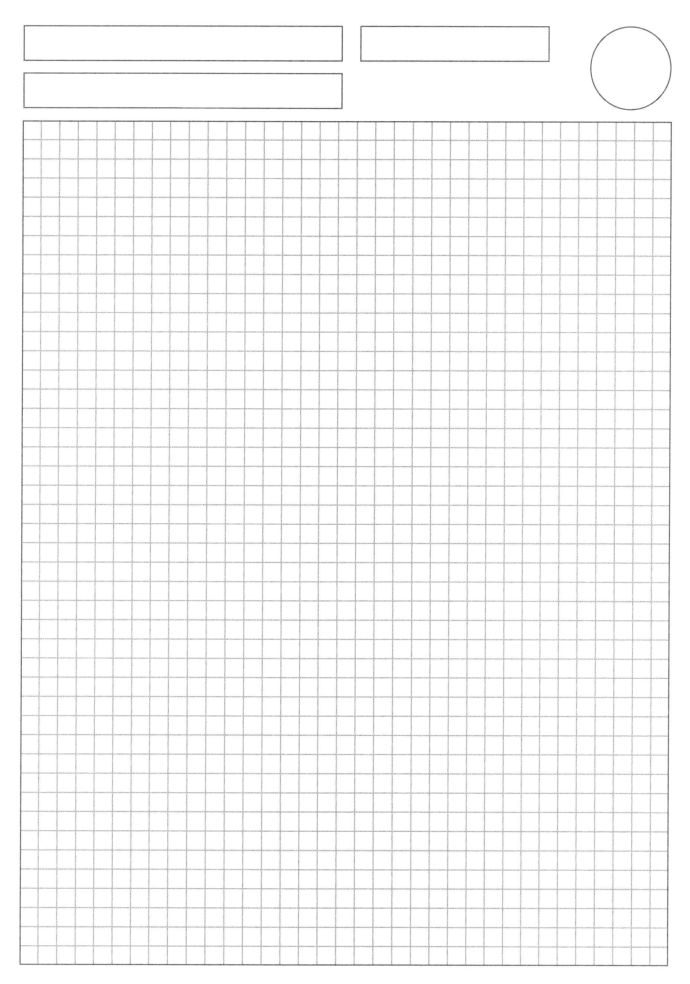

SECTOR 5
BEHAVIORS AND ATTACK
INDICATORS

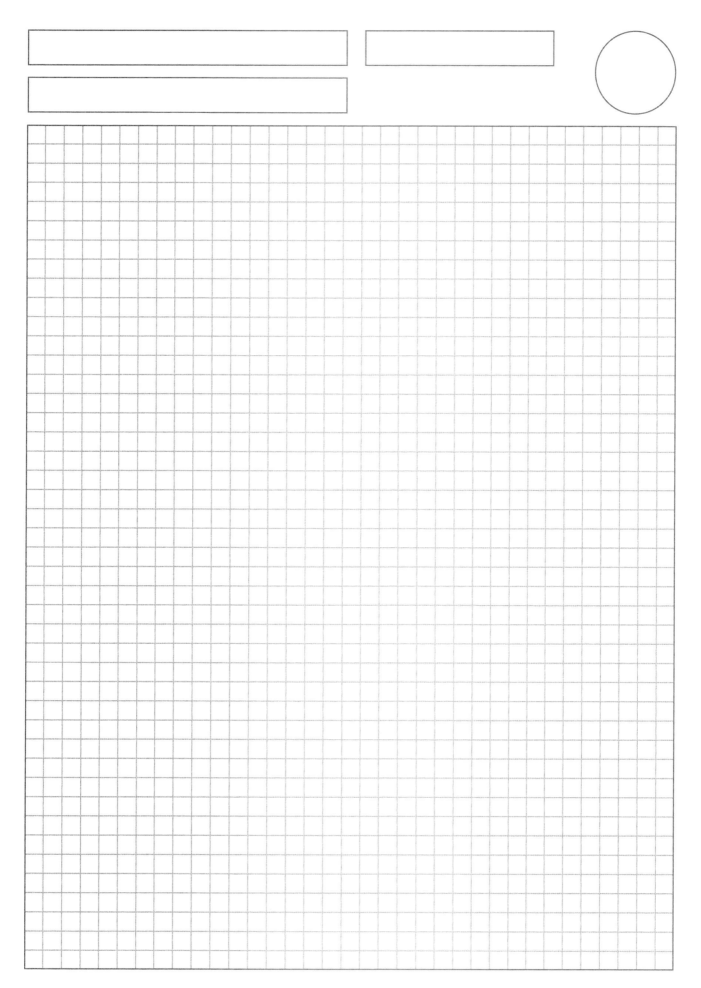

SECTOR 5
SHARED THREATS

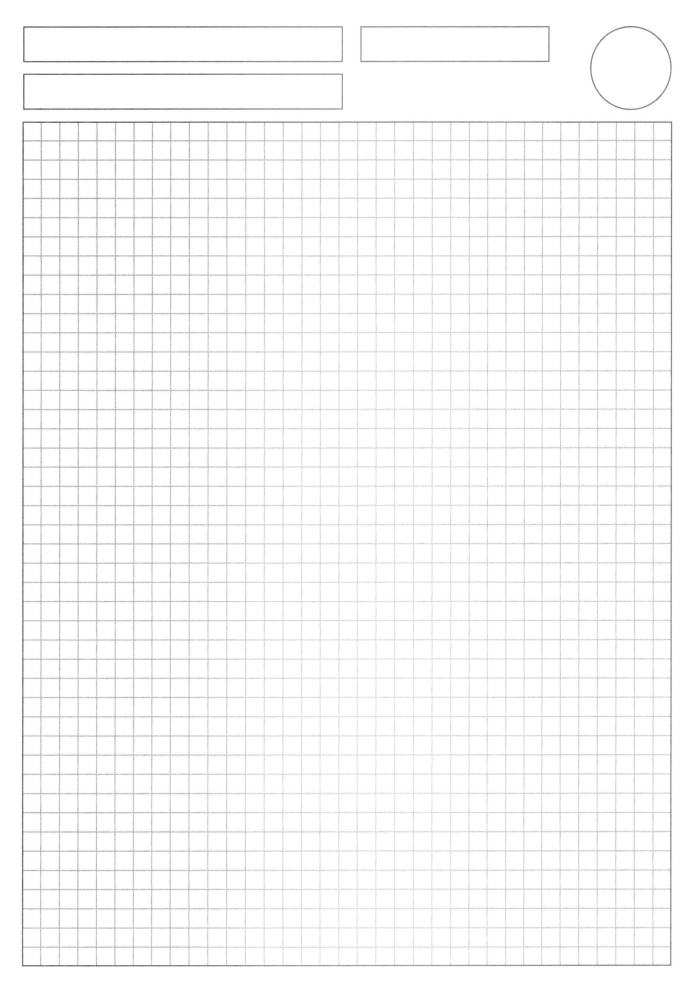

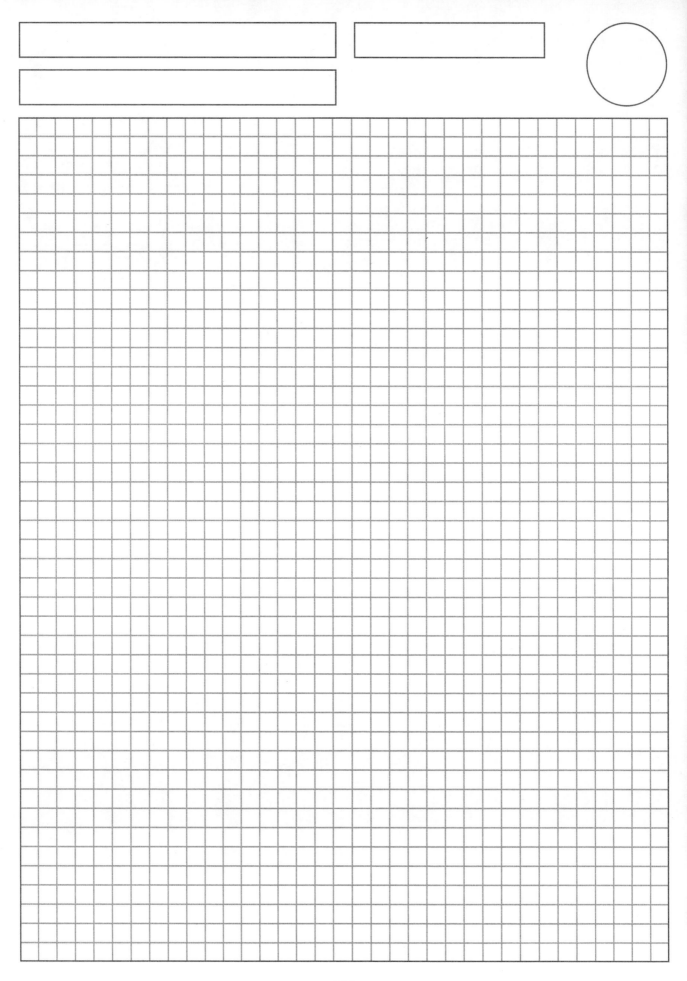

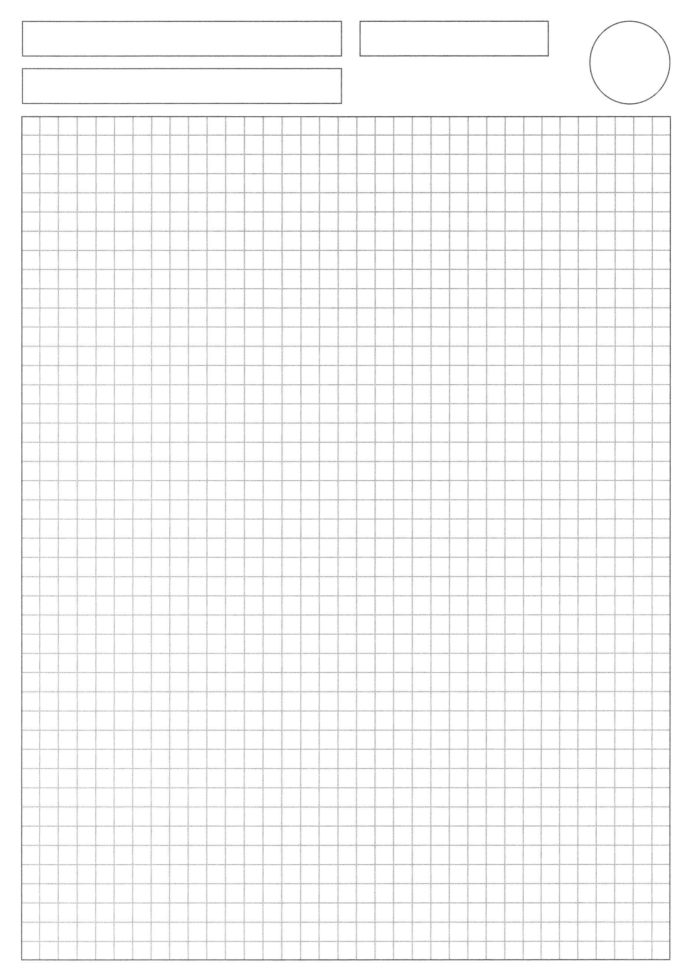

SECTOR 5

TACTICAL PLANS OF ACTION

(WHERE VULNERABILITIES CANNOT BE MITIGATED)

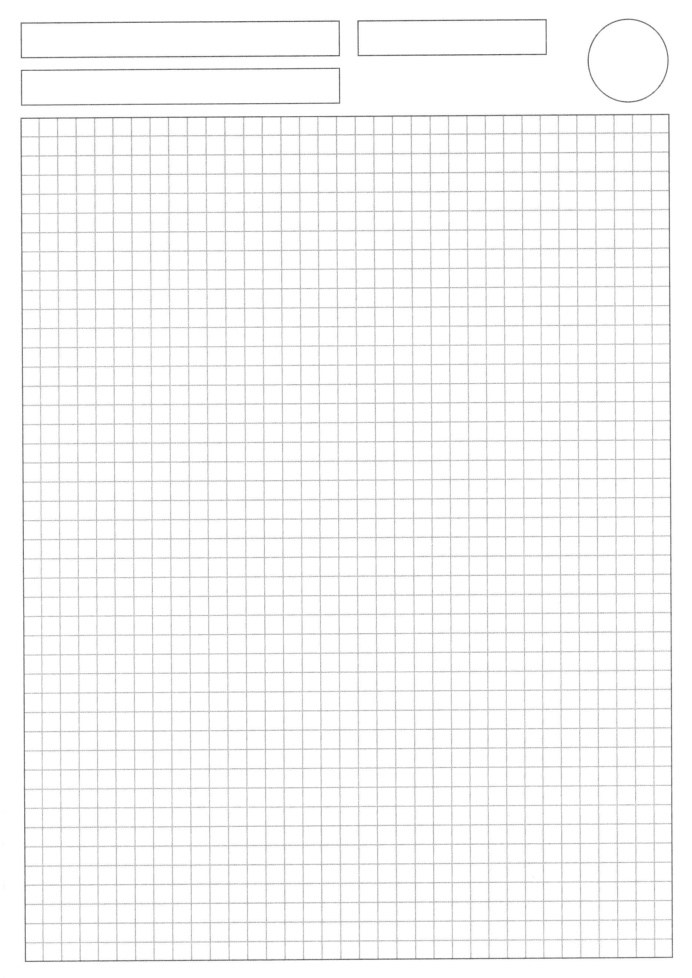

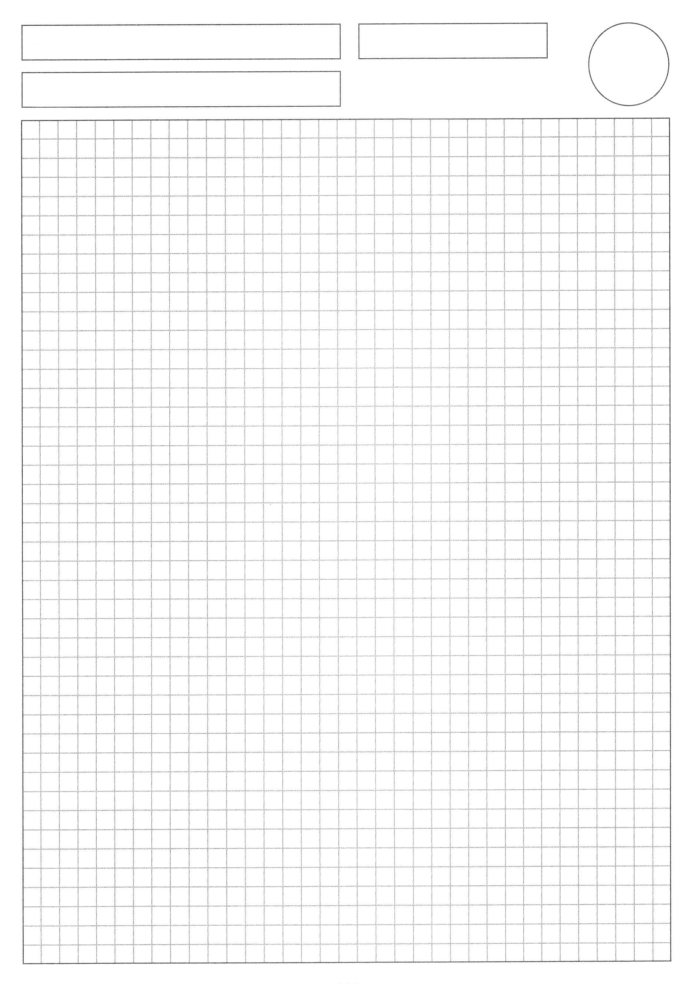

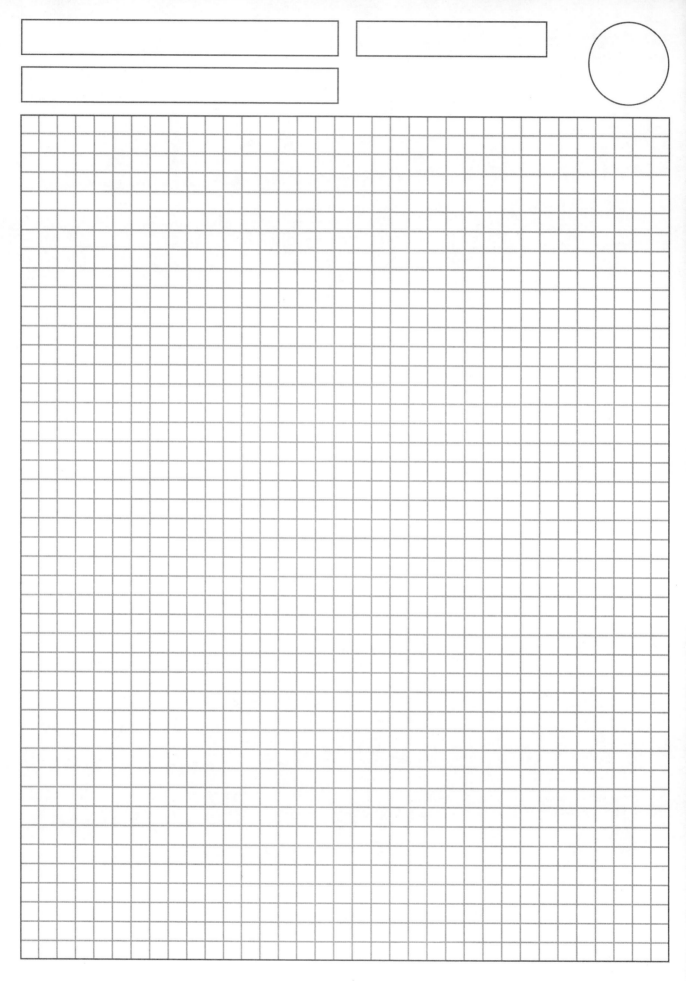

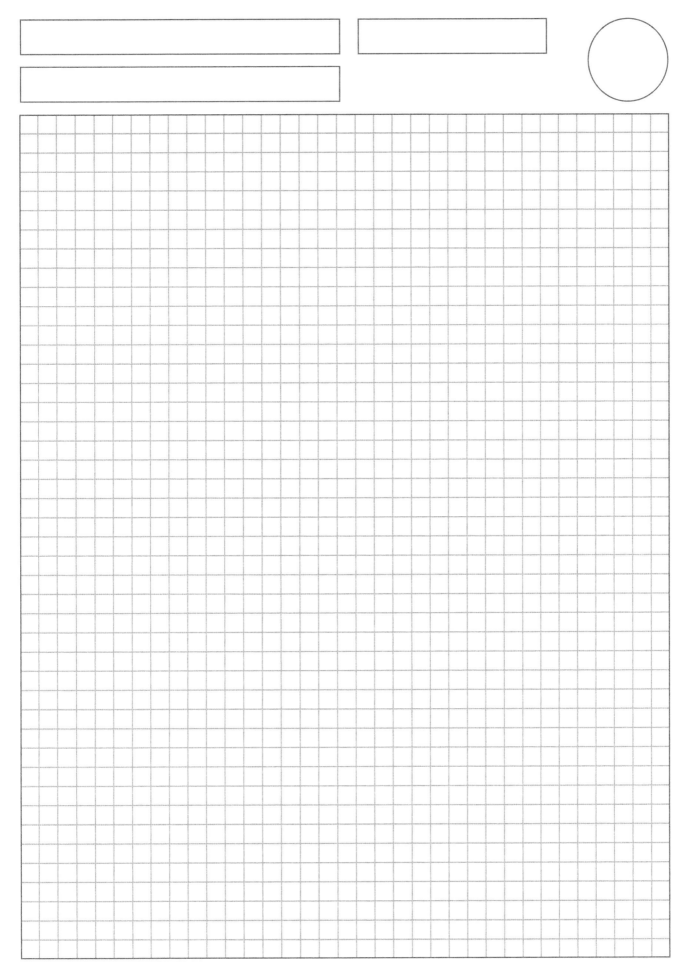

S6

SECTOR 6

SECTOR 6
FIRST RESPONDER OVERVIEW

THREAT ASSESSMENT SECTOR OVERVIEW

Sector:

Date:

Prepared by:

Situation:

Sector Overview:

Note: Make sure you print out map and directions to pertinent police precincts.

Police Departments:

PD Contact Information:

PD Response Times:

Crime Level:

Possible Threat Level:

Known Terror Threats:

Known Criminal Threats:

Note: Make sure you print out map and directions to all trauma centers. Always make the effort to proceed to a level 1 trauma center if the injury is life threatening.

Trauma Centers:

Trauma Center Level (I, II, III):

Response Times:

Weather Conditions:

Spring   Summer   Fall   Winter

RESPONSE RESOURCES
(Specific To This Sector)

Federal

- Department of Homeland Security (DHS)

  _____

  _____

- Federal Emergency Management Agency (FEMA)

  _____

  _____

- Federal Bureau of Investigation (FBI)

  _____

  _____

- Environmental Protection Agency (EPA)

  _____

  _____

- Health and Human Services (HHS)

  _____

  _____

State/Regional

- Emergency Management

  _____

  _____

- State Emergency Operations Center

  _____

  _____

- State Police

  _____

  _____

- National Guard

  _____

  _____

- Joint Terrorism Task Forces (JTTF)

  _____

  _____

> *Note: Make sure you print out map and directions to pertinent police precincts. Always make the effort to proceed to a level 1 trauma center if the injury is life threatening.*

Local First Responders

- Police

  _____

  _____

  - Special Weapons And Tactics (SWAT) Teams

    _____

  - Explosive Ordnance Disposal (EOD)

    _____

- Police

  _____

  _____

  - Special Weapons And Tactics (SWAT) Teams

    _____

  - Explosive Ordnance Disposal (EOD)

    _____

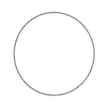

- Police

  _____

  _____

  - Special Weapons And Tactics (SWAT) Teams

    _____

  - Explosive Ordnance Disposal (EOD)

    _____

- Fire

  _____

  _____

  - Rescue / Emergency Medical Services

    _____

  - Hazardous Materials Response Teams

    _____

- Emergency Management

  _____

  _____

Note: Make sure you print out map and directions to all trauma centers. Always make the effort to proceed to a level 1 trauma center if the injury is life threatening.

Hospitals

- Level I Trauma Center

  _____

  _____

- Level II Trauma Center

  _____

  _____

RESPONSE RESOURCES (continued)
(Specific To This Sector)

- Urgent Care

  _____

  _____

- Other Medical Center

  _____

  _____

- Other Medical Center

  _____

  _____

Known Threats

- Crime

  _____

  _____

  _____

  _____

  _____

  _____

- Terror

  _____

  _____

  _____

  _____

  _____

  _____

> _Note: If this sector is a special event or a vacation, take a screen shot of the weather report and attach here_

SECTOR 6
VULNERABILITY MITIGATION

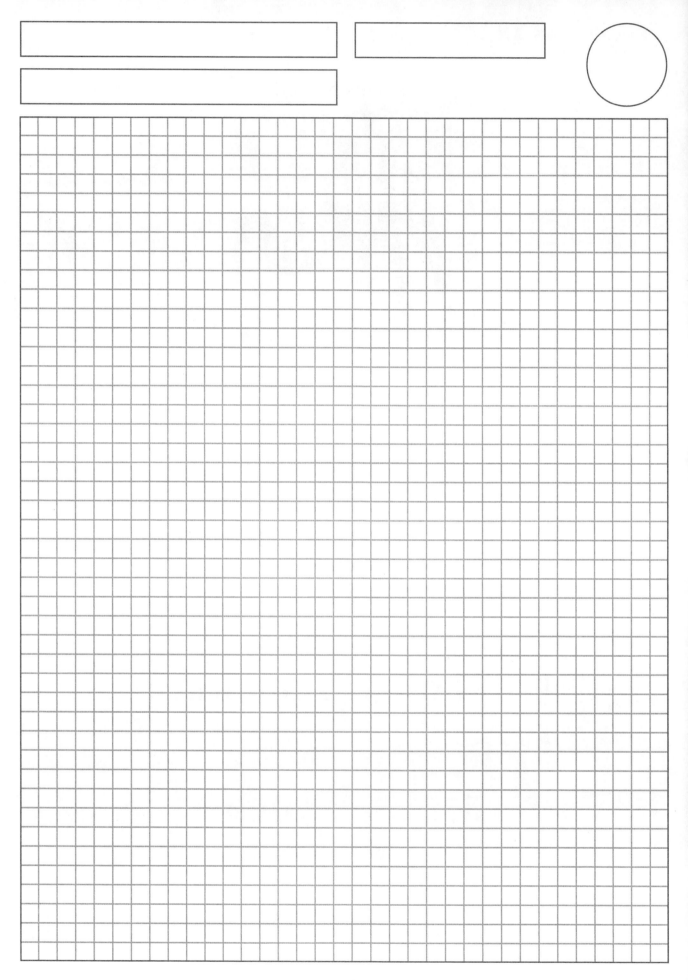

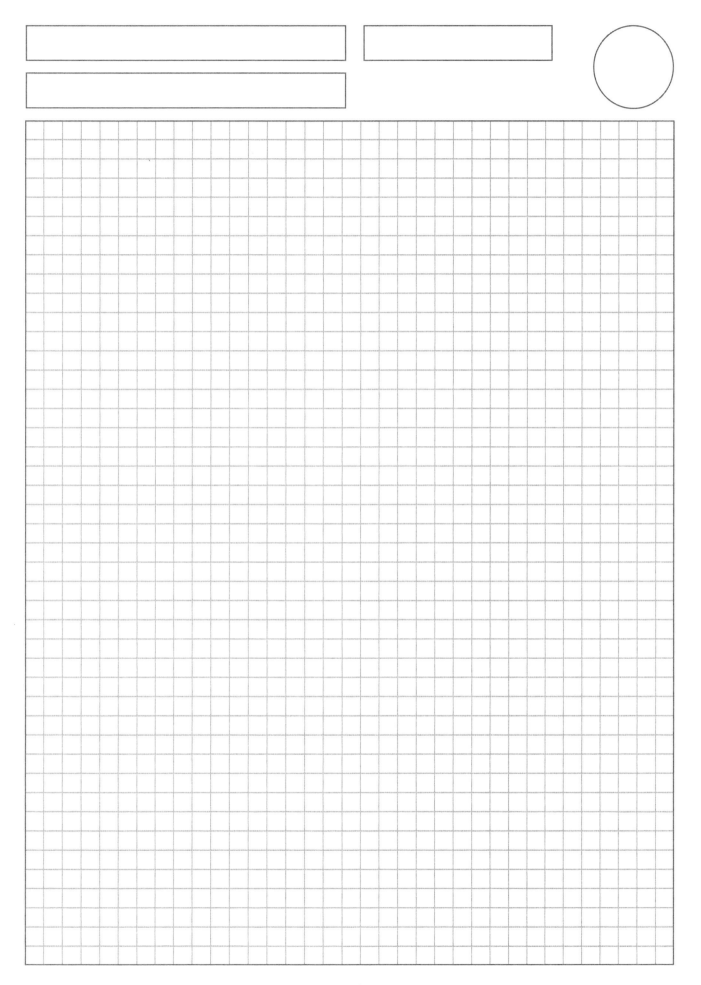

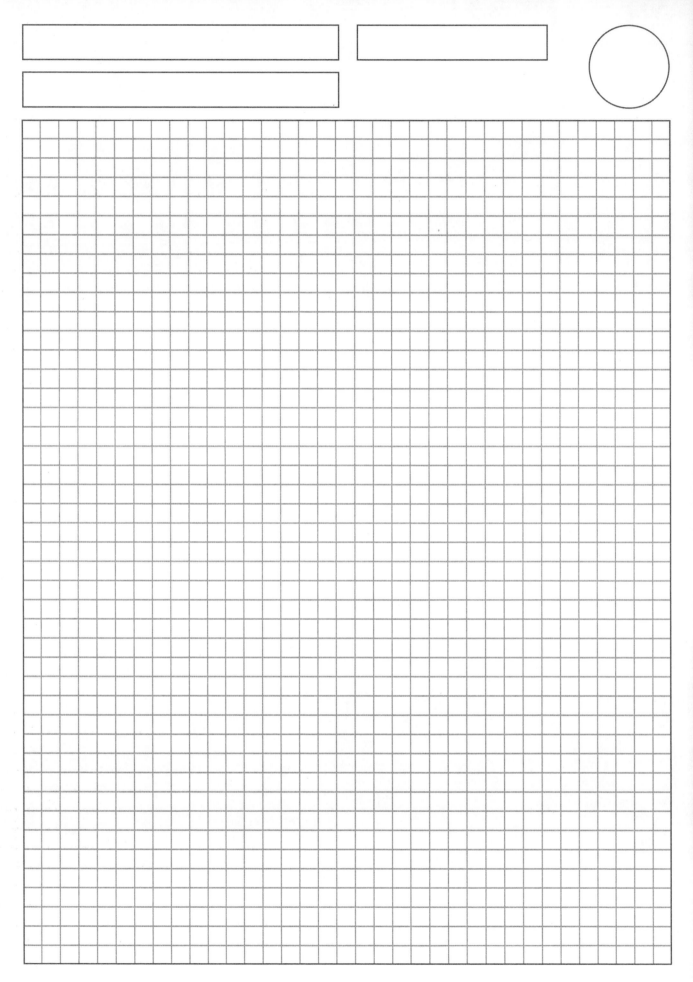

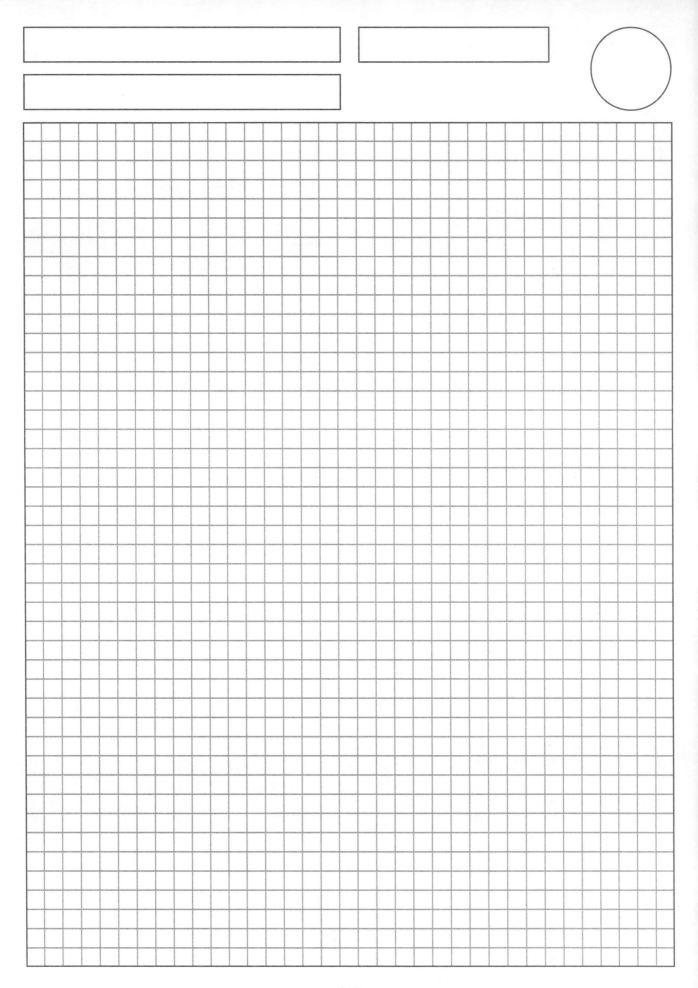

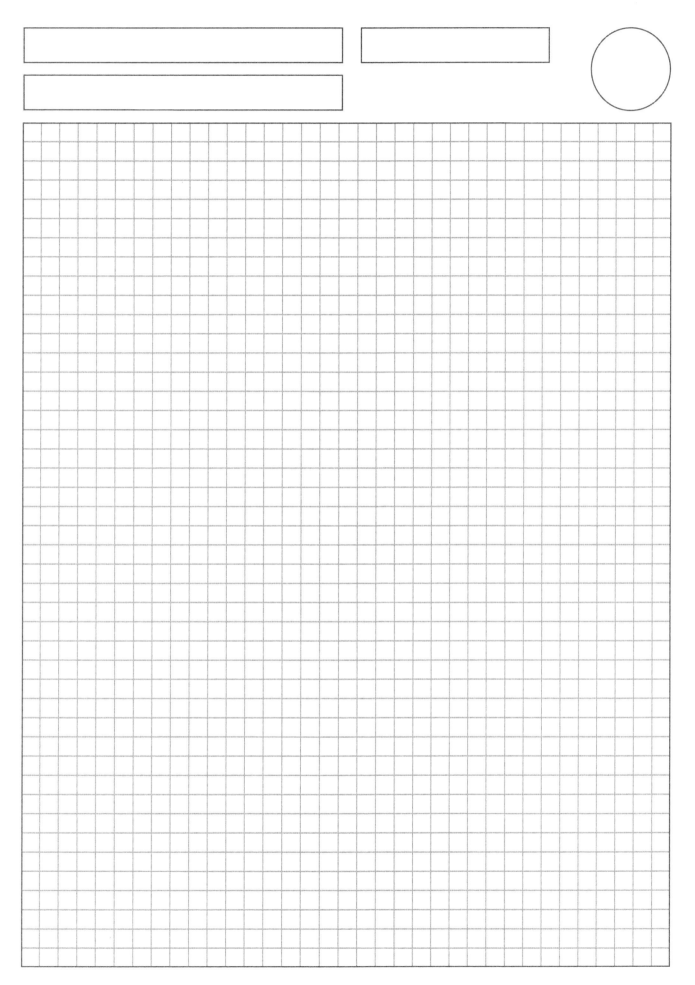

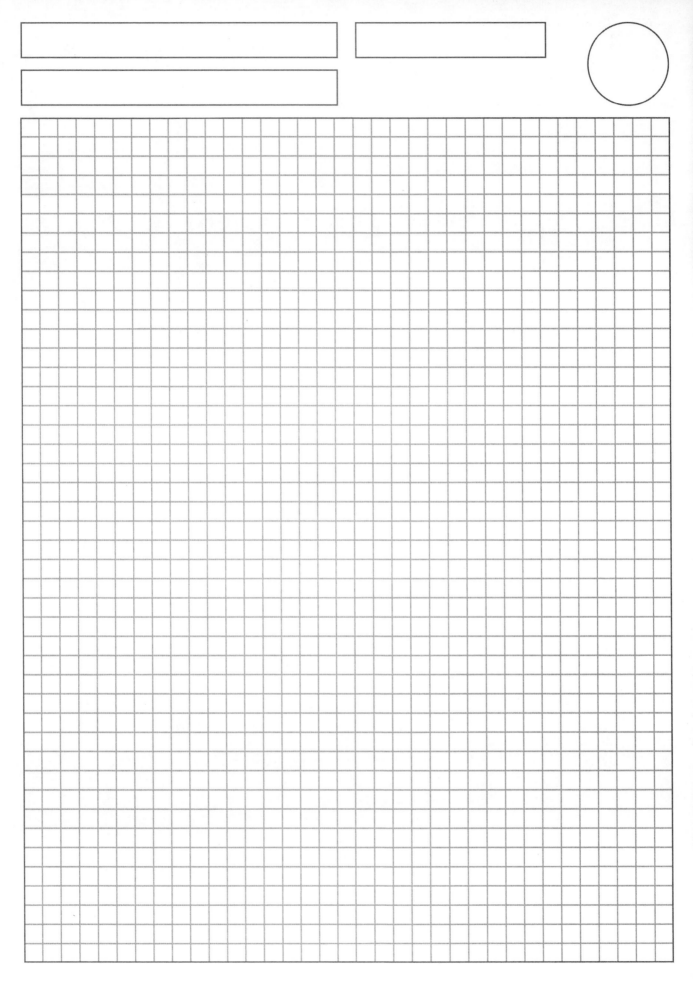

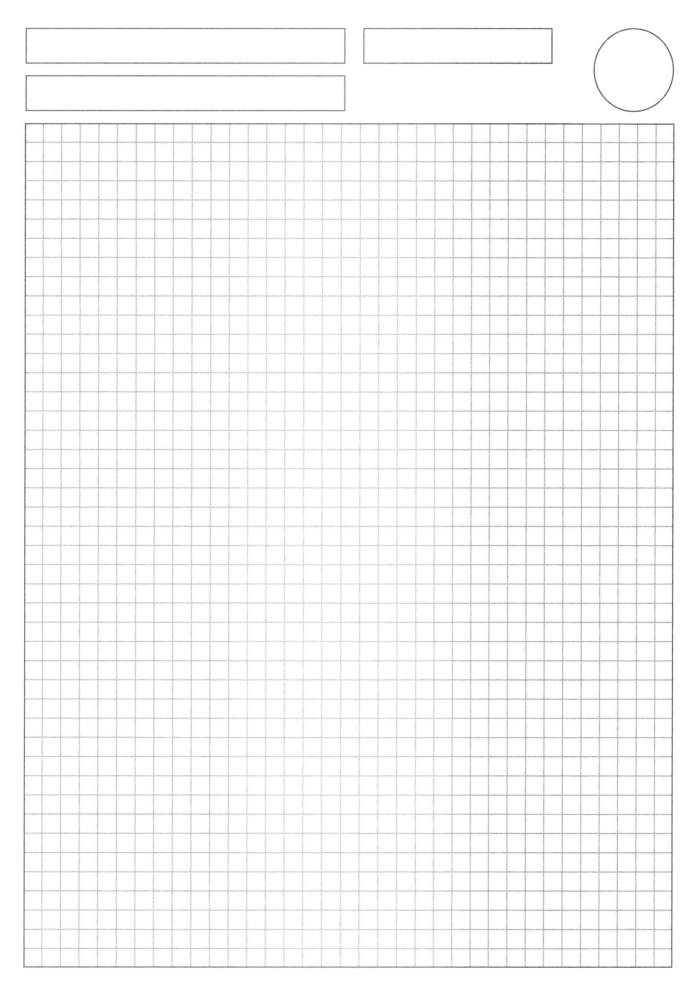

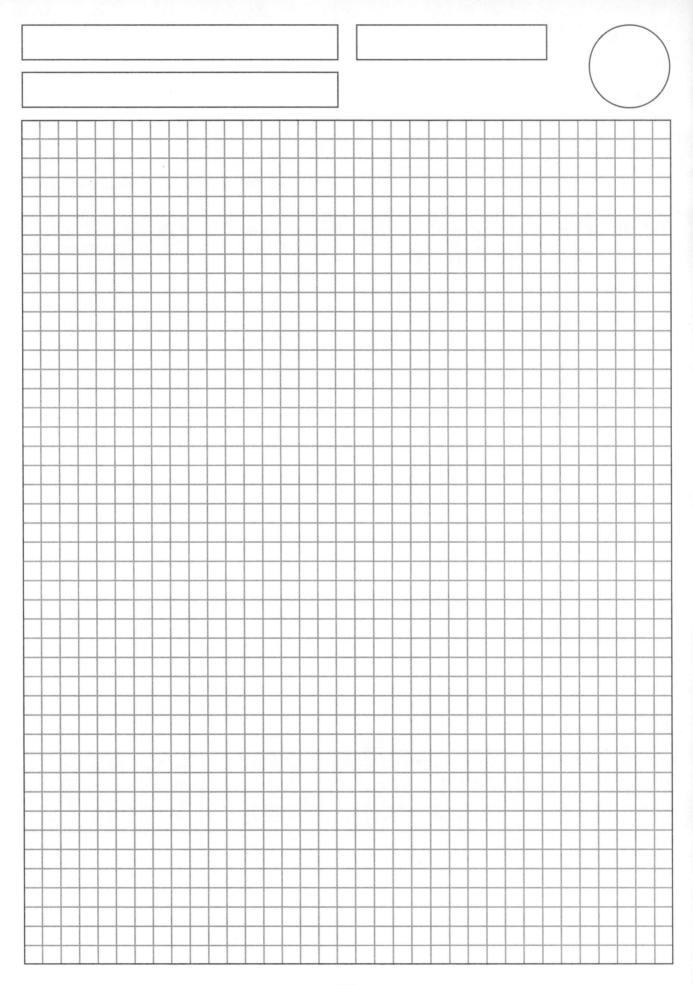

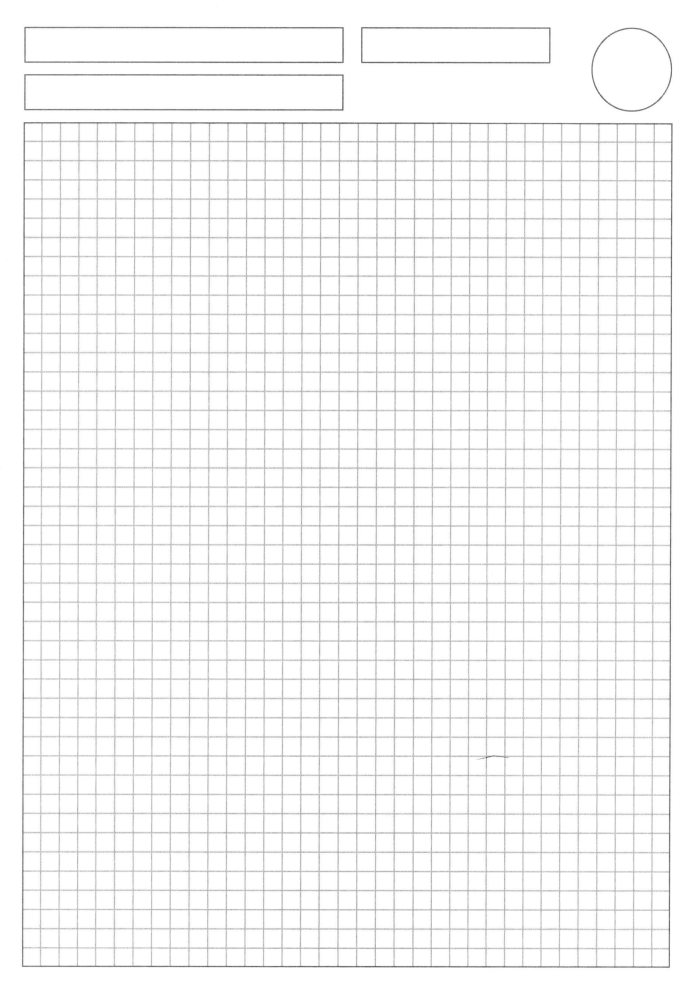

SECTOR 6

IMPLEMENTATION OF PHYSICAL

DEFENSE AND TECHNOLOGY

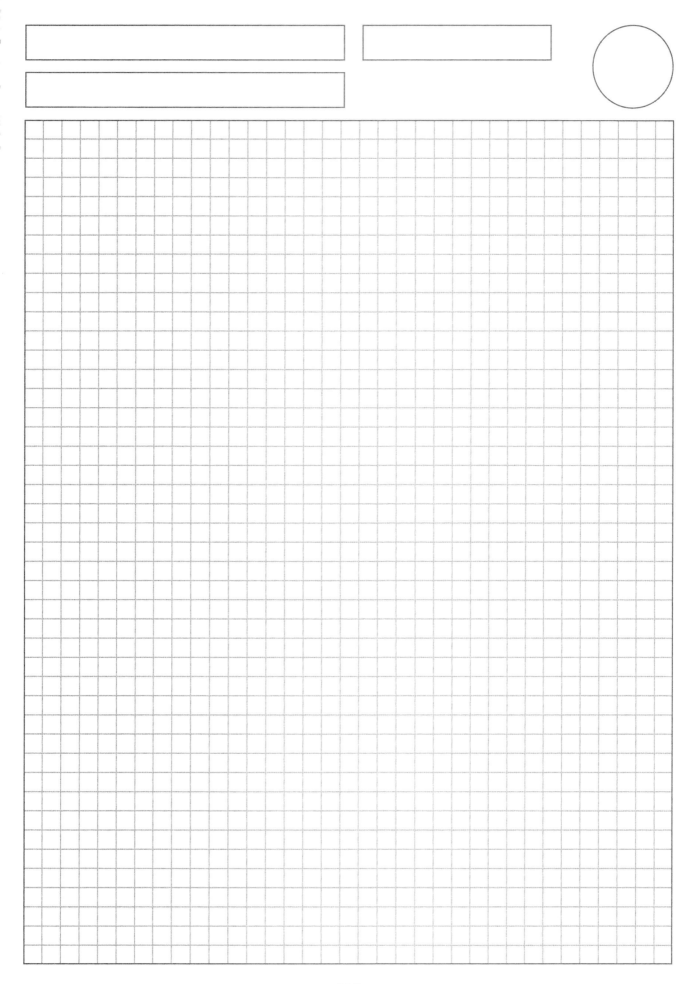

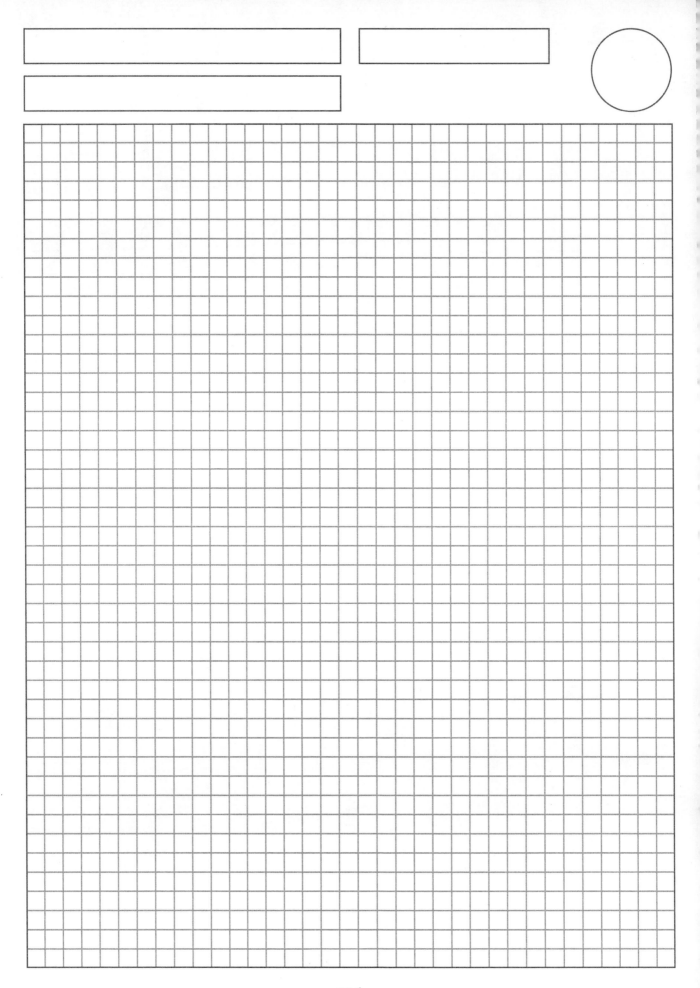

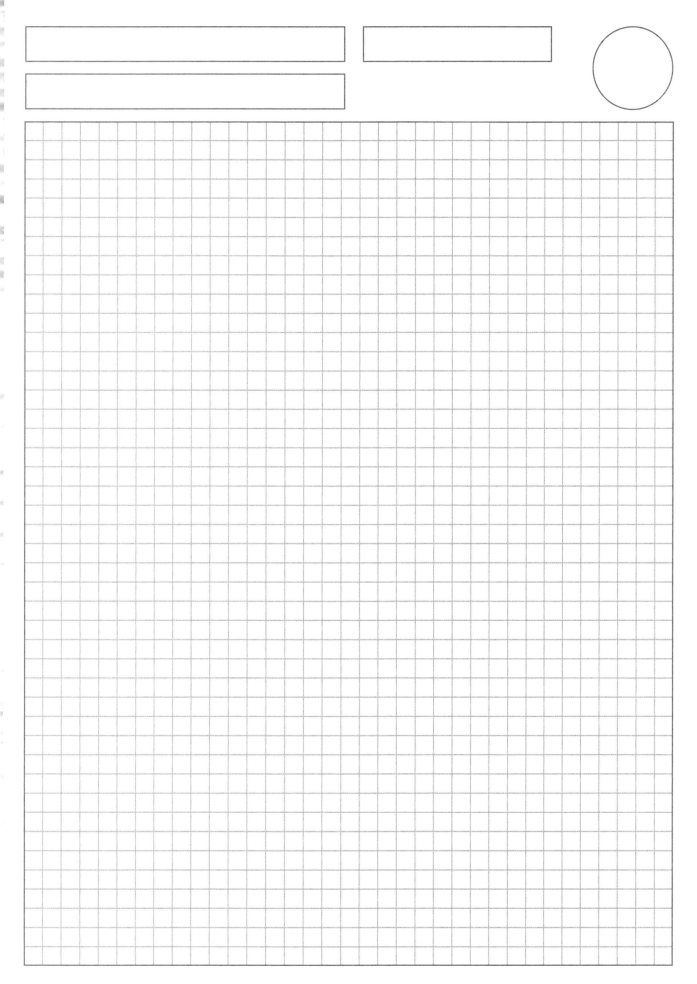

SECTOR 6
BEHAVIORS AND ATTACK
INDICATORS

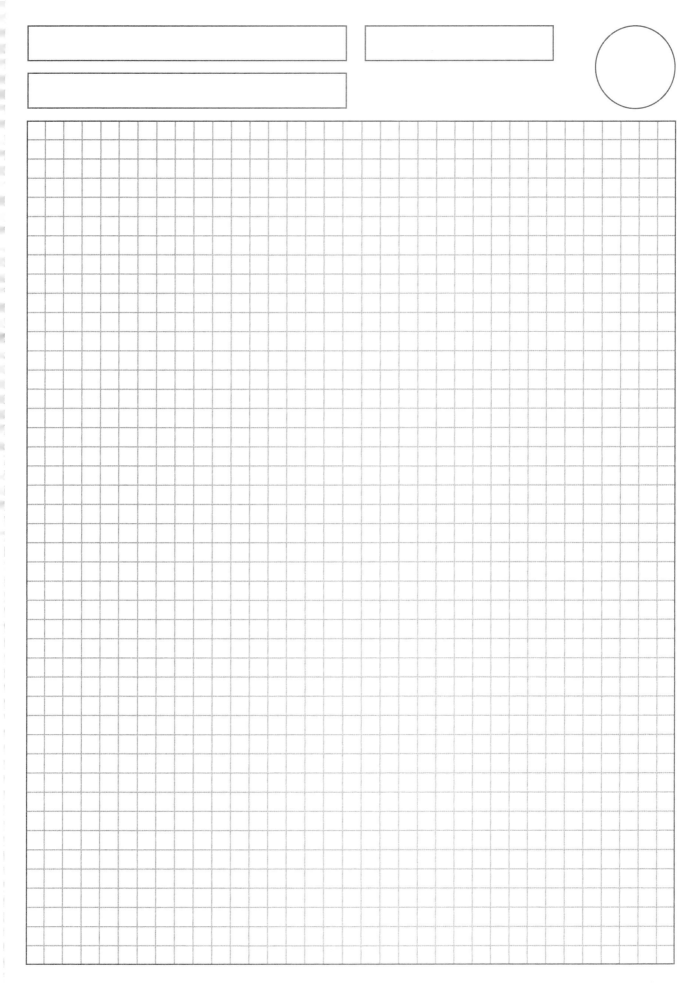

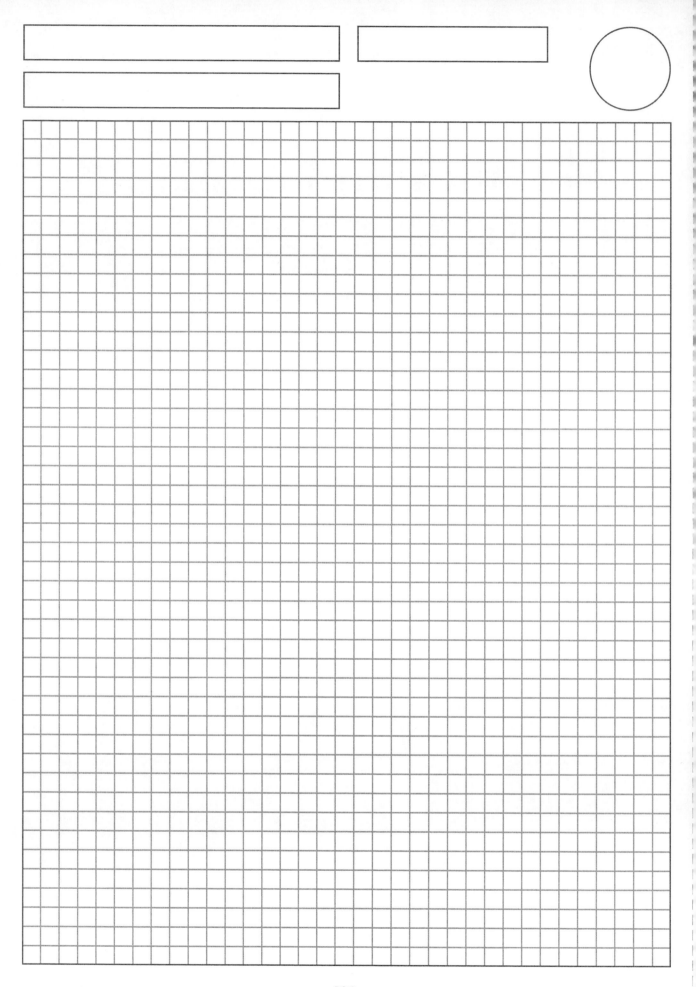

SECTOR 6
SHARED THREATS

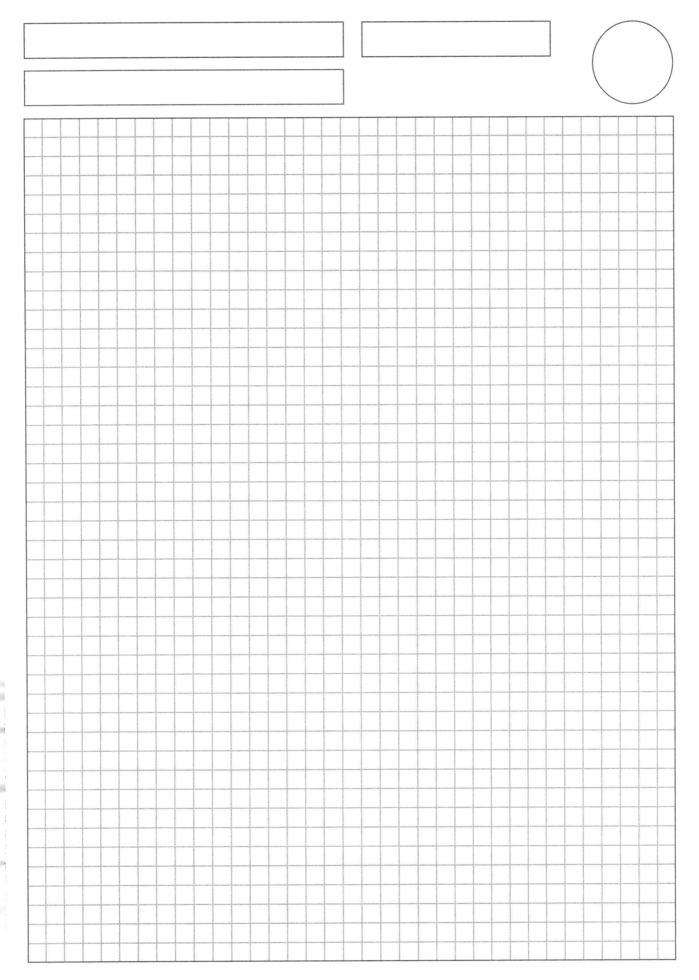

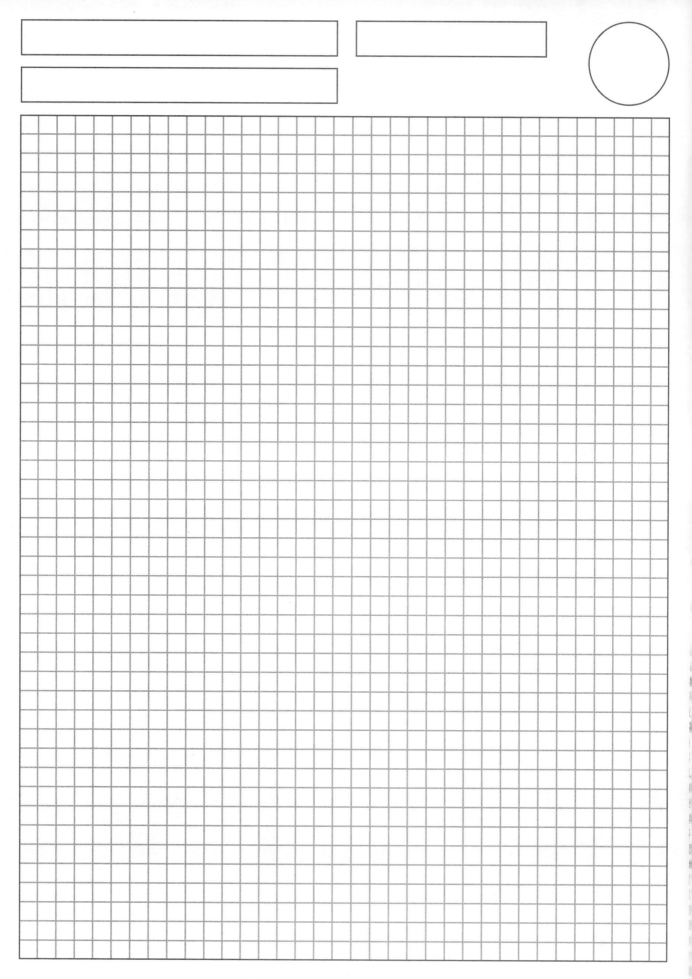

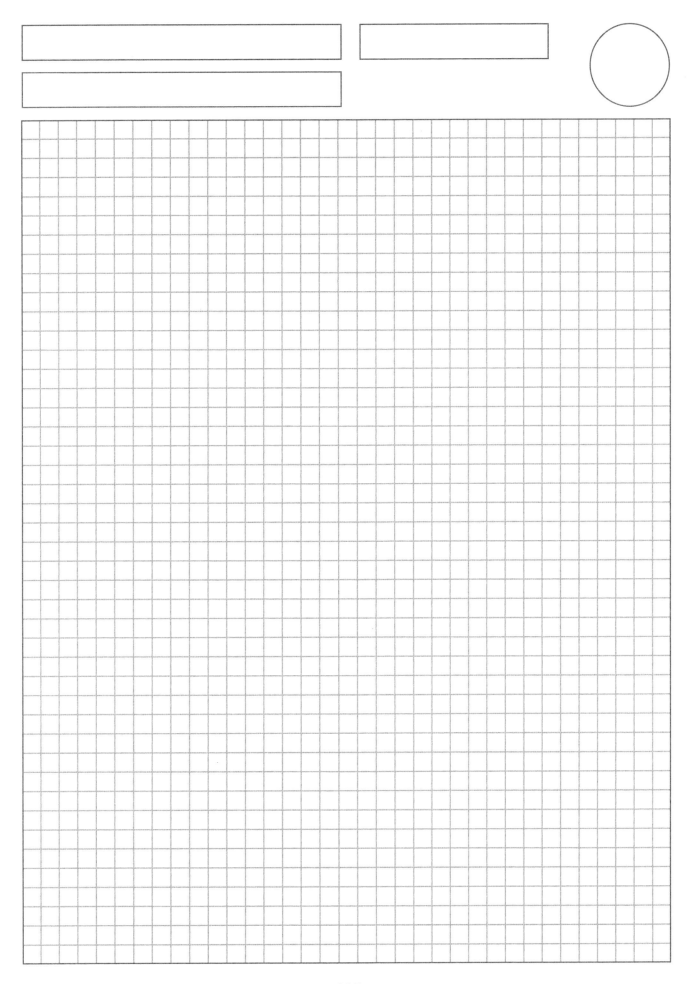

SECTOR 6

TACTICAL PLANS OF ACTION

(WHERE VULNERABILITIES CANNOT BE MITIGATED)

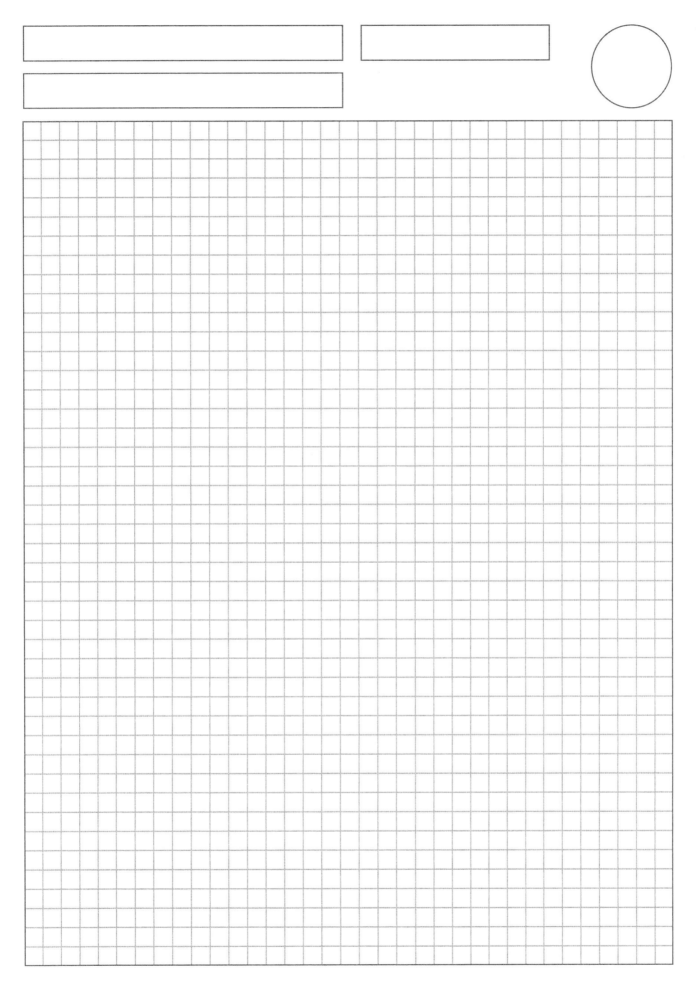

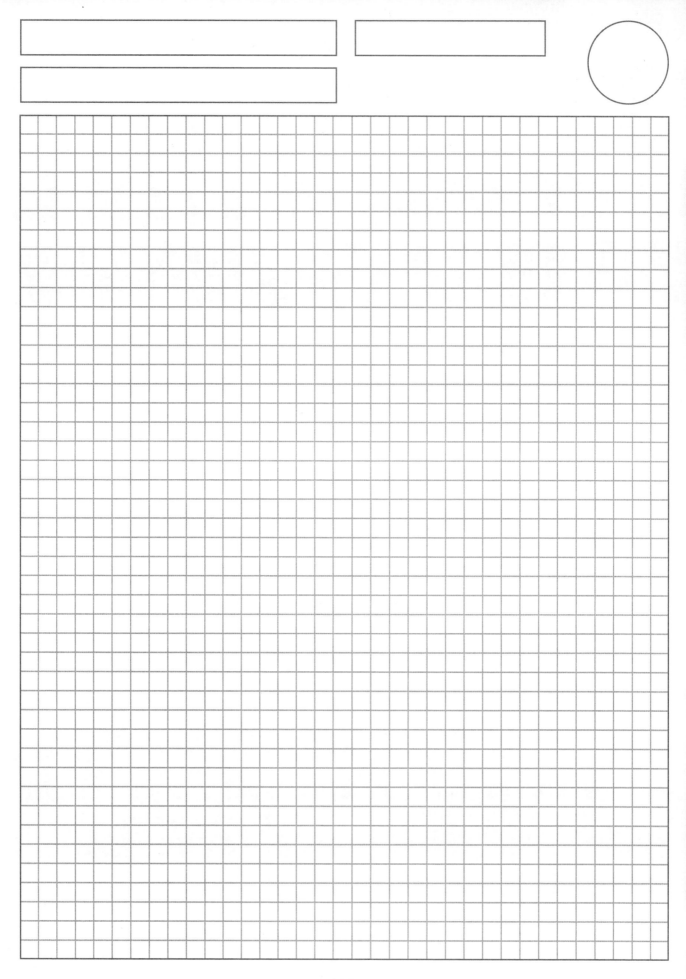

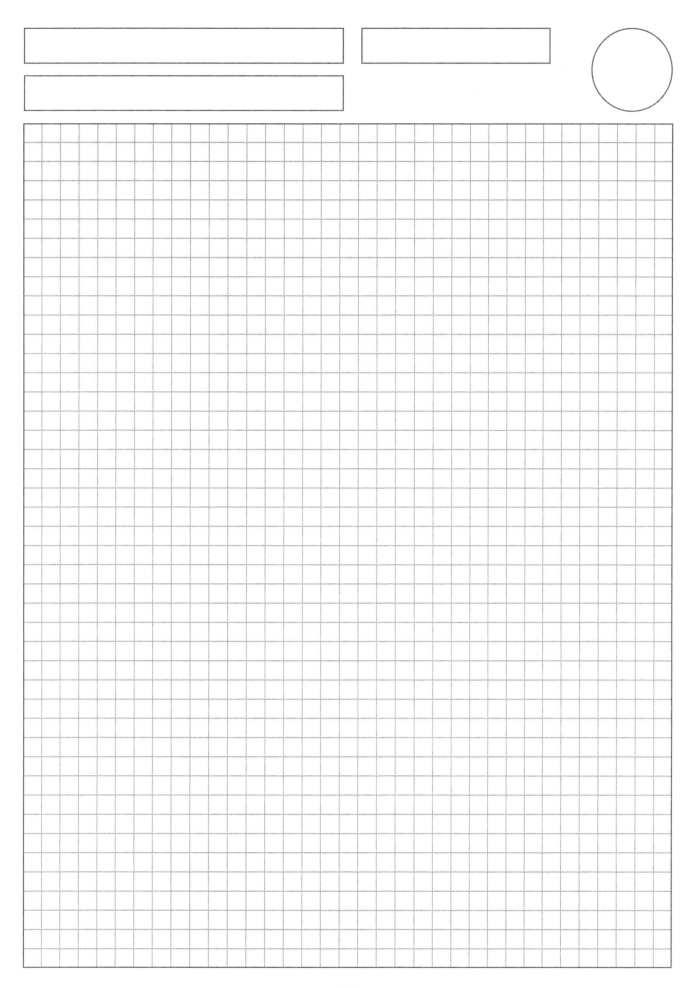

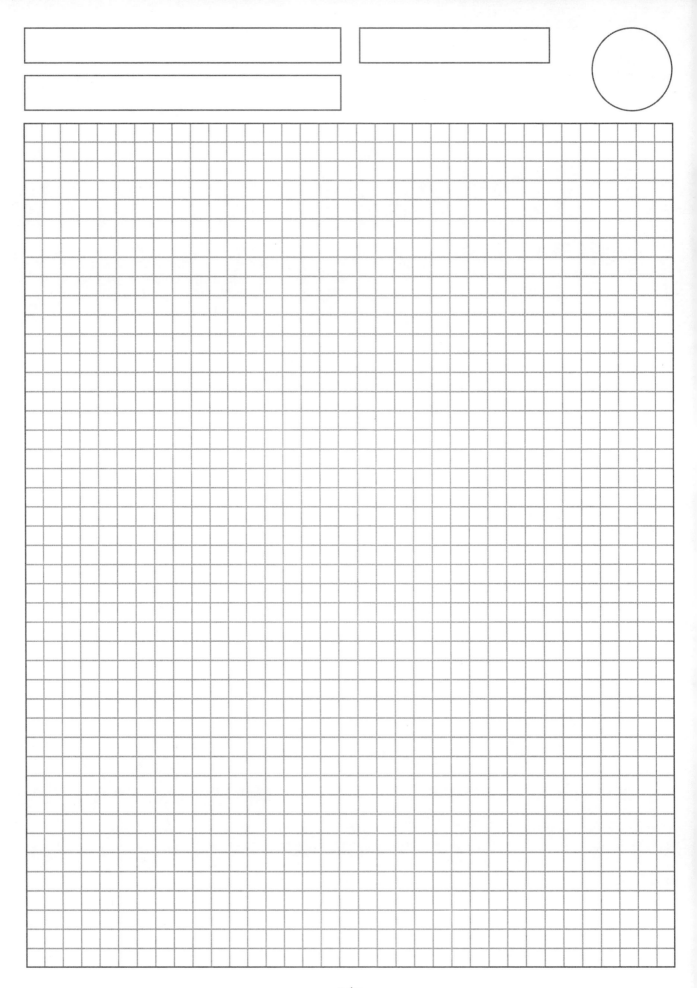

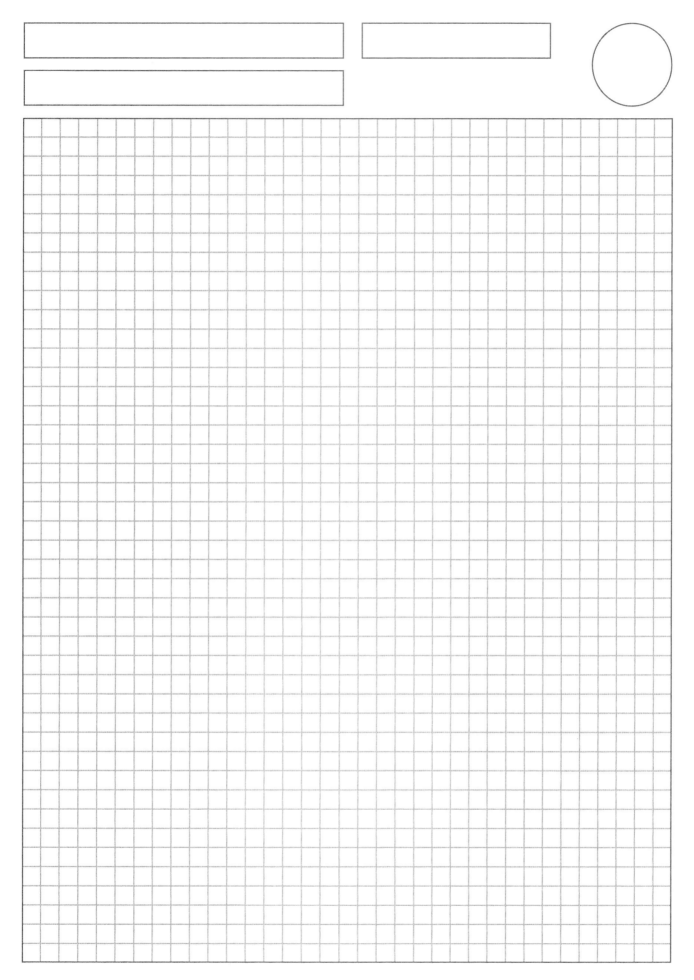

S7

SECTOR 7

SECTOR 7
FIRST RESPONDER OVERVIEW

THREAT ASSESSMENT SECTOR OVERVIEW

Sector:	Date:

Prepared by:

Situation:

Sector Overview:

Note: Make sure you print out map and directions to pertinent police precincts.

Police Departments:	PD Contact Information:	PD Response Times:

Crime Level:	Possible Threat Level:

Known Terror Threats:

Known Criminal Threats:

Note: Make sure you print out map and directions to all trauma centers. Always make the effort to proceed to a level 1 trauma center if the injury is life threatening.

Trauma Centers:	Trauma Center Level (I, II, III):	Response Times:

Weather Conditions:

Spring	Summer	Fall	Winter

RESPONSE RESOURCES
(Specific To This Sector)

Federal

- Department of Homeland Security (DHS)

  _____

  _____

- Federal Emergency Management Agency (FEMA)

  _____

  _____

- Federal Bureau of Investigation (FBI)

  _____

  _____

- Environmental Protection Agency (EPA)

  _____

  _____

- Health and Human Services (HHS)

  _____

  _____

State/Regional

- Emergency Management

  _____

  _____

- State Emergency Operations Center

  _____

  _____

- State Police

  _____

  _____

- National Guard

  _____

  _____

- Joint Terrorism Task Forces (JTTF)

  _____

  _____

> Note: Make sure you print out map and directions to pertinent police precincts. Always make the effort to proceed to a level 1 trauma center if the injury is life threatening.

Local First Responders

- Police

  _____

  _____

  - Special Weapons And Tactics (SWAT) Teams

    _____

  - Explosive Ordnance Disposal (EOD)

    _____

- Police

  _____

  _____

  - Special Weapons And Tactics (SWAT) Teams

    _____

  - Explosive Ordnance Disposal (EOD)

    _____

RESPONSE RESOURCES (continued)
(Specific To This Sector)

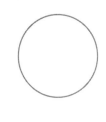

- Police

  _____

  _____

  - Special Weapons And Tactics (SWAT) Teams

    _____

  - Explosive Ordnance Disposal (EOD)

    _____

- Fire

  _____

  _____

  - Rescue / Emergency Medical Services

    _____

  - Hazardous Materials Response Teams

    _____

- Emergency Management

  _____

  _____

Note: Make sure you print out map and directions to all trauma centers. Always make the effort to proceed to a level 1 trauma center if the injury is life threatening.

Hospitals

- Level I Trauma Center

  _____

  _____

- Level II Trauma Center

  _____

  _____

RESPONSE RESOURCES (continued)
(Specific To This Sector)

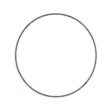

- Urgent Care

  _____

  _____

- Other Medical Center

  _____

  _____

- Other Medical Center

  _____

  _____

Known Threats

- Crime

  _____

  _____

  _____

  _____

  _____

  _____

- Terror

  _____

  _____

  _____

  _____

  _____

  _____

Note: If this sector is a special event or a vacation, take a screen shot
of the weather report and attach here

SECTOR 7
VULNERABILITY MITIGATION

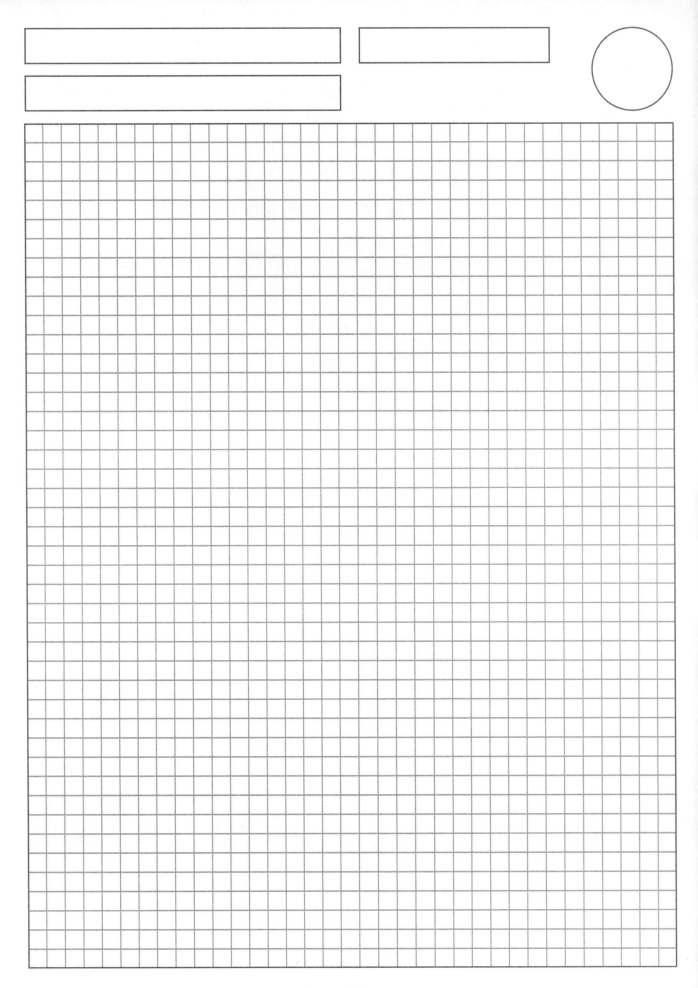

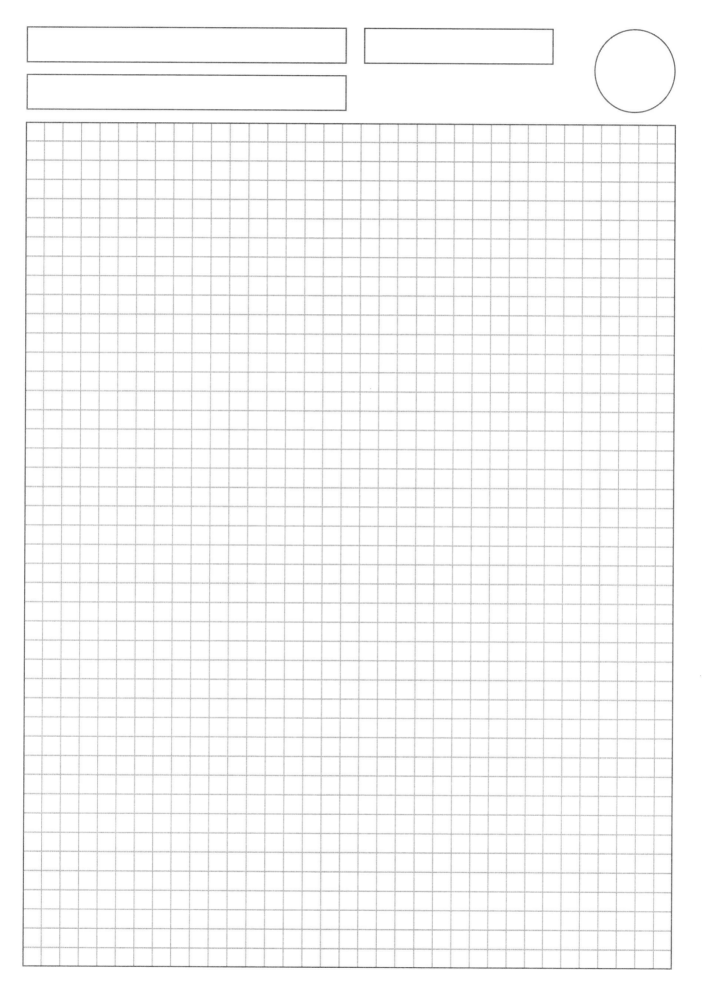

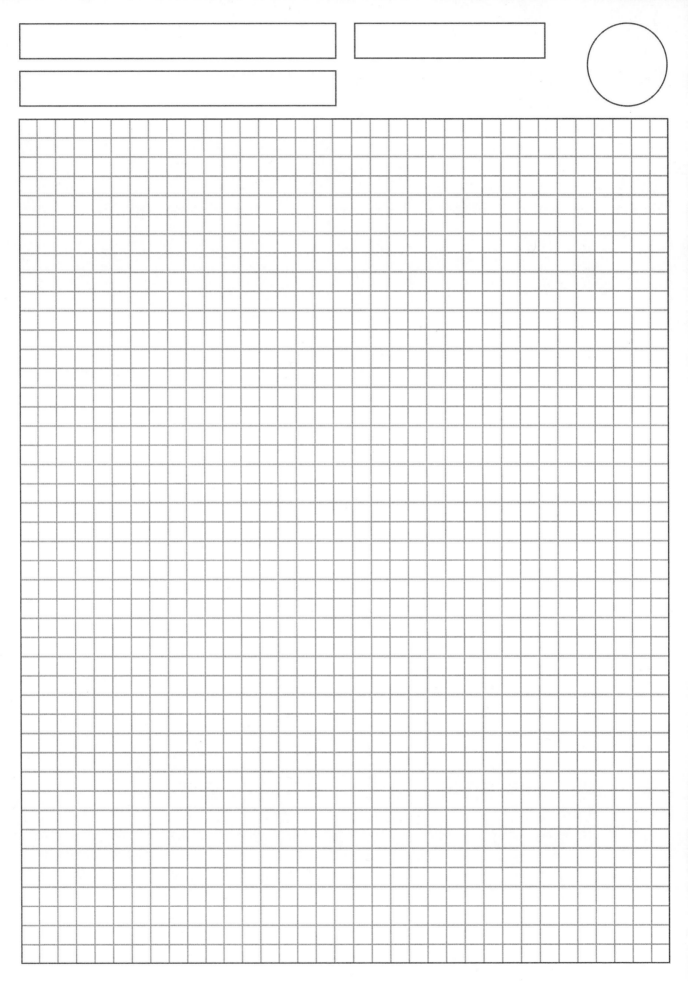

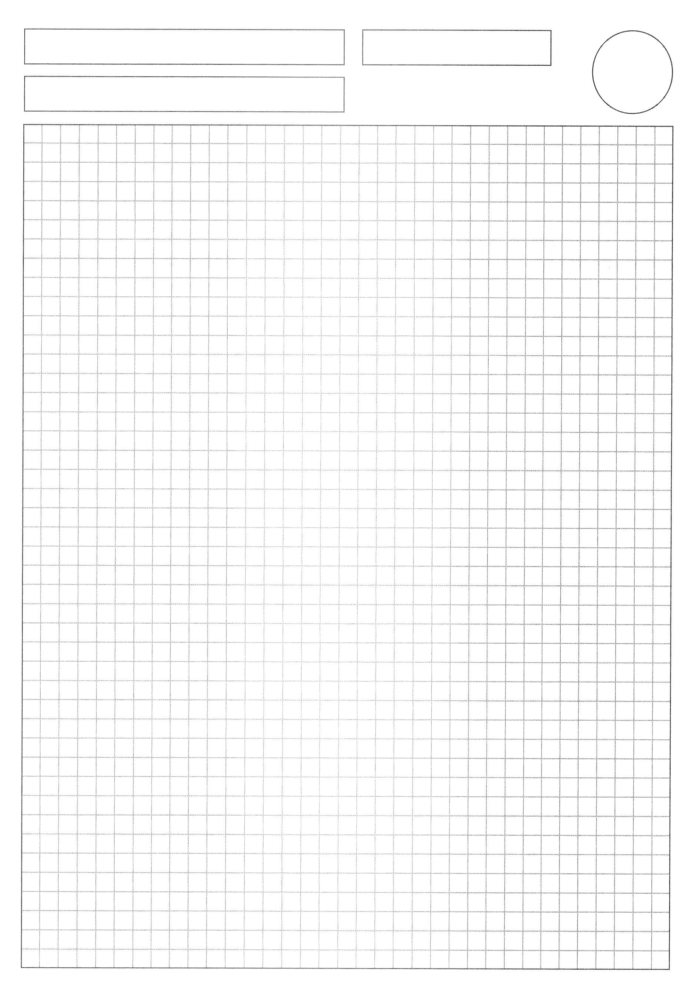

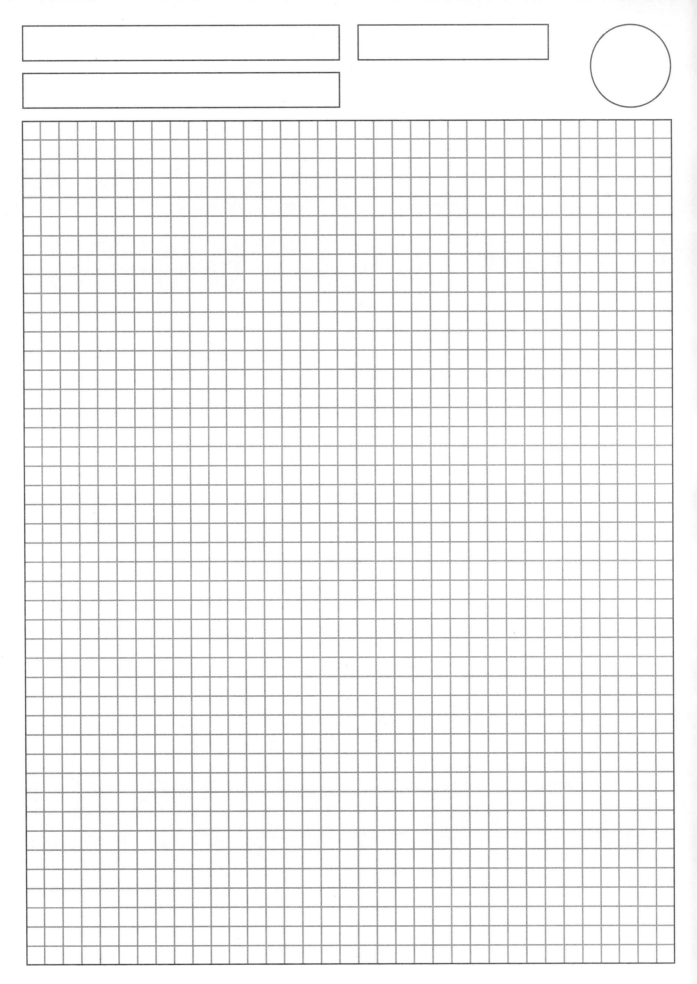

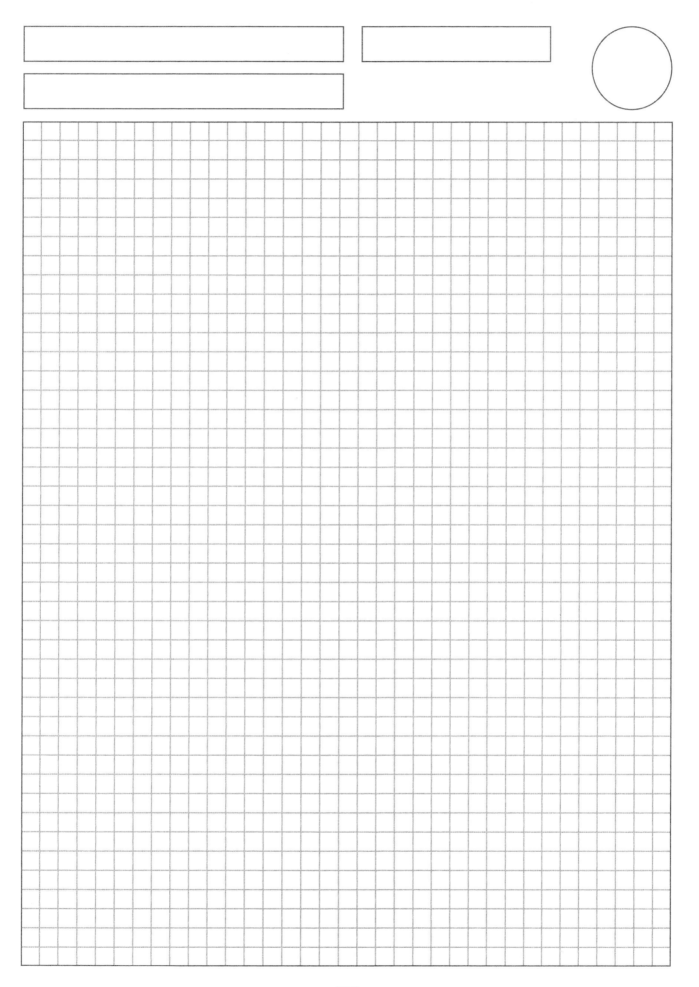

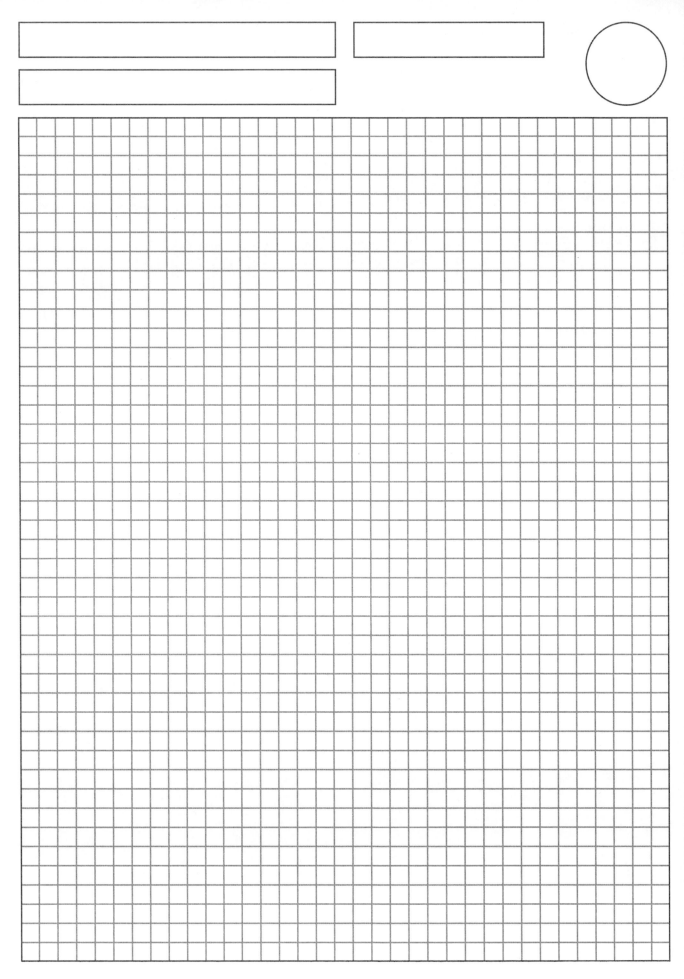

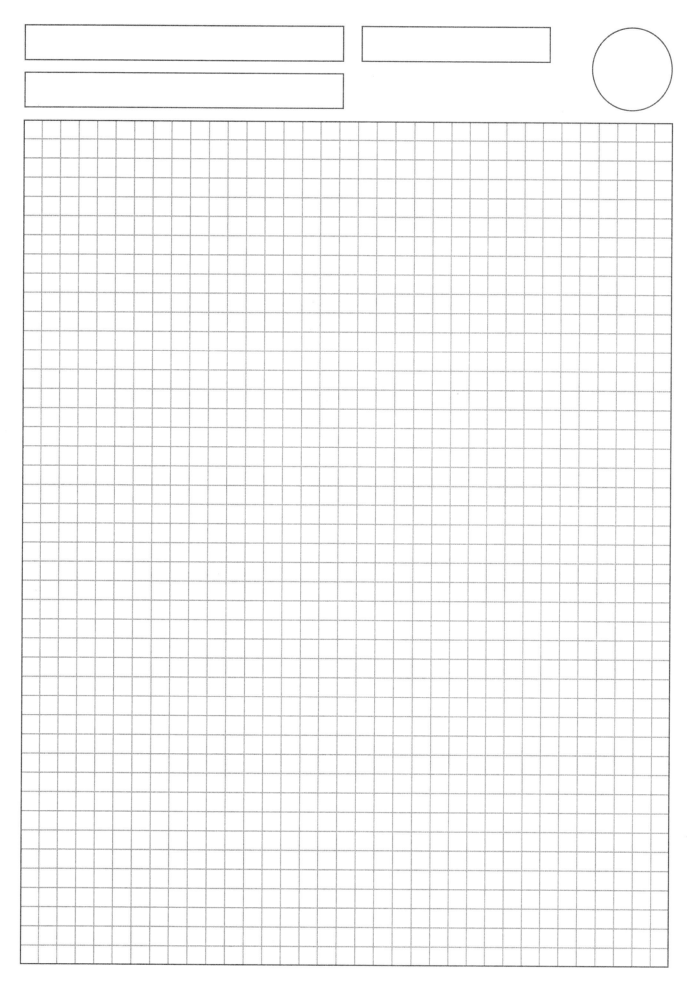

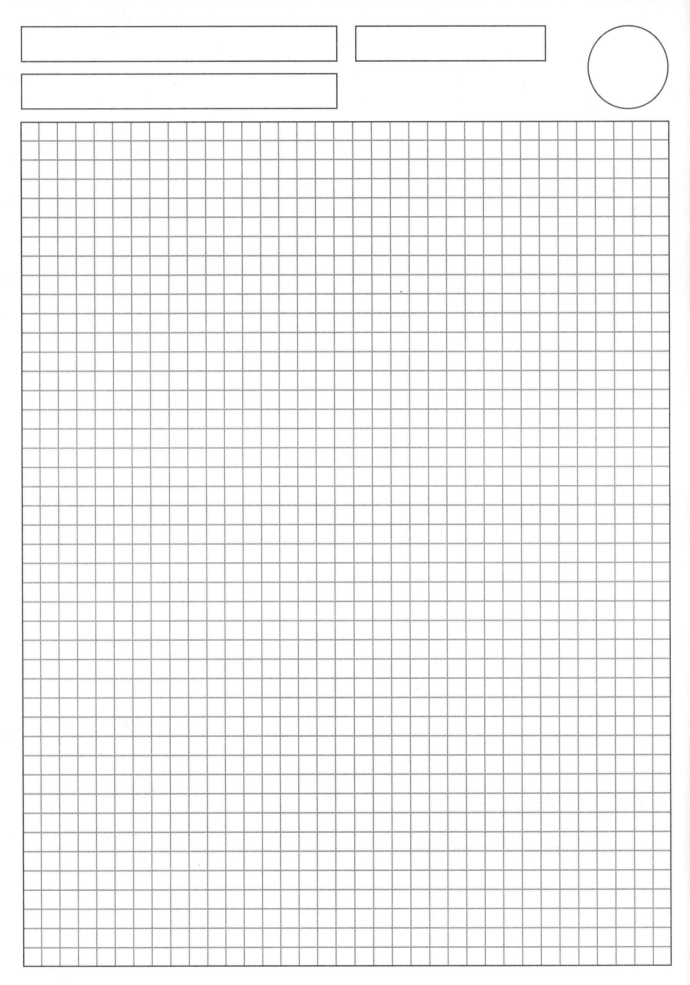

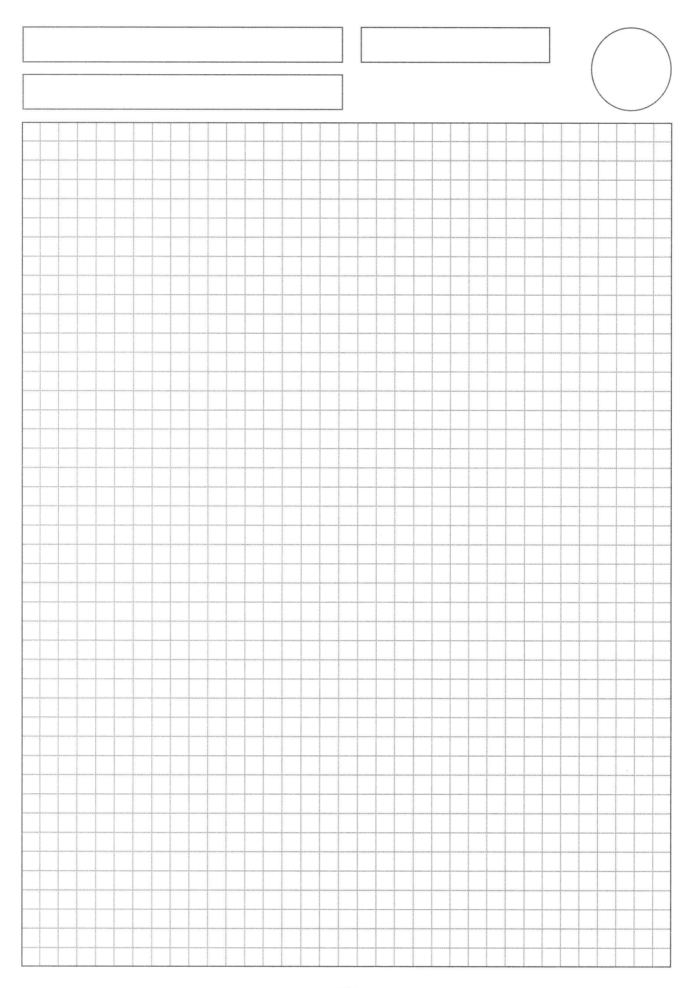

SECTOR 7

IMPLEMENTATION OF PHYSICAL

DEFENSE AND TECHNOLOGY

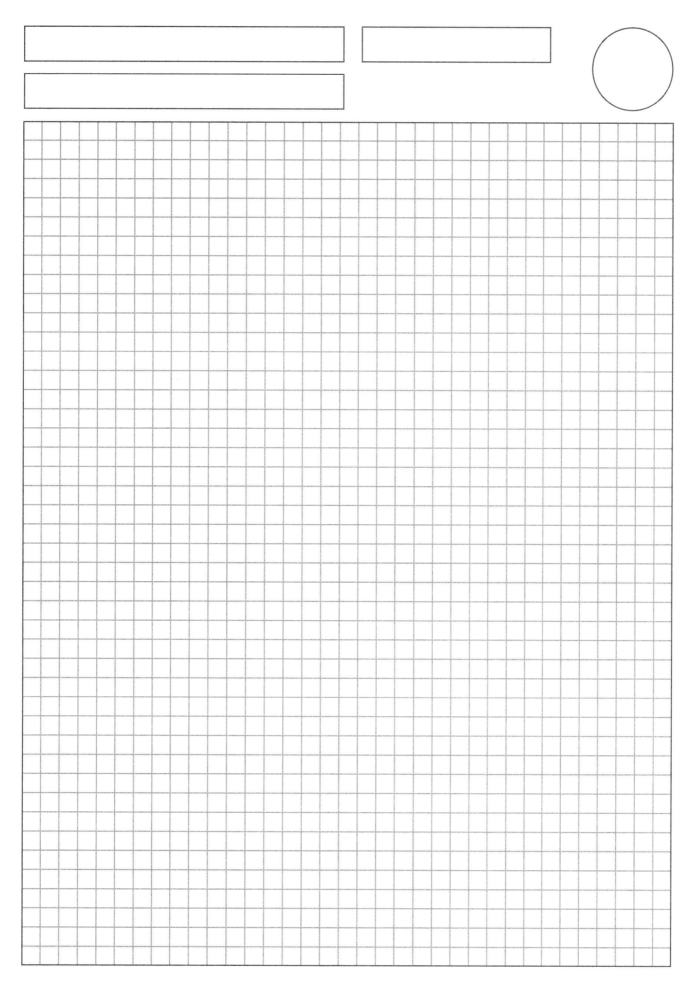

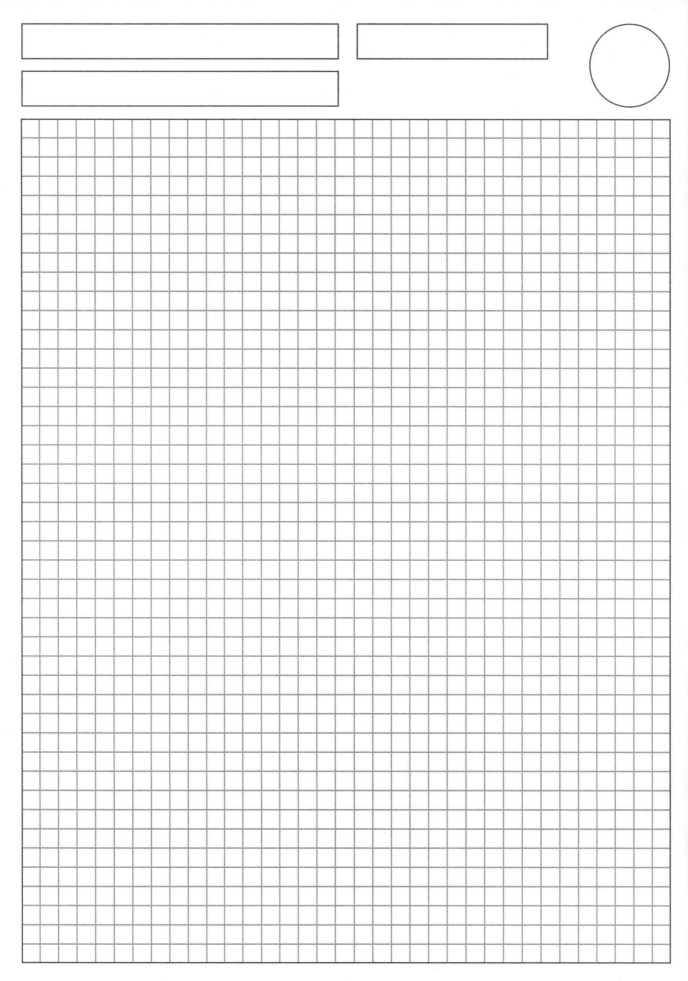

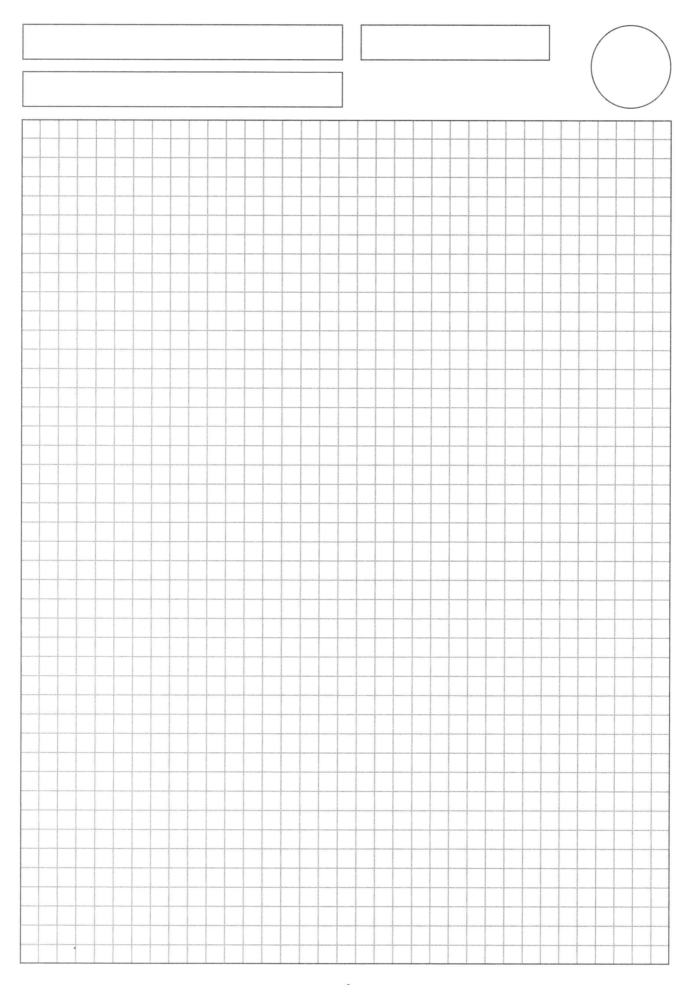

SECTOR 7
BEHAVIORS AND ATTACK
INDICATORS

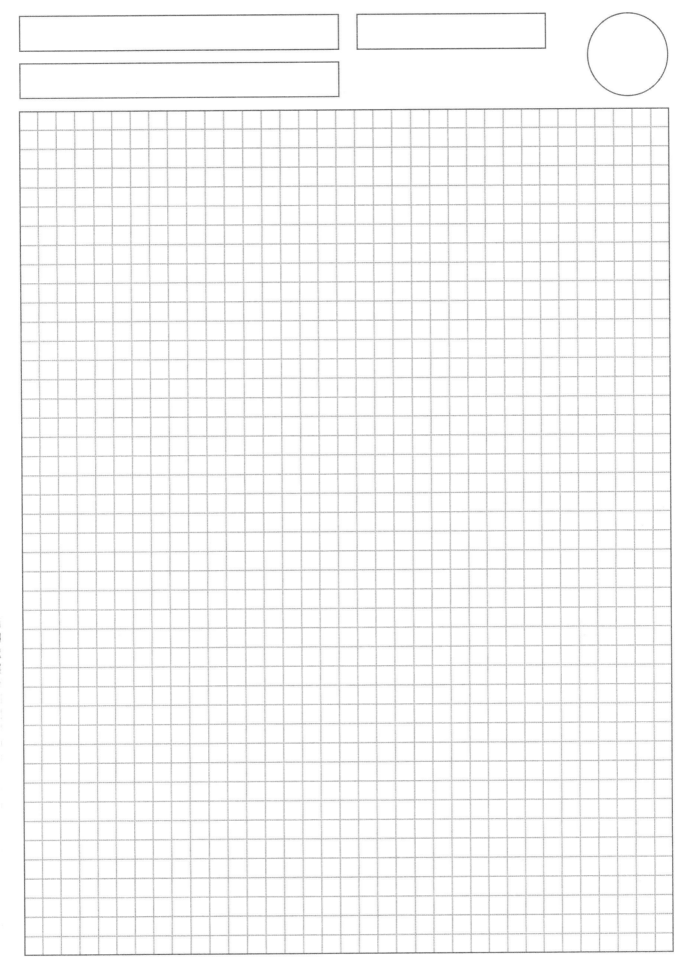

265

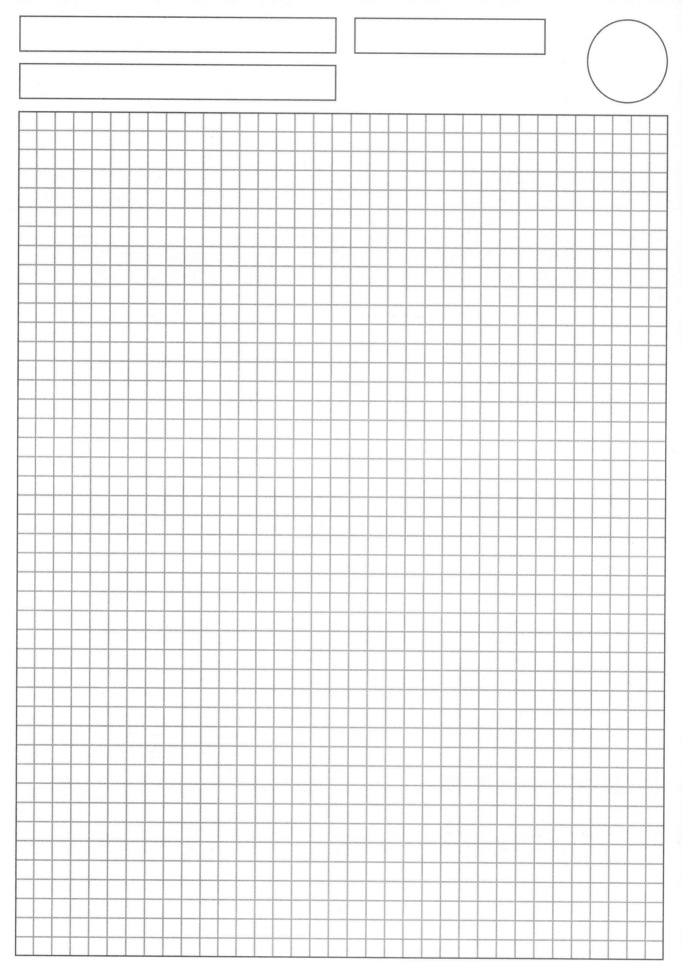

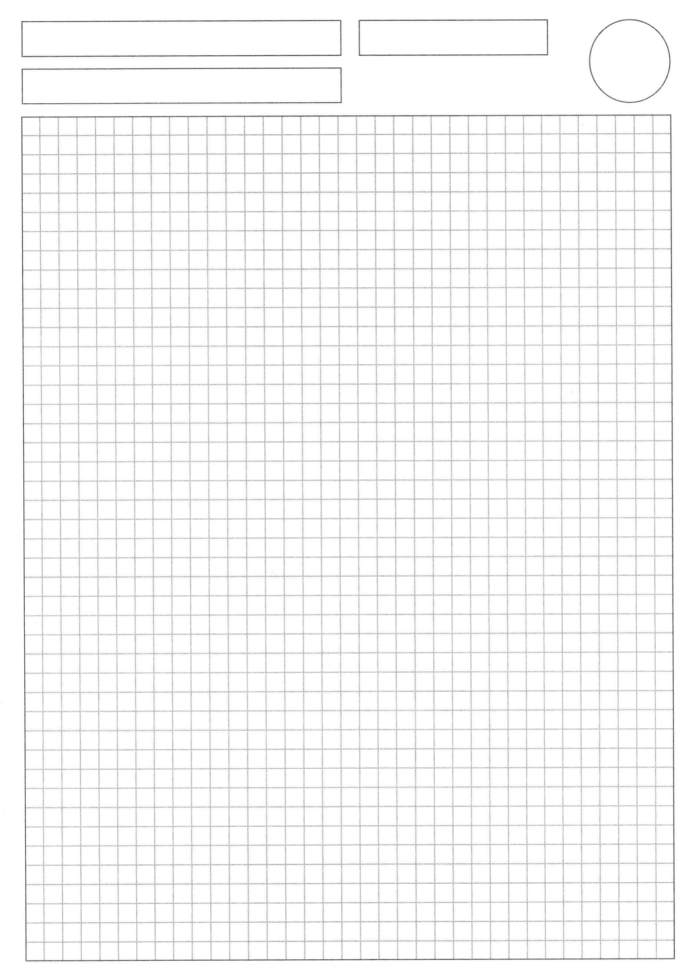

SECTOR 7
SHARED THREATS

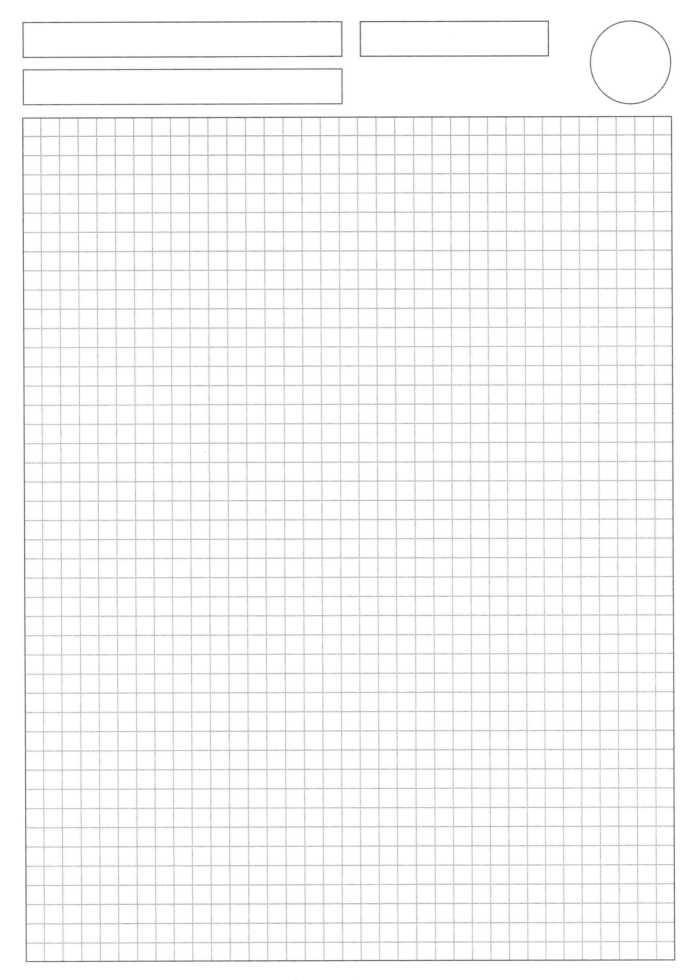

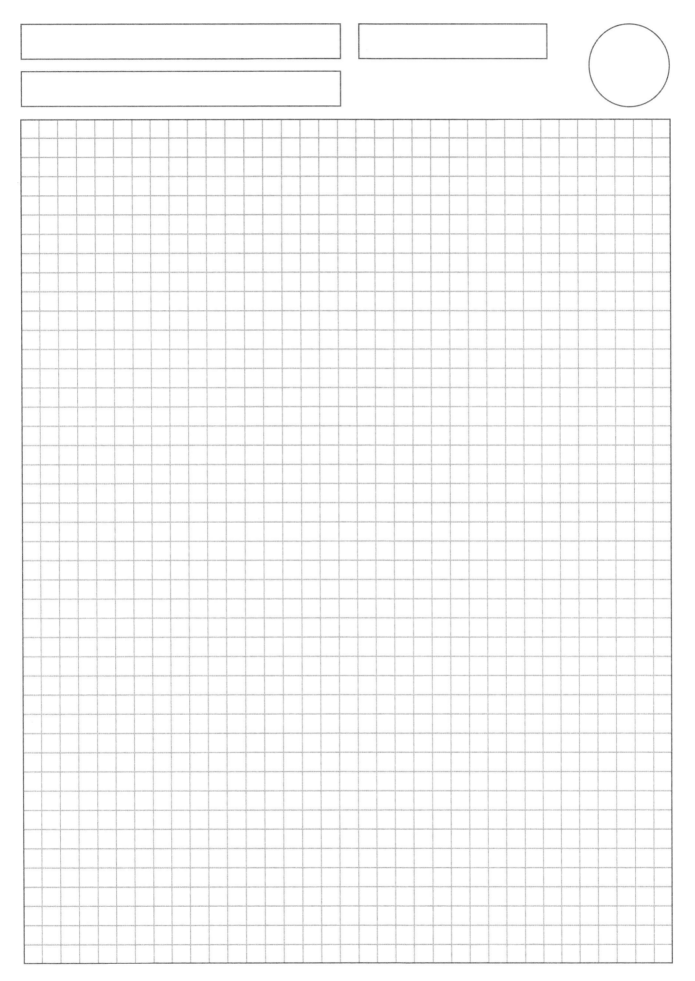

SECTOR 7
TACTICAL PLANS OF ACTION
(WHERE VULNERABILITIES CANNOT BE MITIGATED)

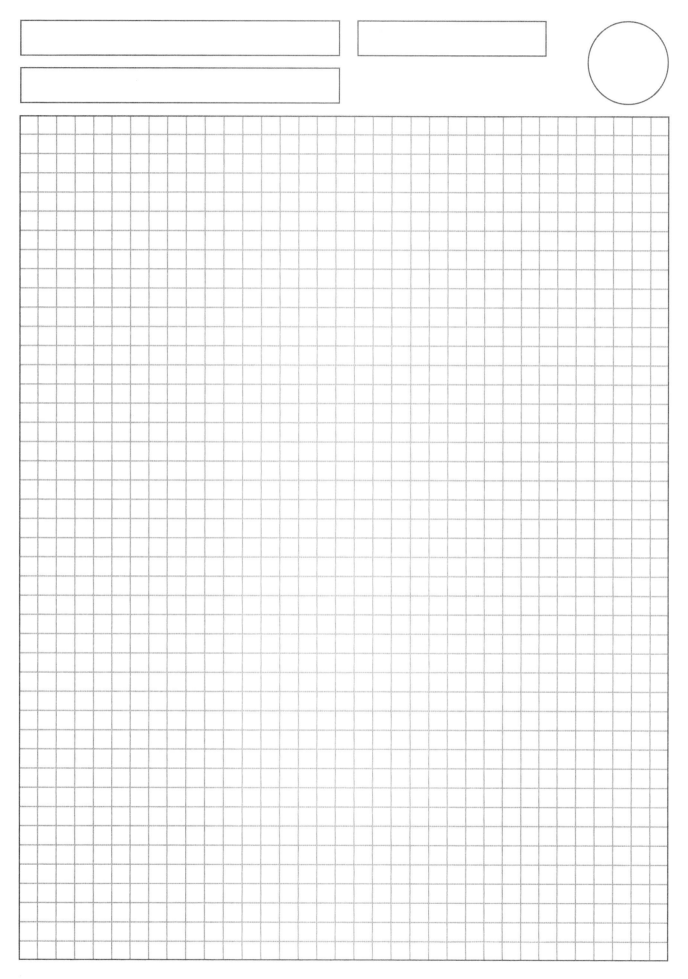

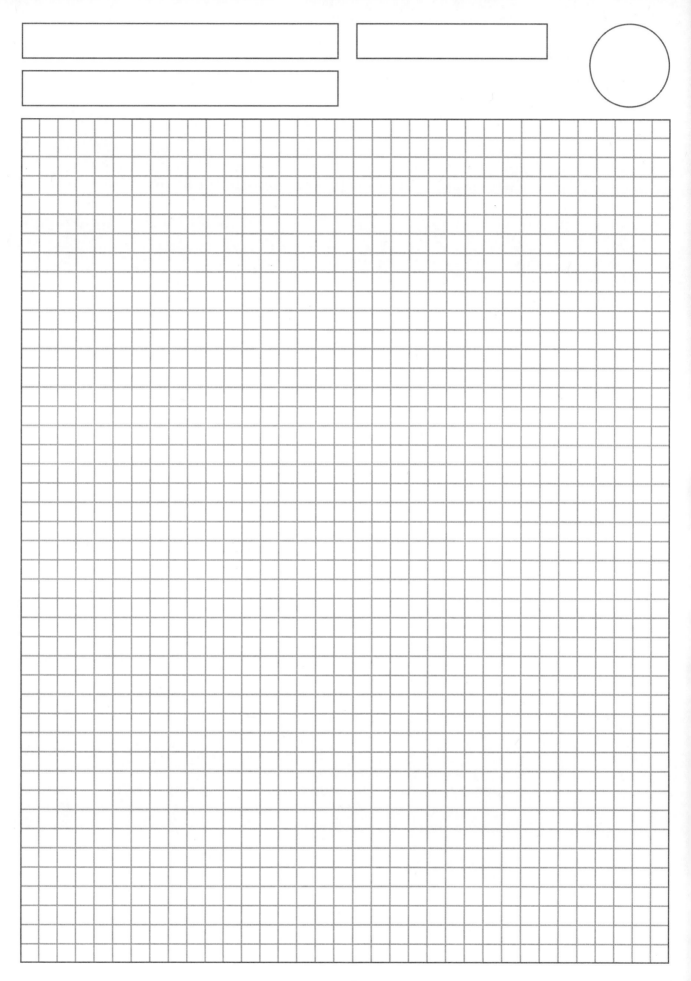

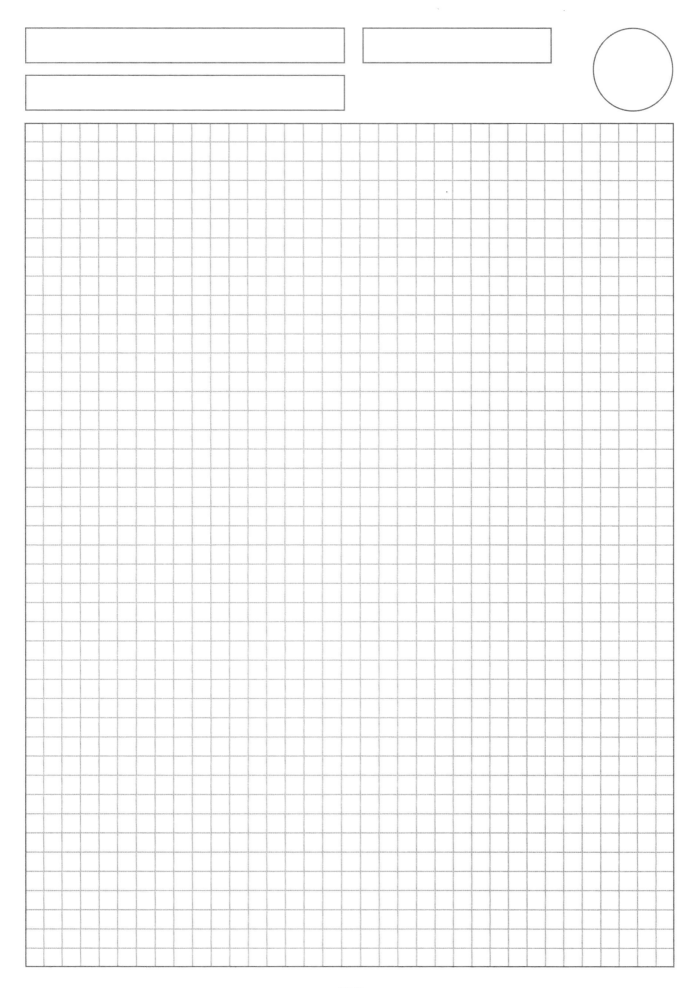

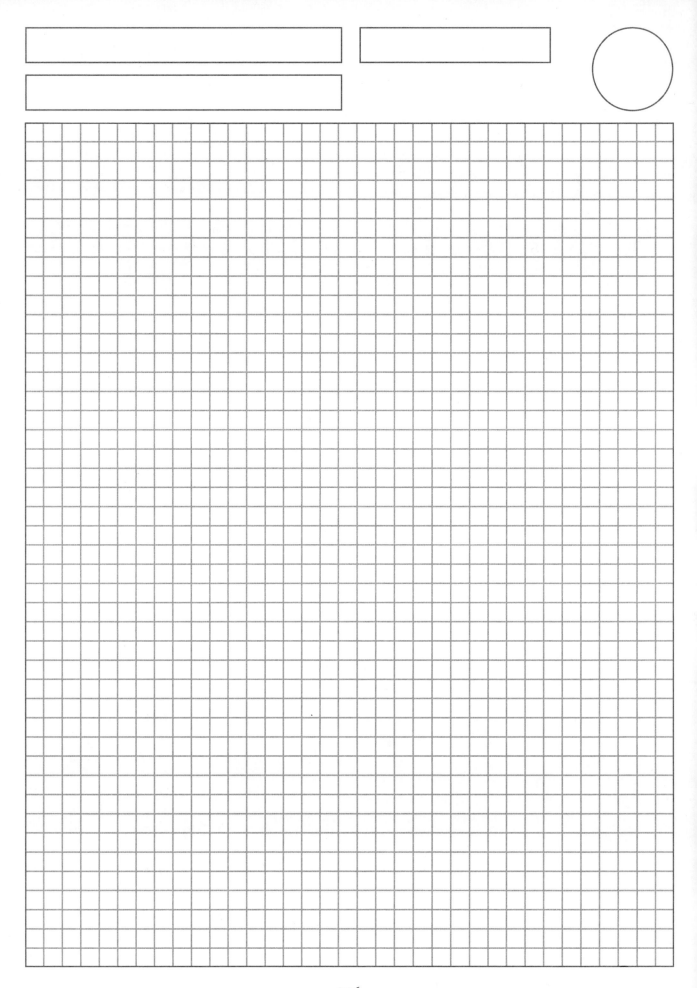

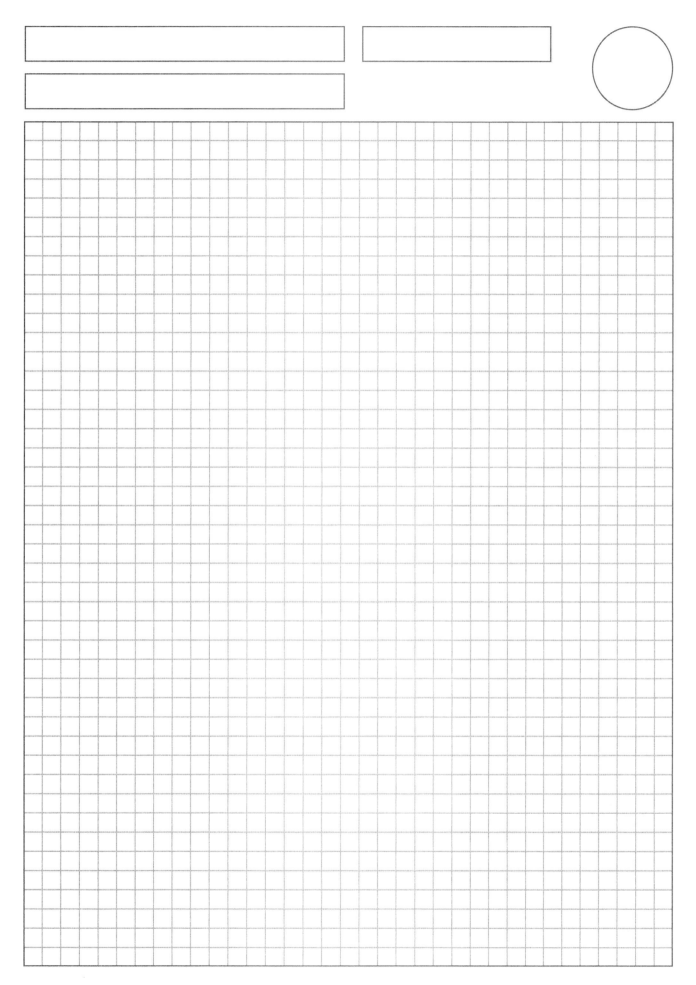

S8

SECTOR 8

SECTOR 8
FIRST RESPONDER OVERVIEW

THREAT ASSESSMENT SECTOR OVERVIEW

Sector:

Date:

Prepared by:

Situation:

Sector Overview:

Note: Make sure you print out map and directions to pertinent police precincts.

Police Departments:

PD Contact Information:

PD Response Times:

Crime Level:

Possible Threat Level:

Known Terror Threats:

Known Criminal Threats:

Note: Make sure you print out map and directions to all trauma centers. Always make the effort to proceed to a level 1 trauma center if the injury is life threatening.

Trauma Centers:

Trauma Center Level (I, II, III):

Response Times:

Weather Conditions:

Spring   Summer   Fall   Winter

Sector:

Date:

Prepared by:

RESPONSE RESOURCES

(Specific To This Sector)

Federal

- Department of Homeland Security (DHS)

  ____

  ____

- Federal Emergency Management Agency (FEMA)

  ____

  ____

- Federal Bureau of Investigation (FBI)

  ____

  ____

- Environmental Protection Agency (EPA)

  ____

  ____

- Health and Human Services (HHS)

  ____

  ____

State/Regional

- Emergency Management

  ____

  ____

- State Emergency Operations Center

  ____

  ____

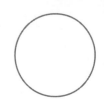

- State Police

_____

_____

- National Guard

_____

_____

- Joint Terrorism Task Forces (JTTF)

_____

_____

> *Note: Make sure you print out map and directions to pertinent police precincts. Always make the effort to proceed to a level 1 trauma center if the injury is life threatening.*

Local First Responders

- Police

_____

_____

  - Special Weapons And Tactics (SWAT) Teams

_____

  - Explosive Ordnance Disposal (EOD)

_____

- Police

_____

_____

  - Special Weapons And Tactics (SWAT) Teams

_____

  - Explosive Ordnance Disposal (EOD)

_____

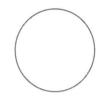

- Police

  _____

  _____

  - Special Weapons And Tactics (SWAT) Teams

    _____

  - Explosive Ordnance Disposal (EOD)

    _____

- Fire

  _____

  _____

  - Rescue / Emergency Medical Services

    _____

  - Hazardous Materials Response Teams

    _____

- Emergency Management

  _____

  _____

Note: Make sure you print out map and directions to all trauma centers. Always make the effort to proceed to a level 1 trauma center if the injury is life threatening.

Hospitals

- Level I Trauma Center

  _____

  _____

- Level II Trauma Center

  _____

  _____

RESPONSE RESOURCES (continued)
(Specific To This Sector)

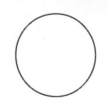

- Urgent Care

  _____

  _____

- Other Medical Center

  _____

  _____

- Other Medical Center

  _____

  _____

Known Threats

- Crime

  _____

  _____

  _____

  _____

  _____

  _____

- Terror

  _____

  _____

  _____

  _____

  _____

Note: If this sector is a special event or a vacation, take a screen shot of the weather report and attach here

SECTOR 8
VULNERABILITY MITIGATION

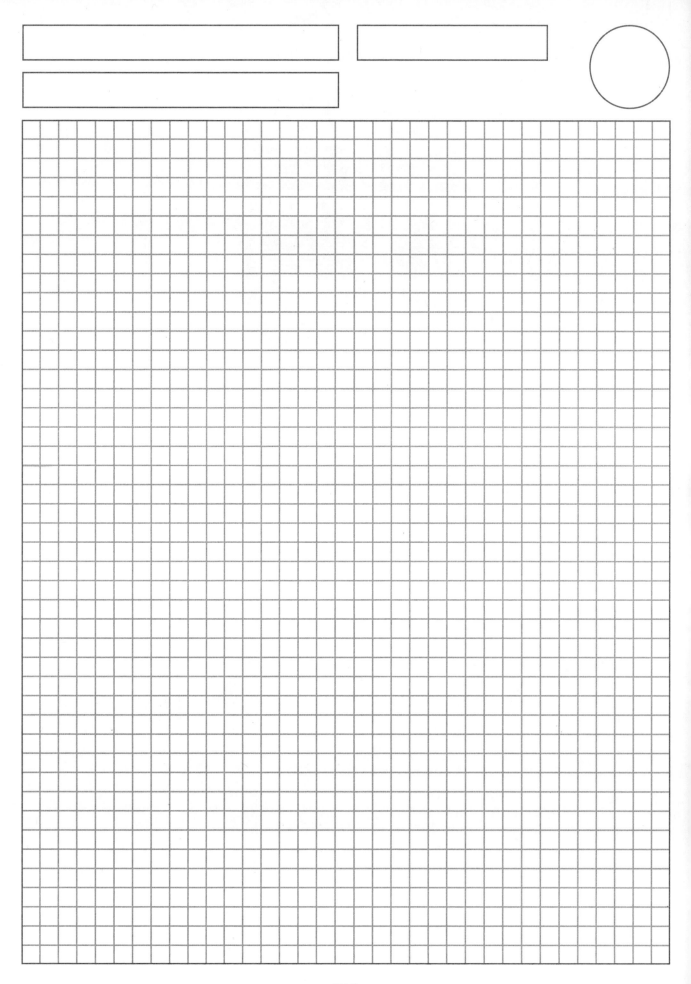

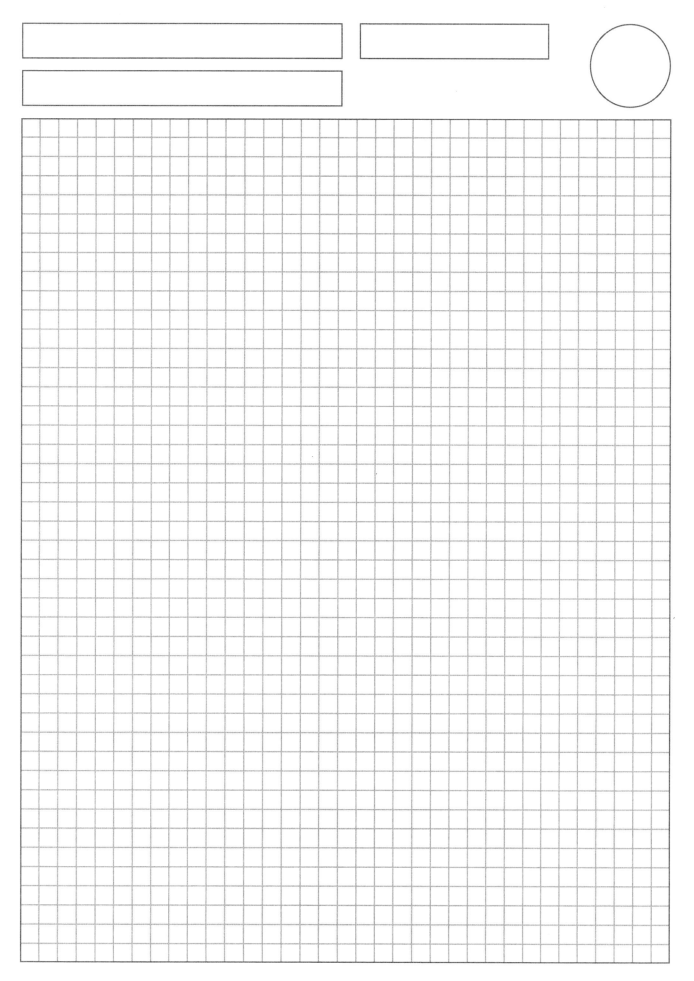

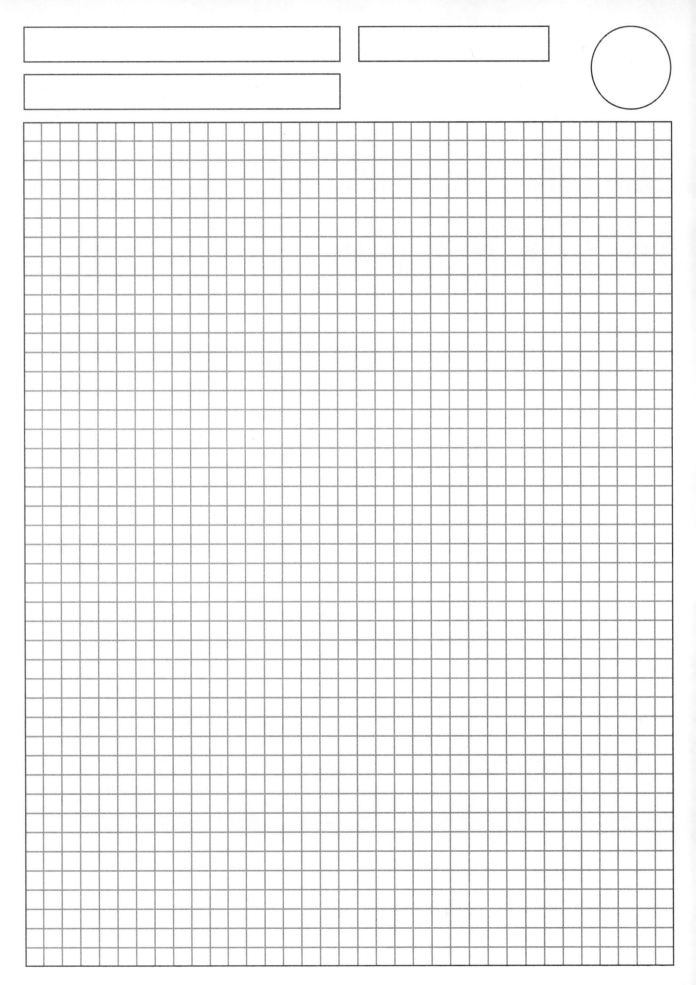

288

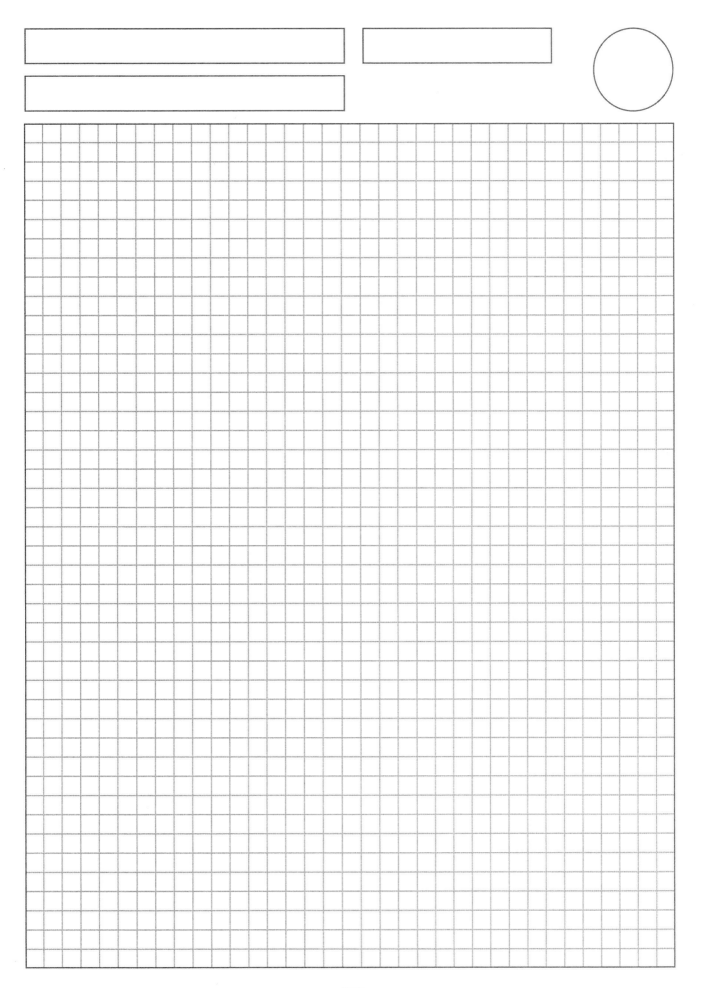

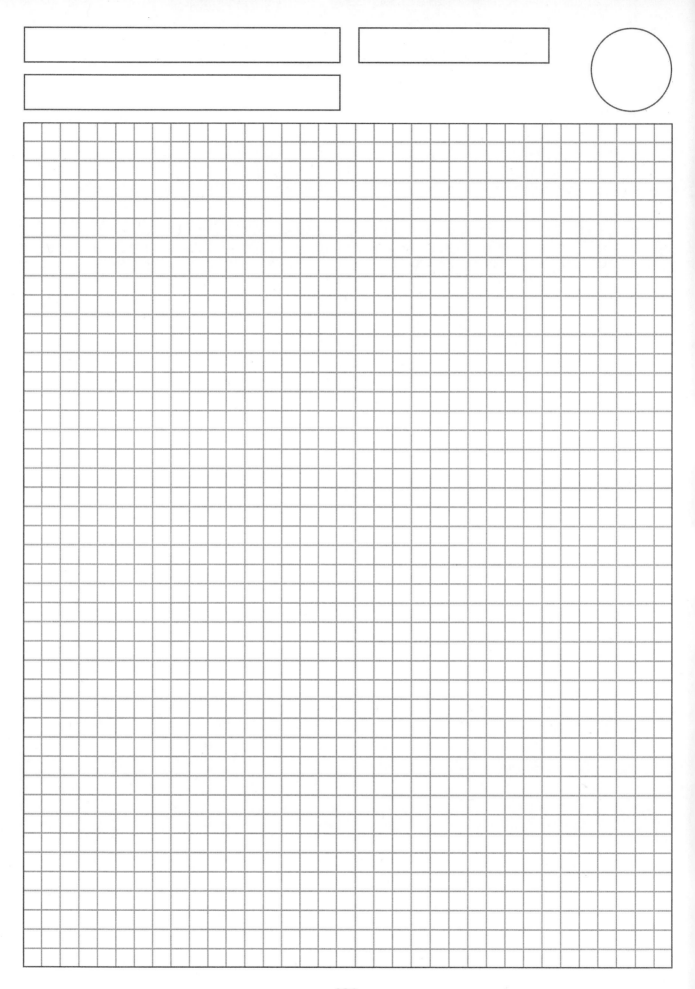

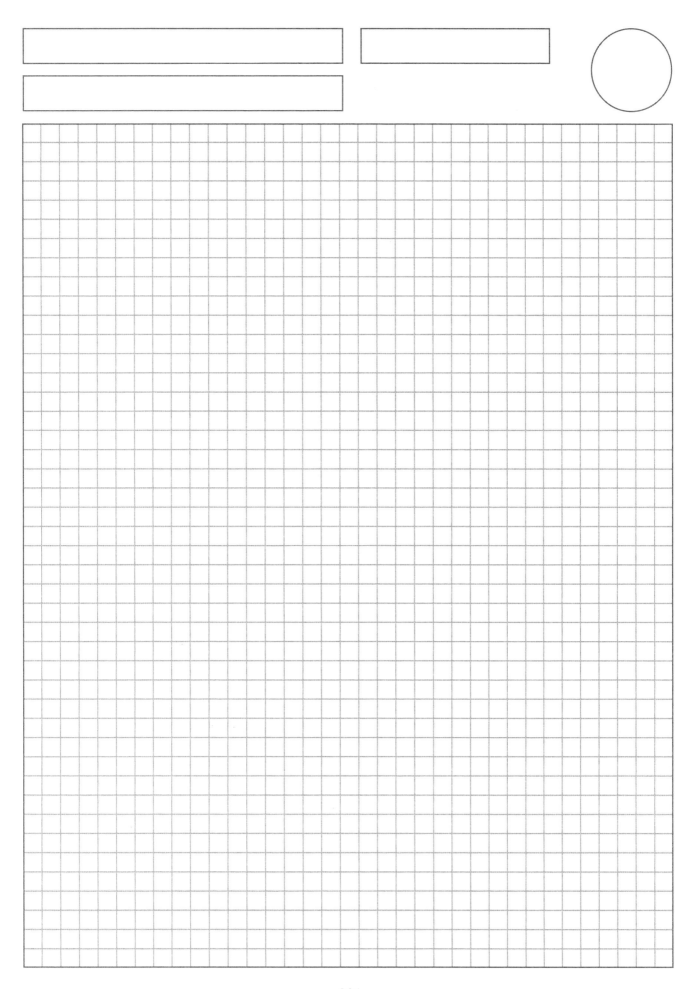

291

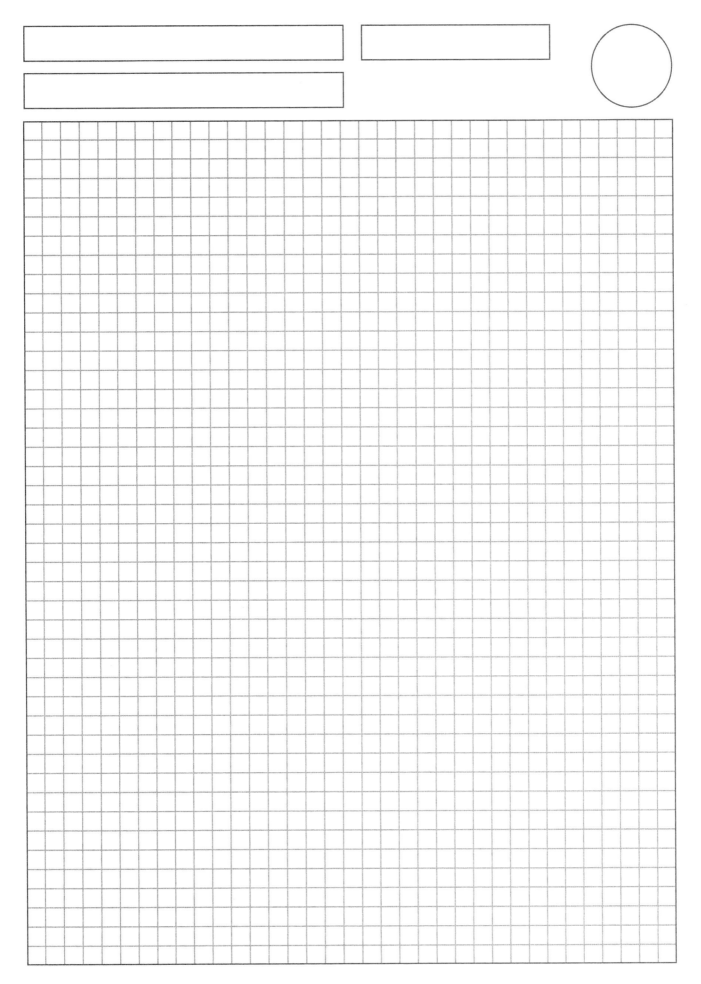

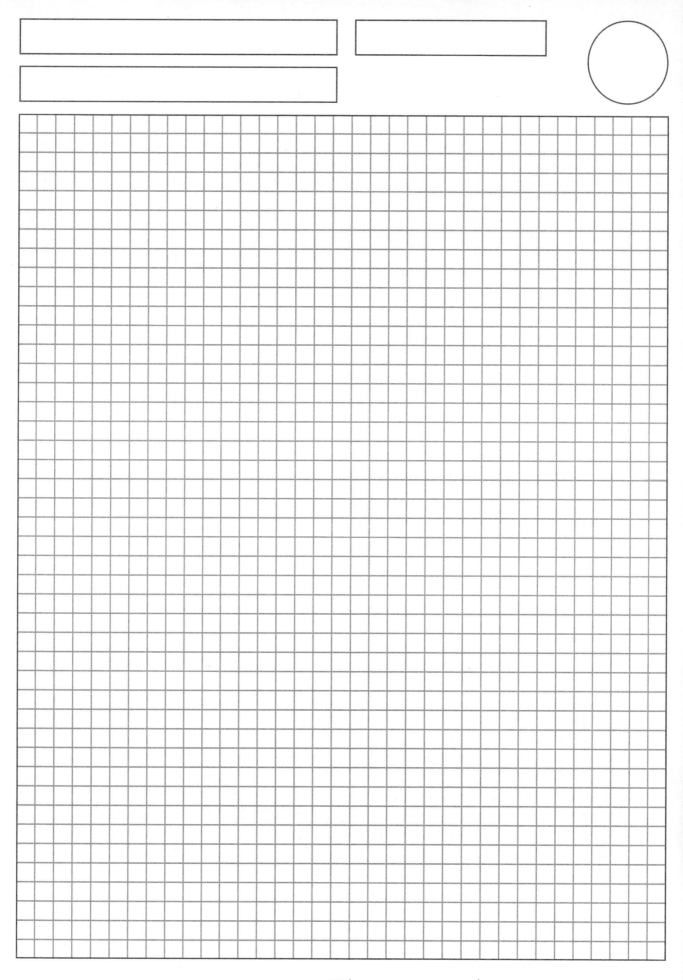

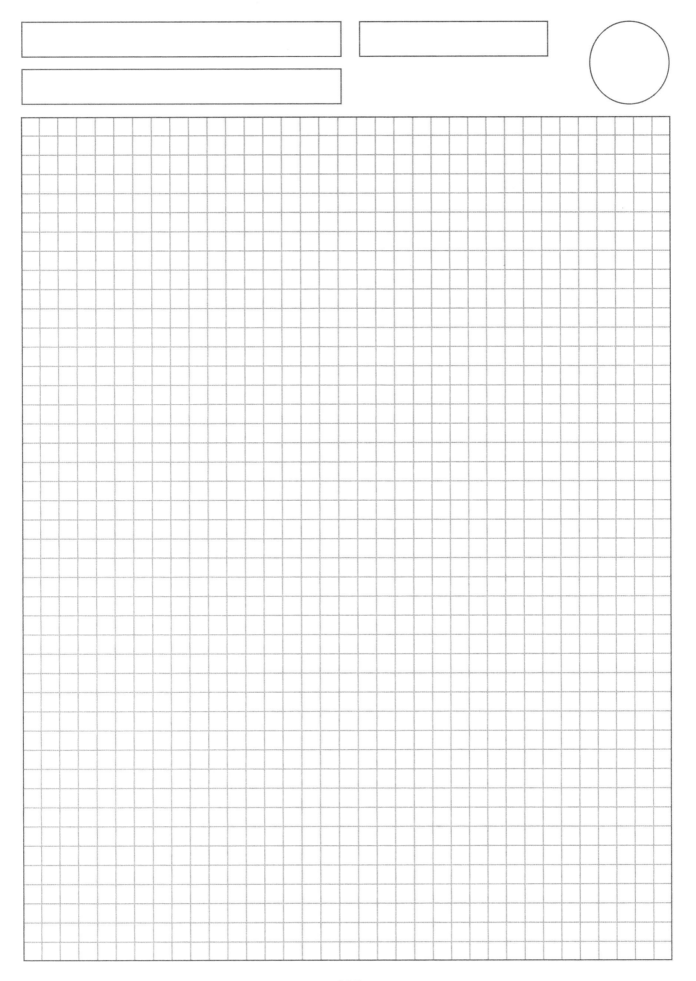

SECTOR 8

IMPLEMENTATION OF PHYSICAL

DEFENSE AND TECHNOLOGY

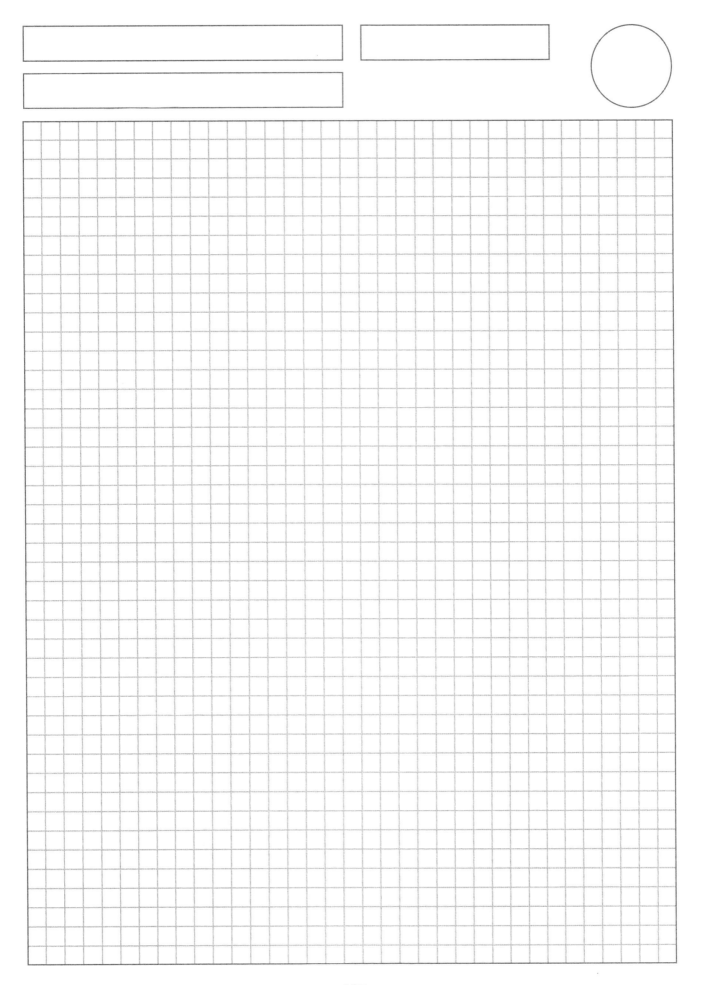

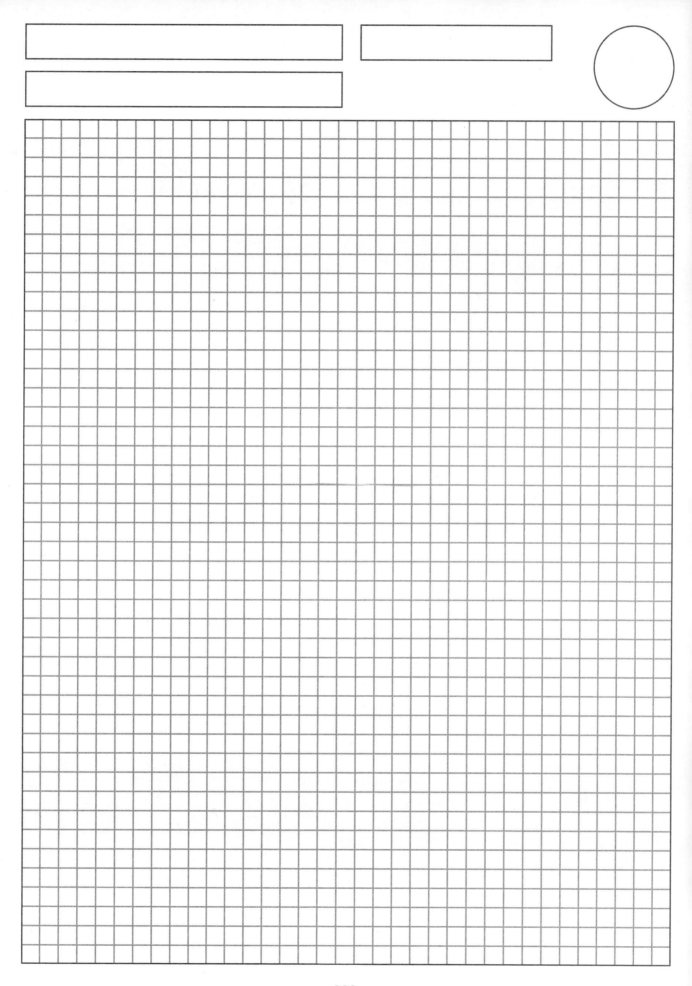

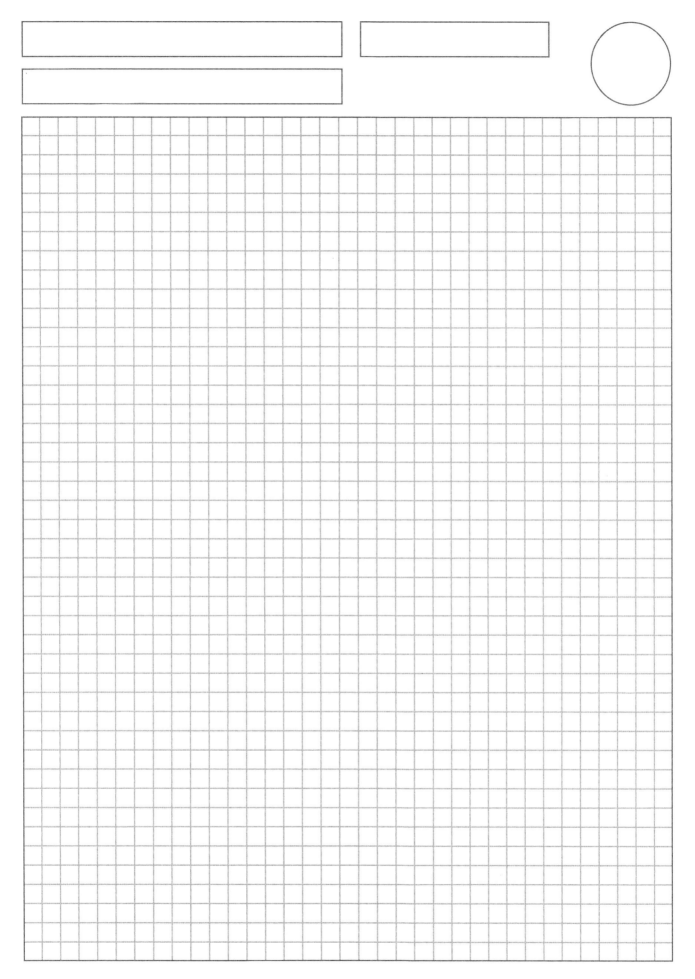

SECTOR 8

BEHAVIORS AND ATTACK

INDICATORS

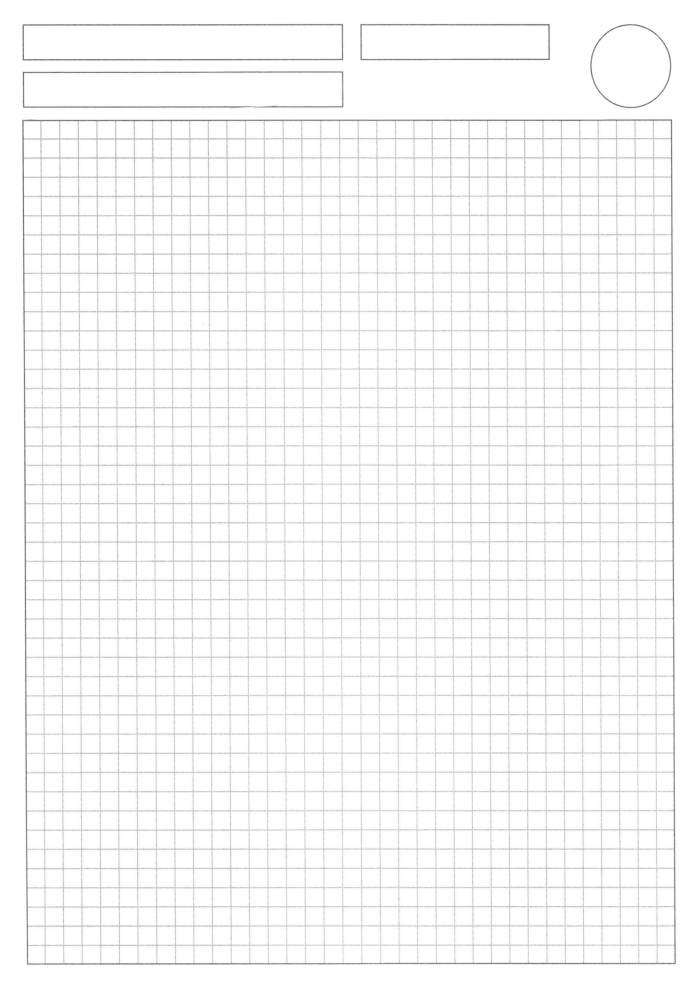

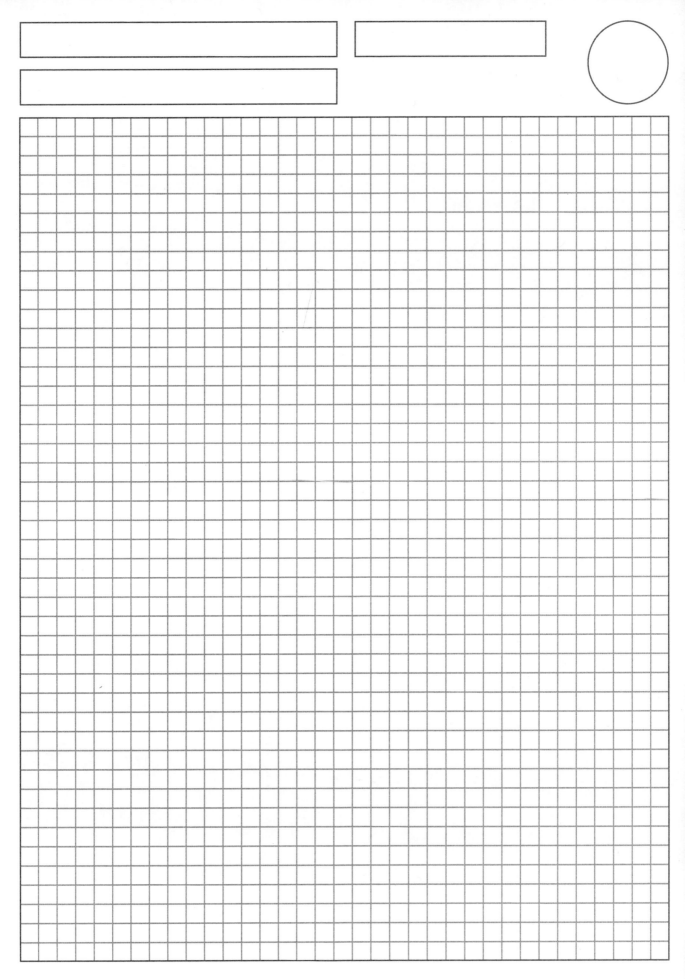

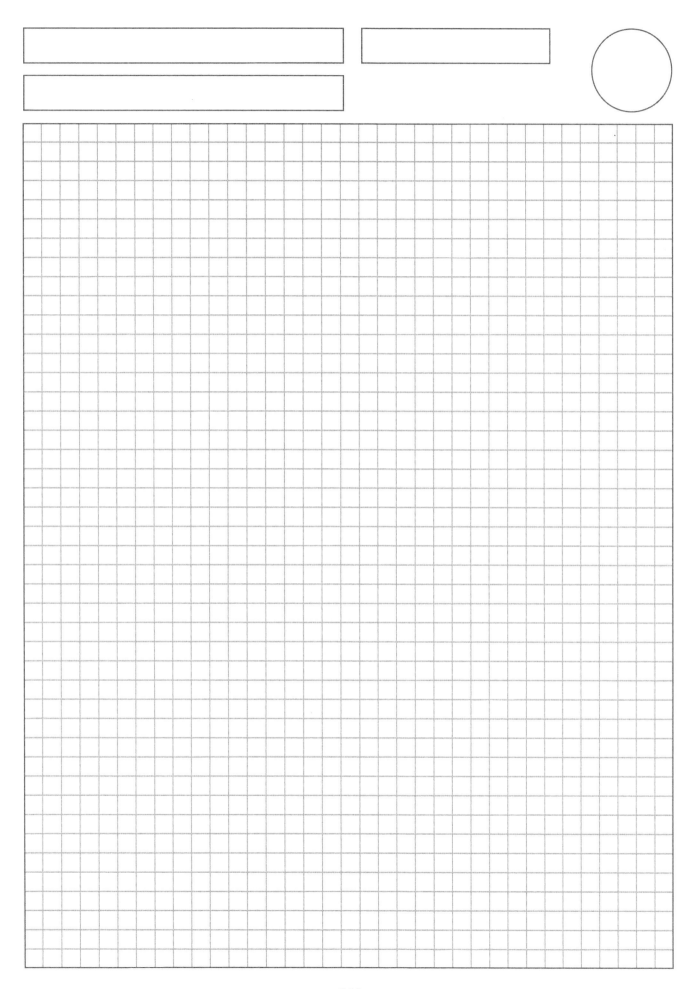

SECTOR 8

SHARED THREATS

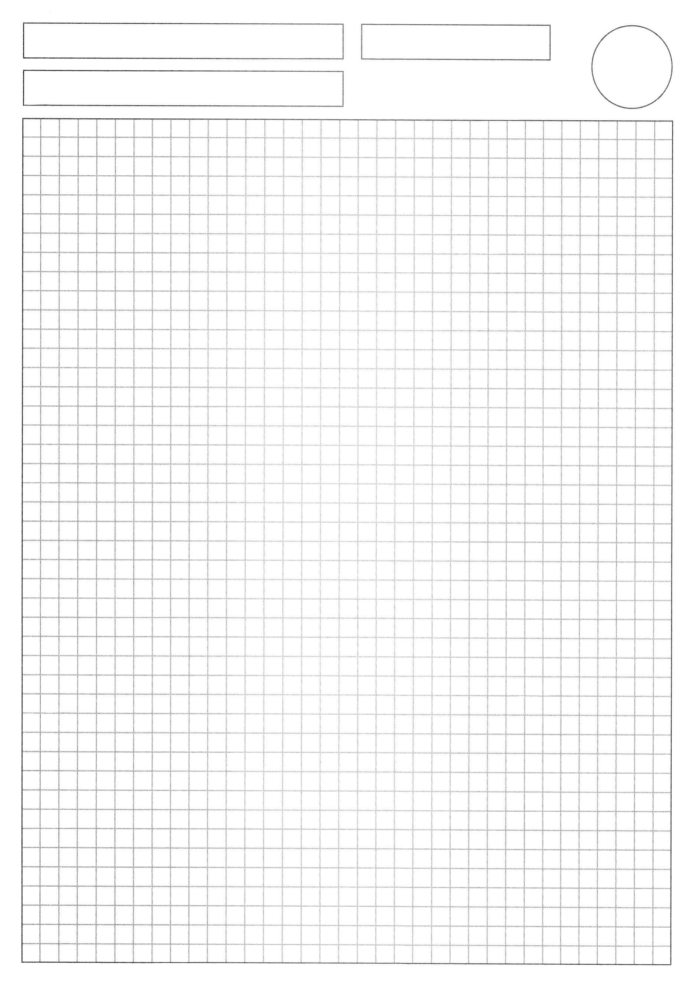

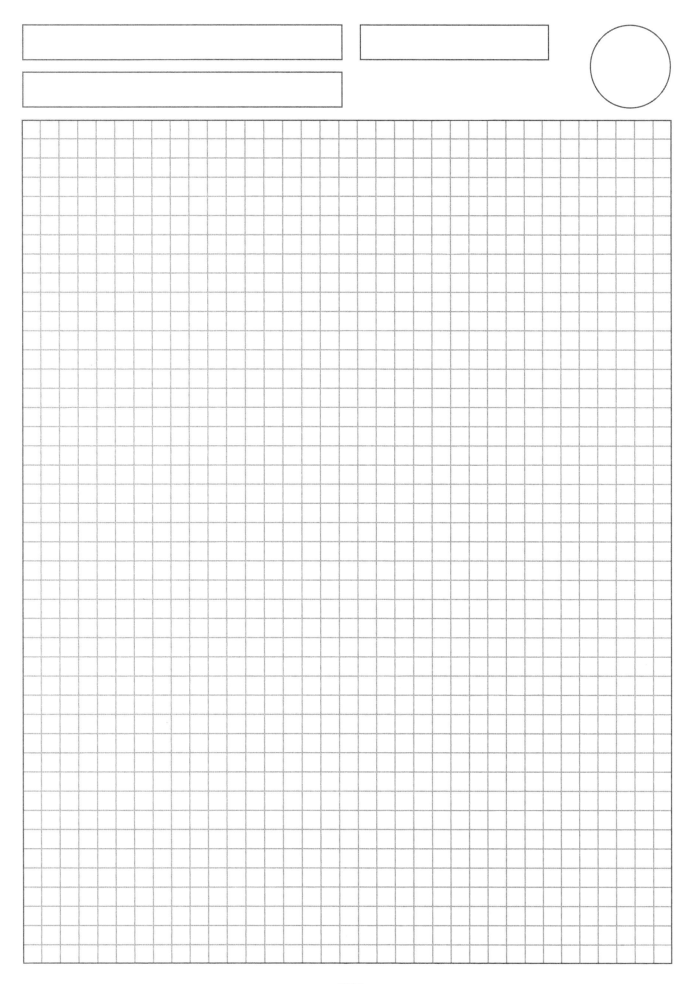

SECTOR 8

TACTICAL PLANS OF ACTION

(WHERE VULNERABILITIES CANNOT BE MITIGATED)

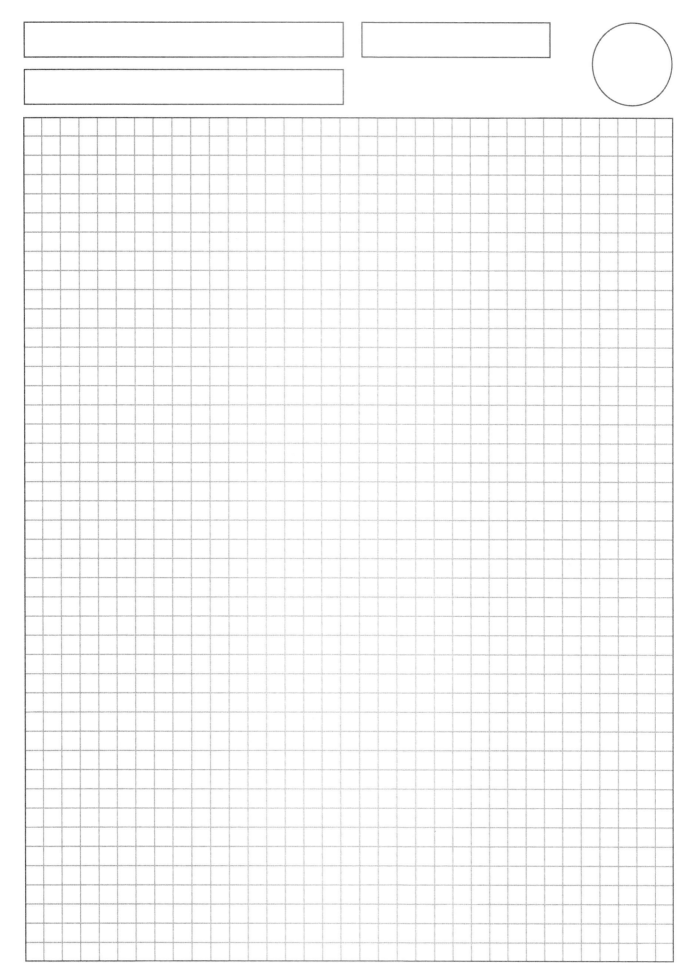

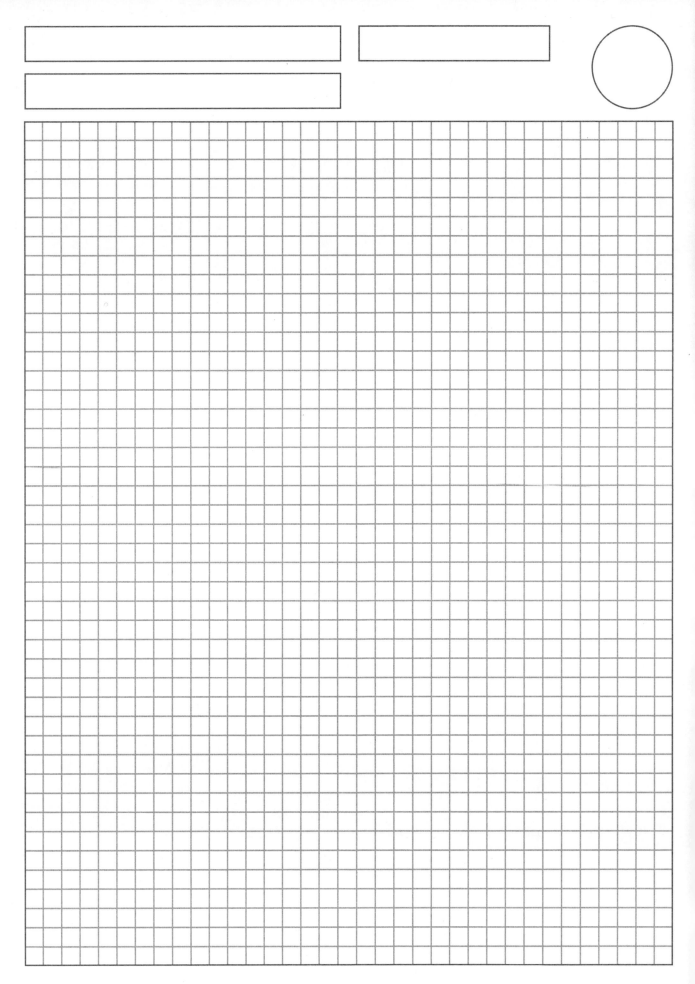

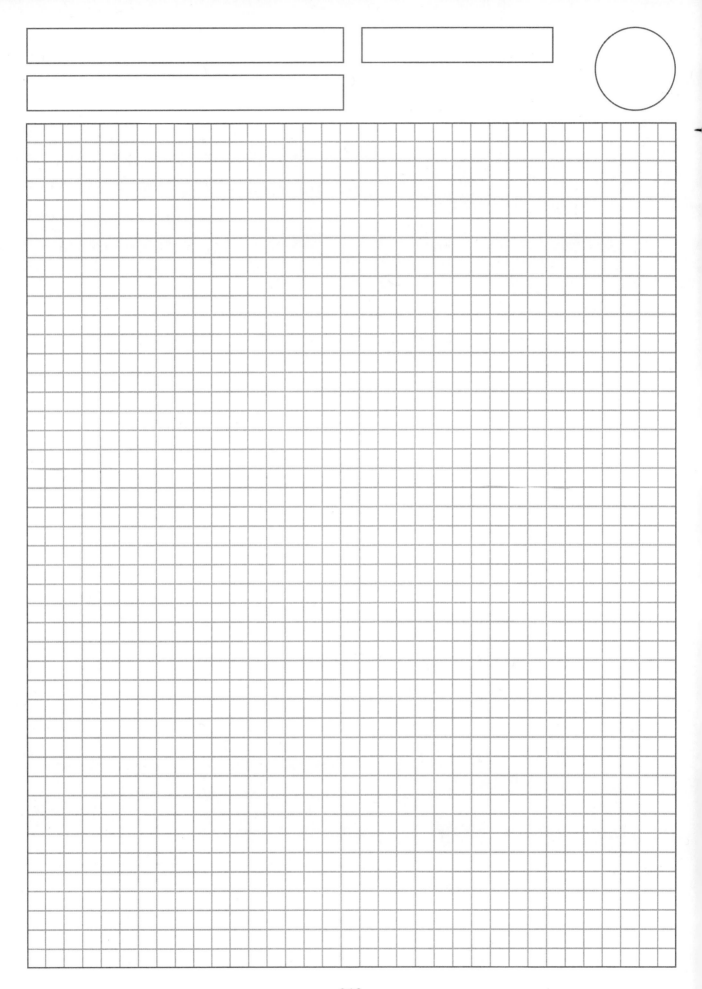

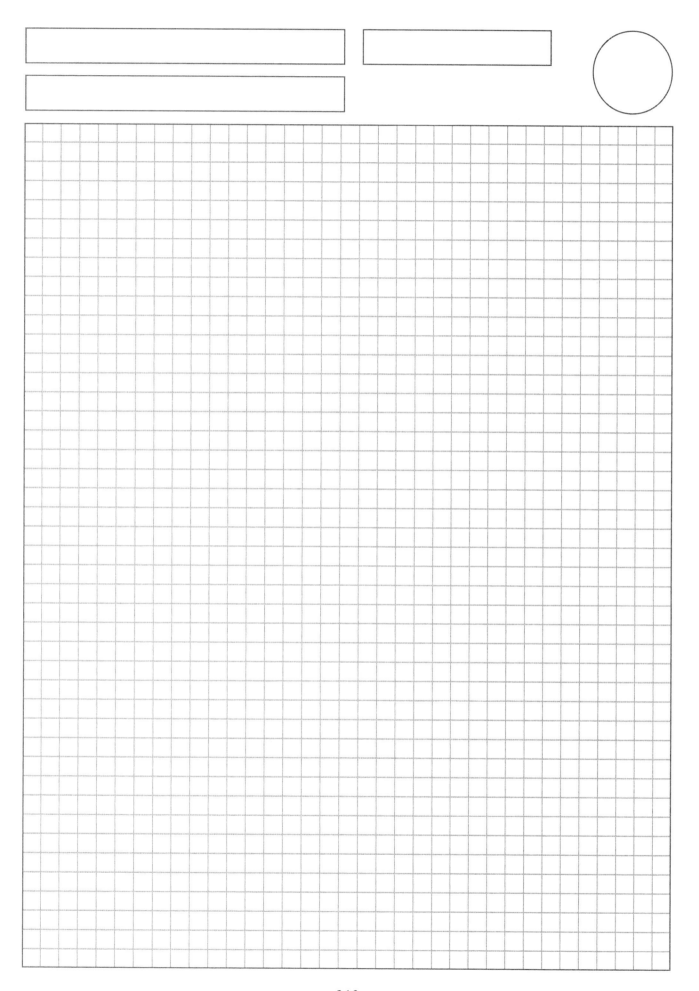

S9

SECTOR 9

SECTOR 9
FIRST RESPONDER OVERVIEW

THREAT ASSESSMENT SECTOR OVERVIEW

Sector:

Date:

Prepared by:

Situation:

Sector Overview:

Note: Make sure you print out map and directions to pertinent police precincts.

Police Departments:

PD Contact Information:

PD Response Times:

Crime Level:

Possible Threat Level:

Known Terror Threats:

Known Criminal Threats:

Note: Make sure you print out map and directions to all trauma centers. Always make the effort to proceed to a level 1 trauma center if the injury is life threatening.

Trauma Centers:

Trauma Center Level (I, II, III):

Response Times:

Weather Conditions:

| Spring | Summer | Fall | Winter |

RESPONSE RESOURCES
(Specific To This Sector)

Federal

- Department of Homeland Security (DHS)

  _____

  _____

- Federal Emergency Management Agency (FEMA)

  _____

  _____

- Federal Bureau of Investigation (FBI)

  _____

  _____

- Environmental Protection Agency (EPA)

  _____

  _____

- Health and Human Services (HHS)

  _____

  _____

State/Regional

- Emergency Management

  _____

  _____

- State Emergency Operations Center

  _____

  _____

- State Police

  _____

  _____

- National Guard

  _____

  _____

- Joint Terrorism Task Forces (JTTF)

  _____

  _____

Note: Make sure you print out map and directions to pertinent police precincts. Always make the effort to proceed to a level 1 trauma center if the injury is life threatening.

Local First Responders

- Police

  _____

  _____

  - Special Weapons And Tactics (SWAT) Teams

    _____

  - Explosive Ordnance Disposal (EOD)

    _____

- Police

  _____

  _____

  - Special Weapons And Tactics (SWAT) Teams

    _____

  - Explosive Ordnance Disposal (EOD)

    _____

RESPONSE RESOURCES (continued)
(Specific To This Sector)

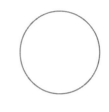

- Police

  _____

  _____

  - Special Weapons And Tactics (SWAT) Teams

    _____

  - Explosive Ordnance Disposal (EOD)

    _____

- Fire

  _____

  _____

  - Rescue / Emergency Medical Services

    _____

  - Hazardous Materials Response Teams

    _____

- Emergency Management

  _____

  _____

Note: Make sure you print out map and directions to all trauma centers. Always make the effort to proceed to a level 1 trauma center if the injury is life threatening.

Hospitals

- Level I Trauma Center

  _____

  _____

- Level II Trauma Center

  _____

  _____

- Urgent Care

  _____

  _____

- Other Medical Center

  _____

  _____

- Other Medical Center

  _____

  _____

Known Threats

- Crime

  _____

  _____

  _____

  _____

  _____

  _____

- Terror

  _____

  _____

  _____

  _____

  _____

*Note: If this sector is a special event or a vacation, take a screen shot
of the weather report and attach here*

SECTOR 9
VULNERABILITY MITIGATION

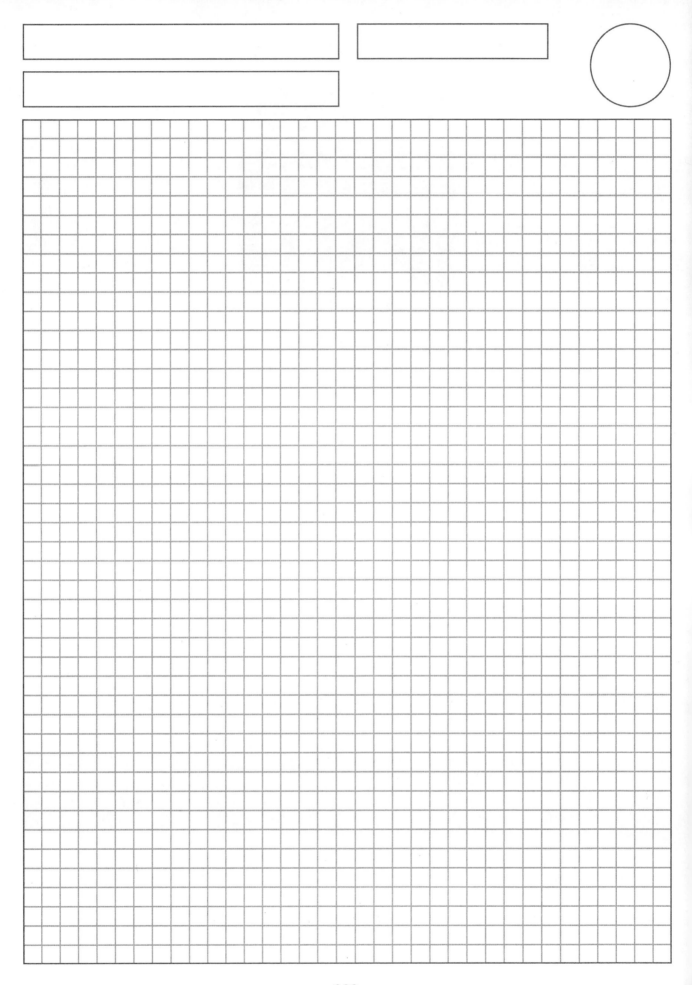

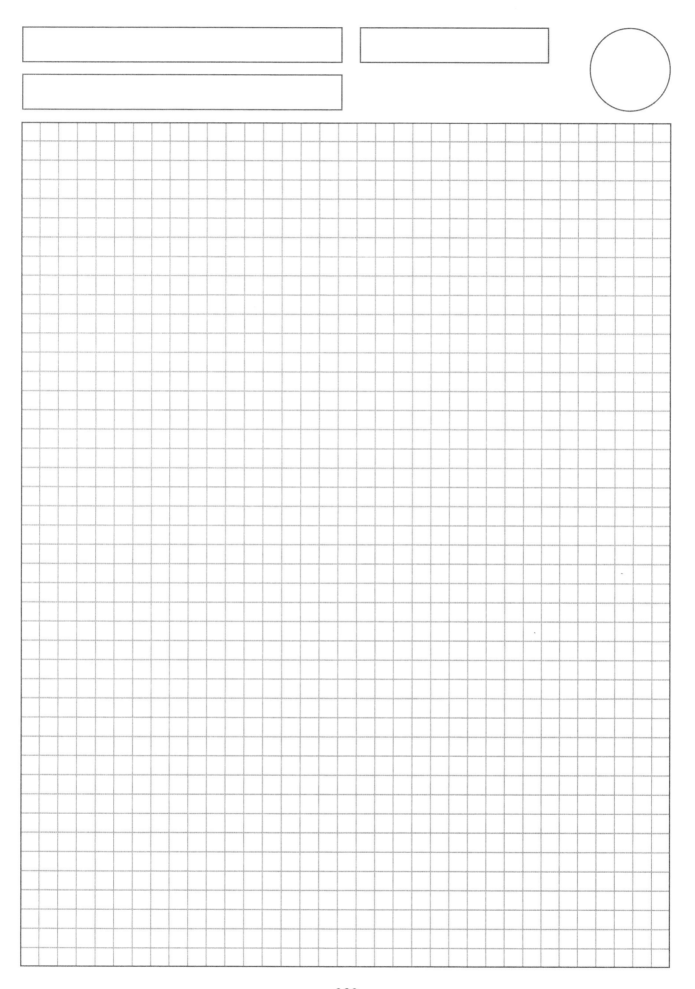

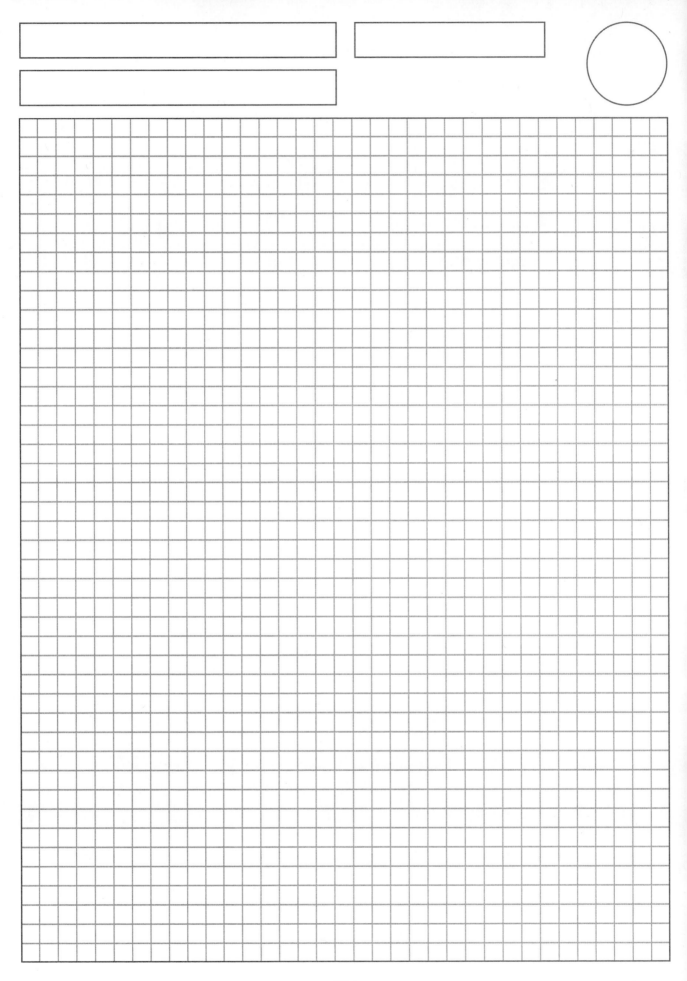

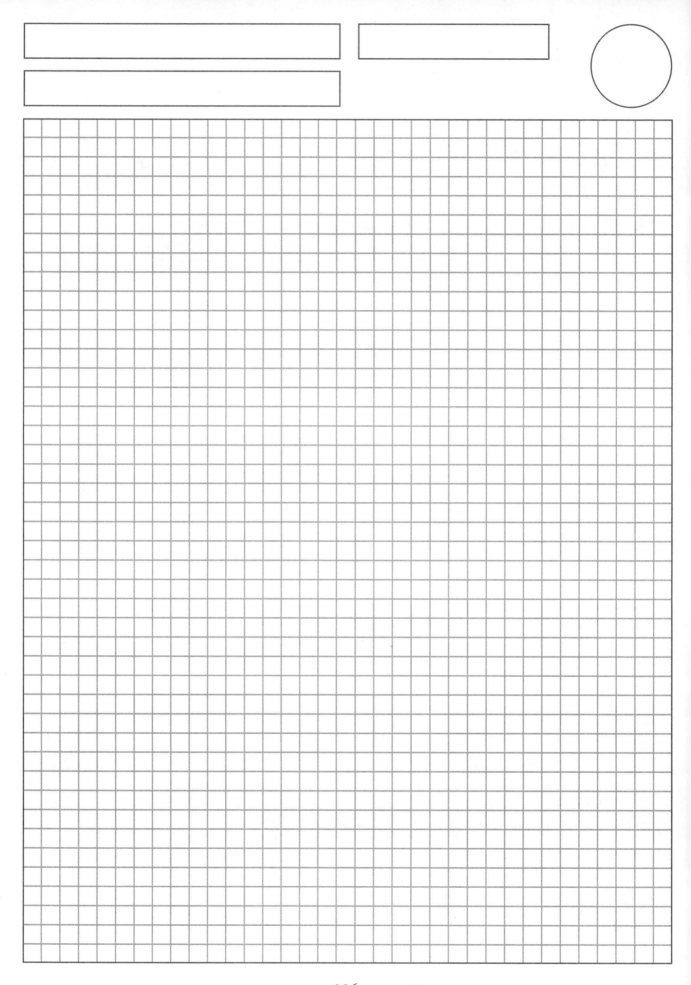

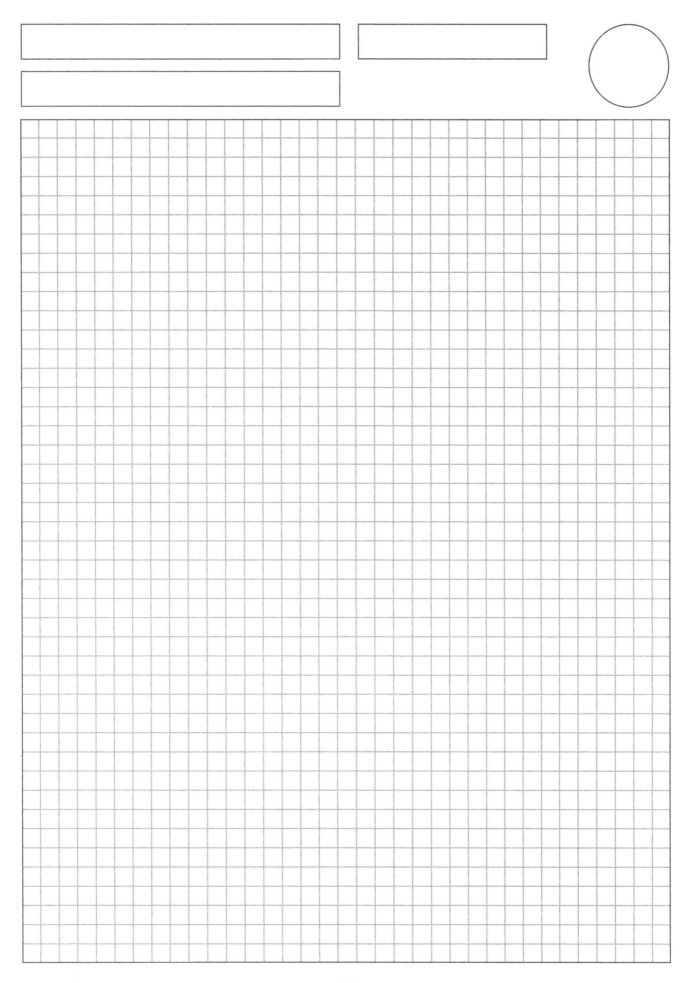

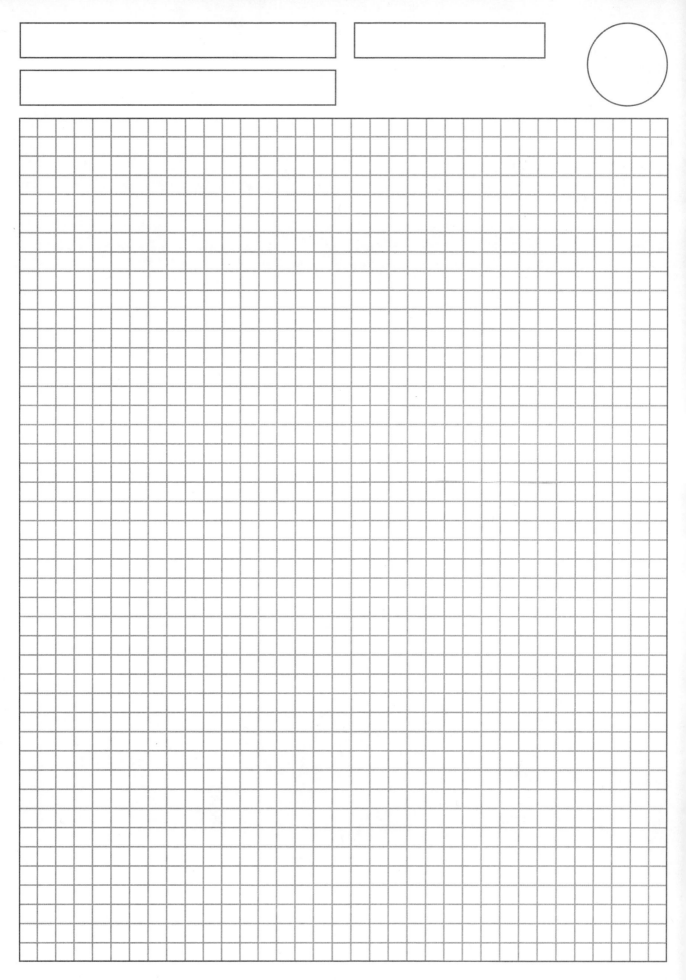

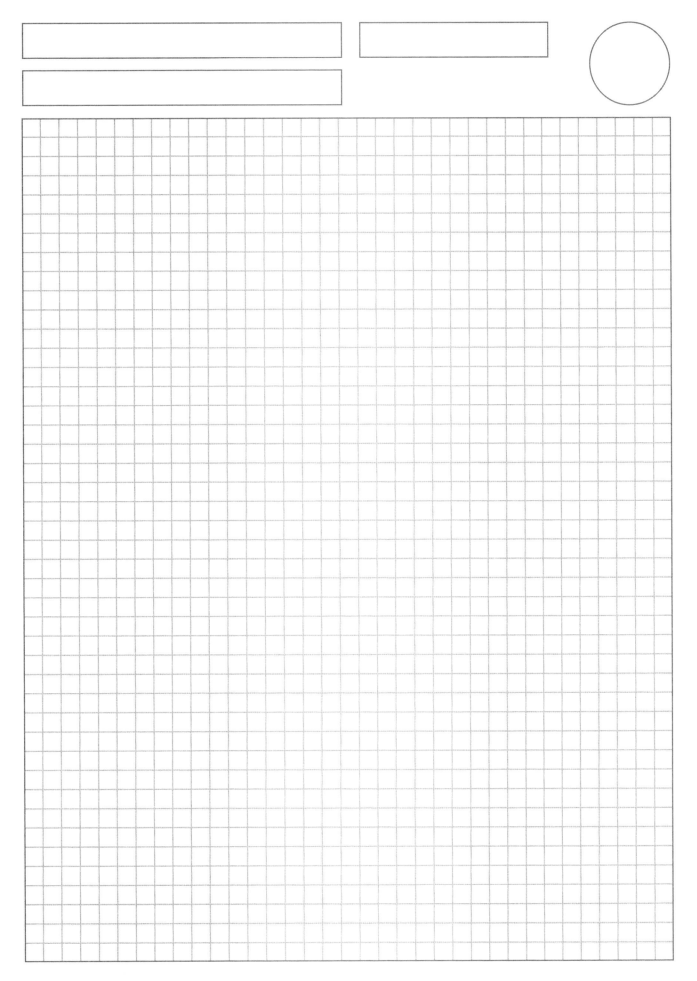

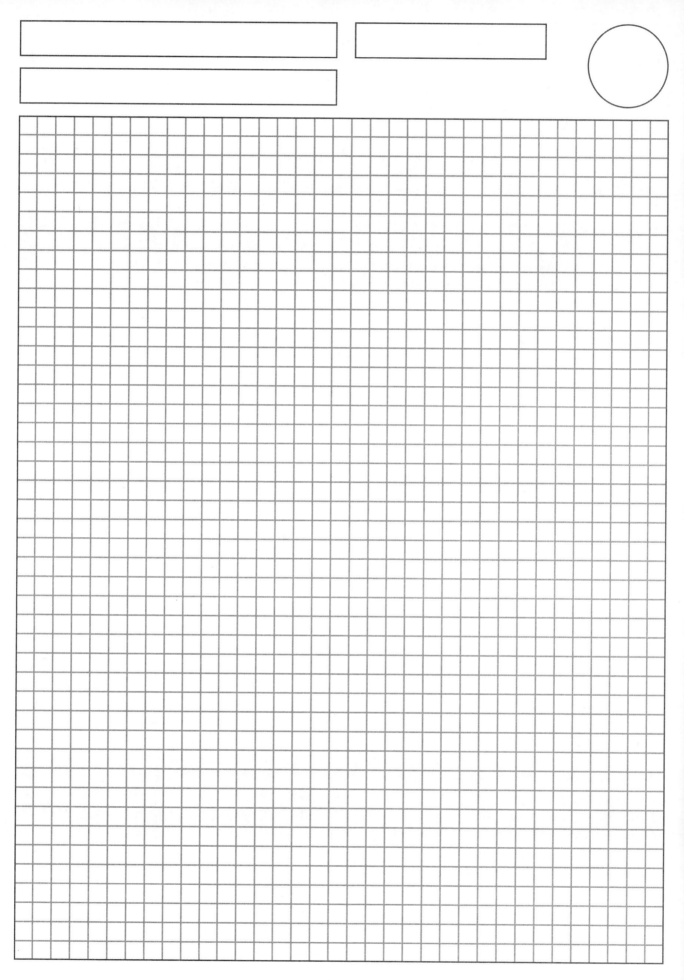

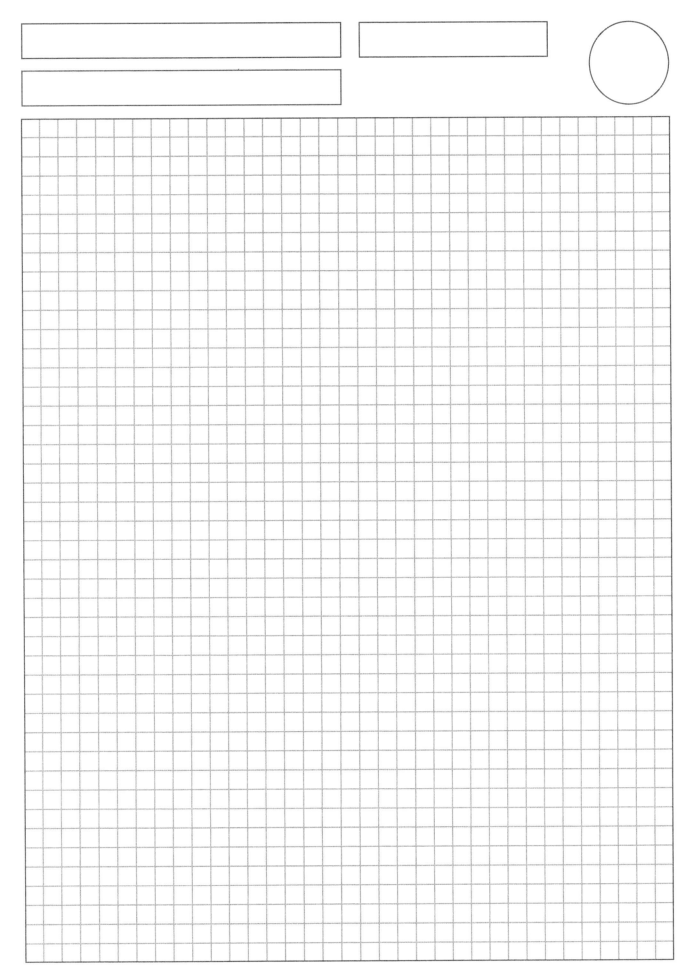

SECTOR 9

IMPLEMENTATION OF PHYSICAL

DEFENSE AND TECHNOLOGY

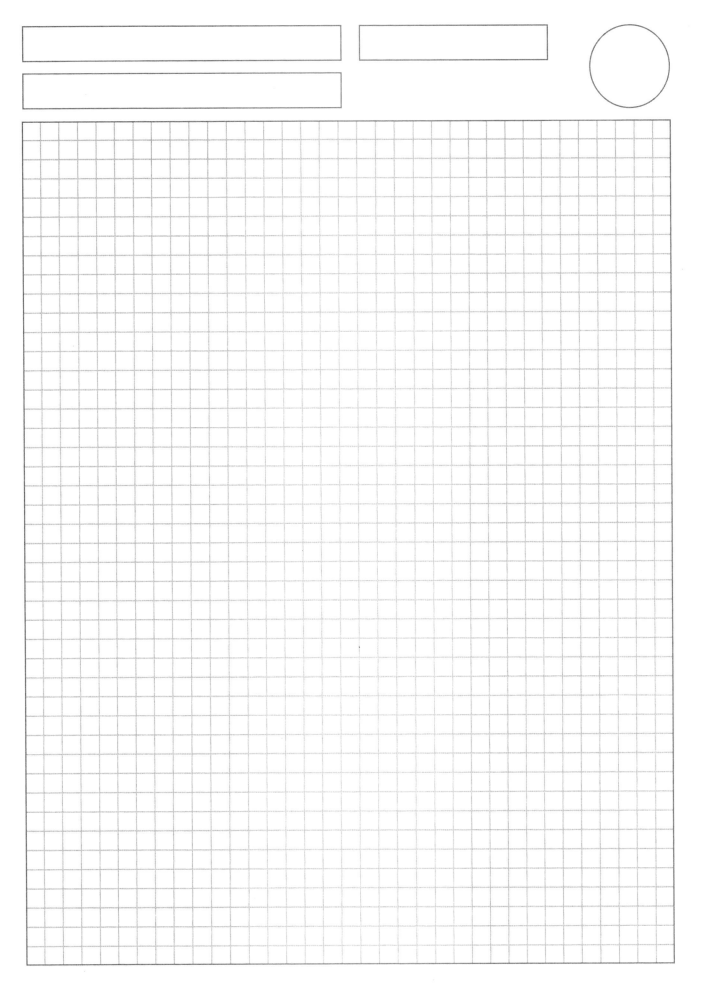

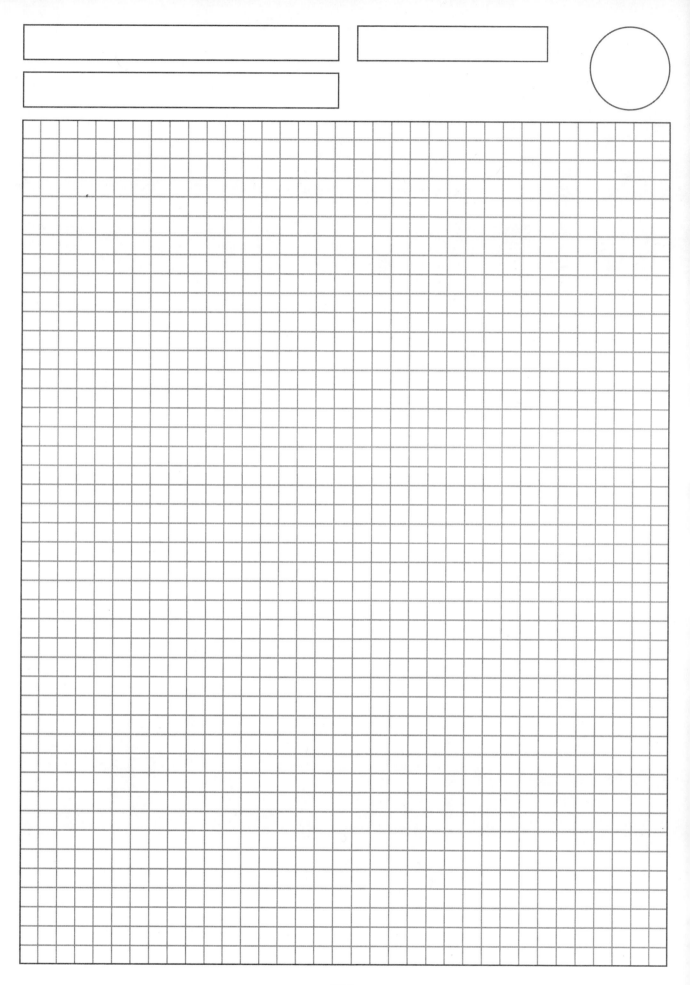

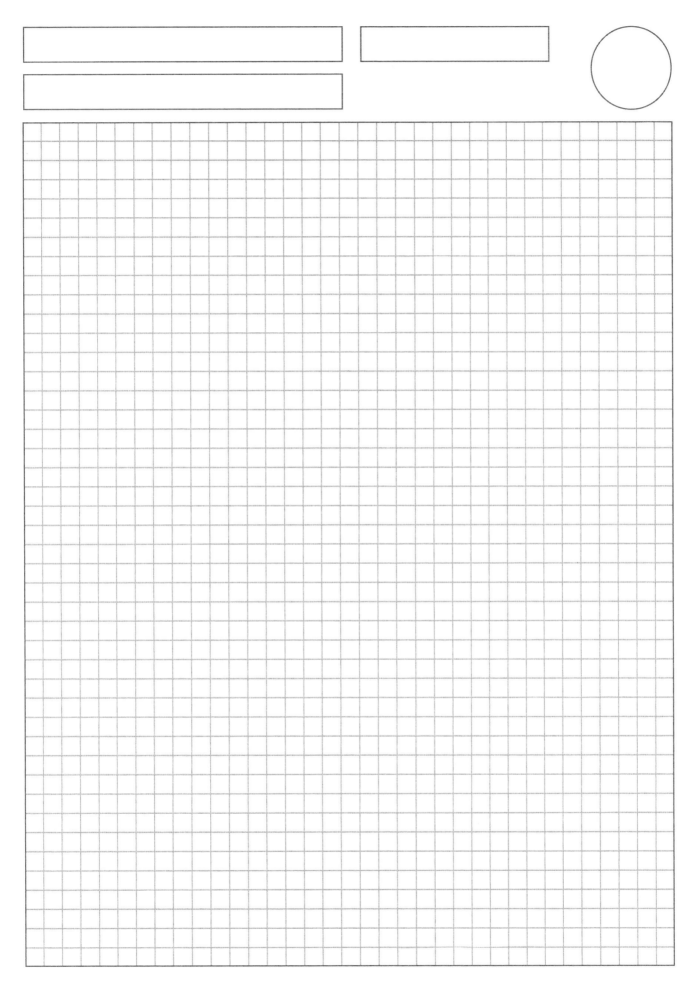

SECTOR 9
BEHAVIORS AND ATTACK
INDICATORS

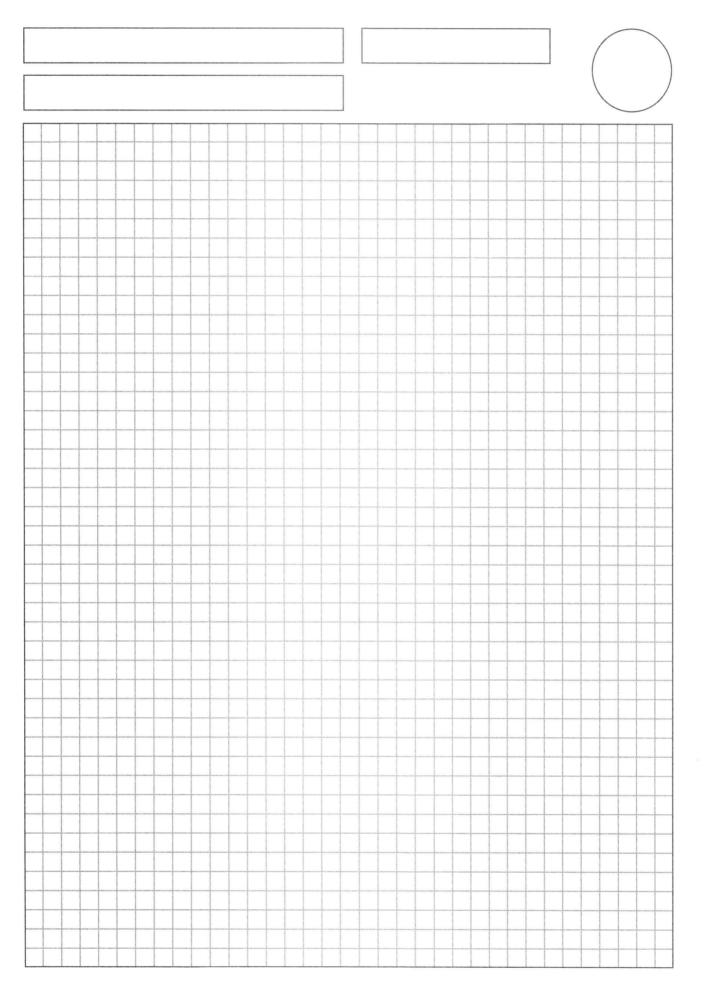

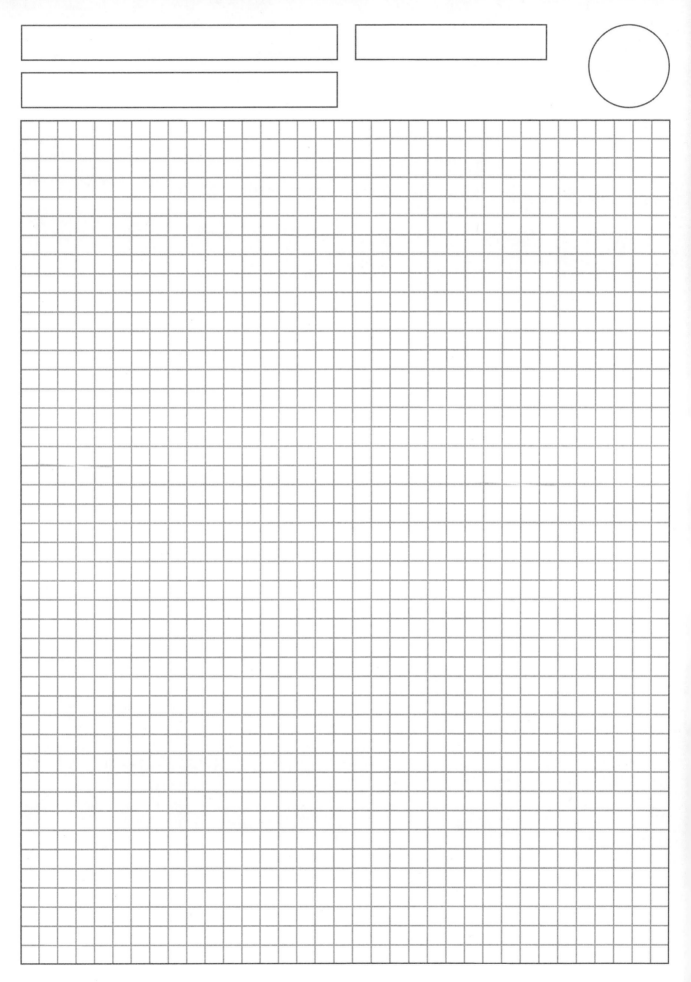

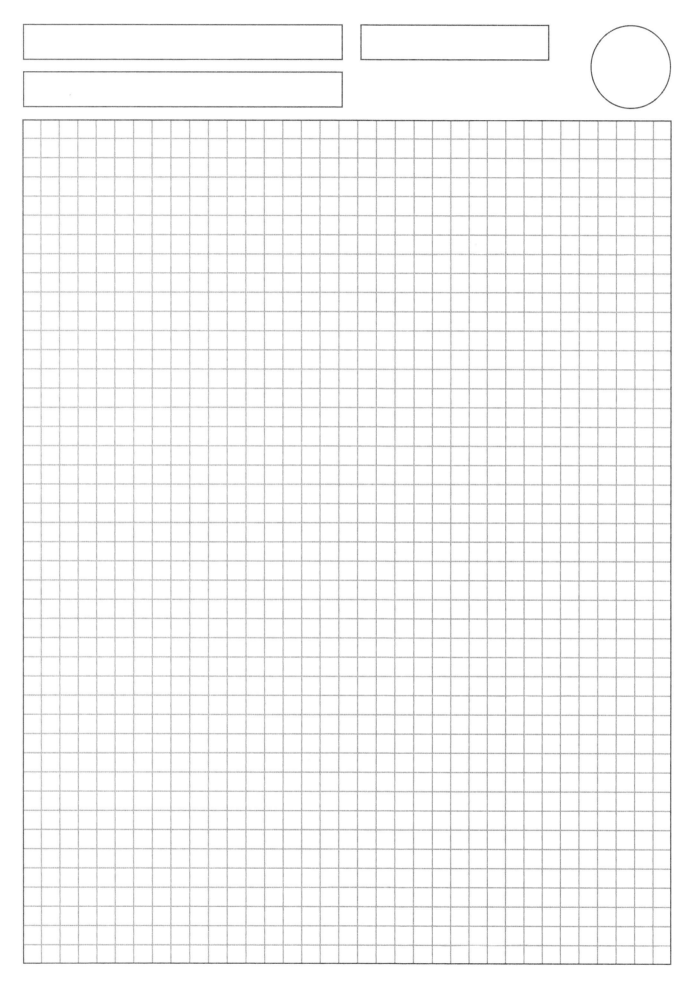

SECTOR 9

SHARED THREATS

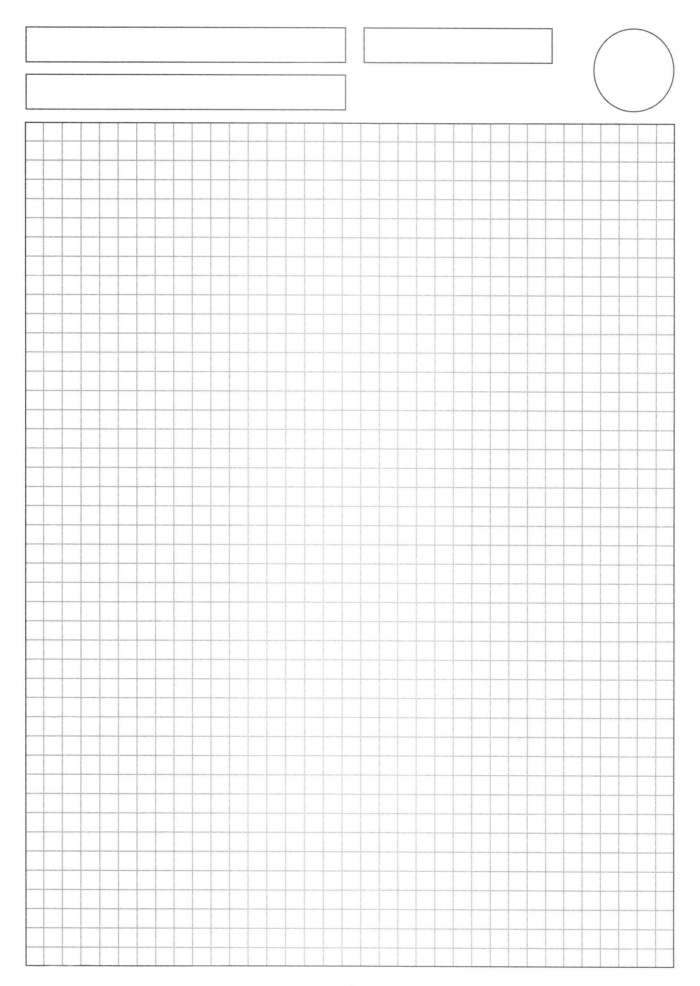

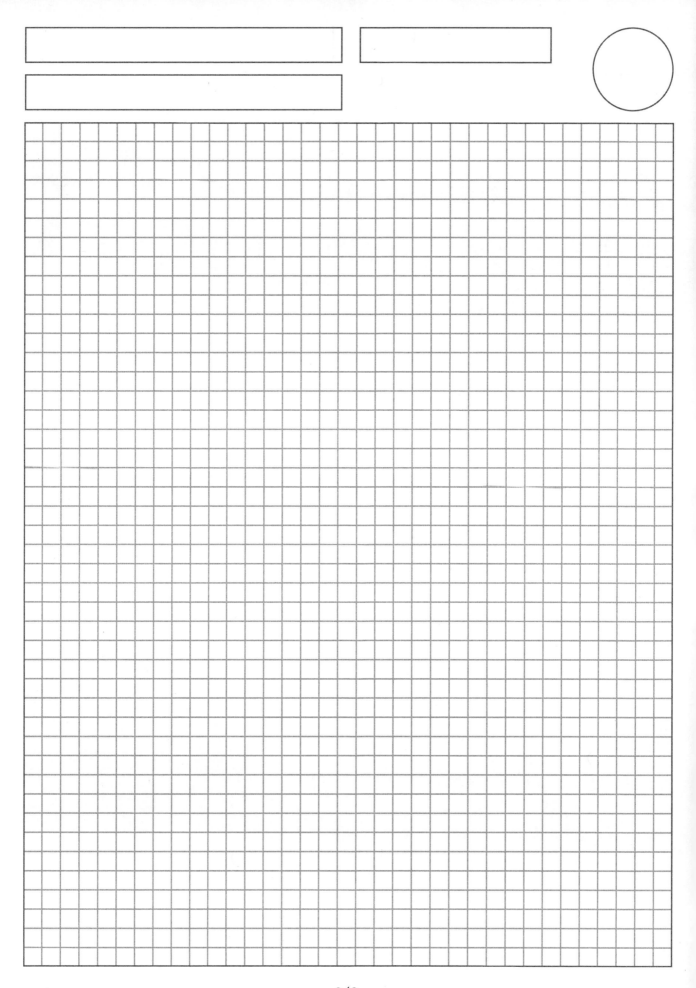

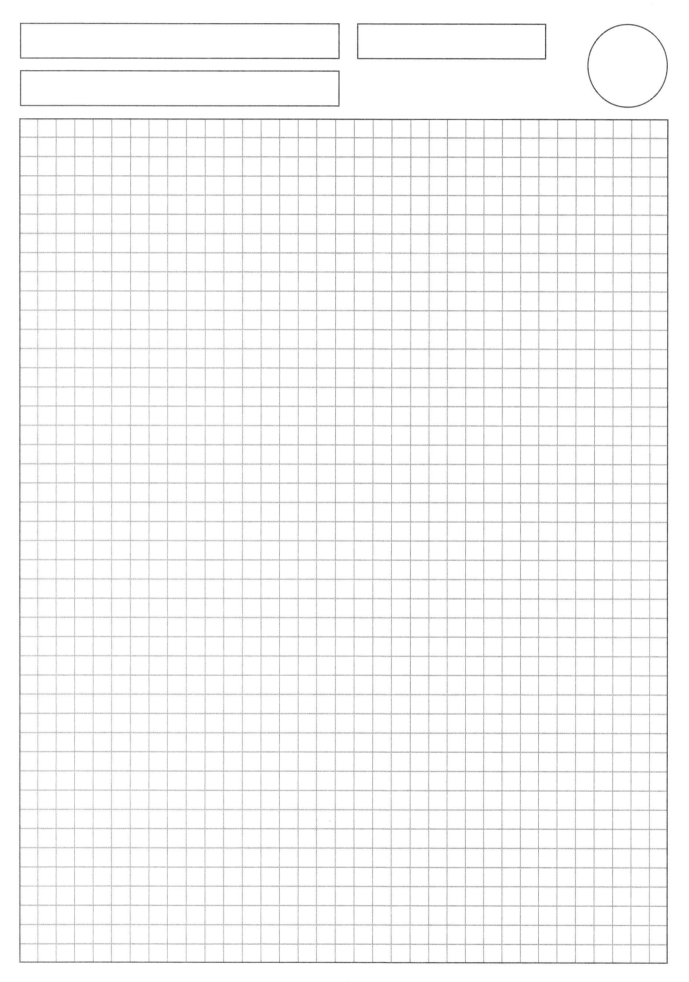

SECTOR 9

TACTICAL PLANS OF ACTION

(WHERE VULNERABILITIES CANNOT BE MITIGATED)

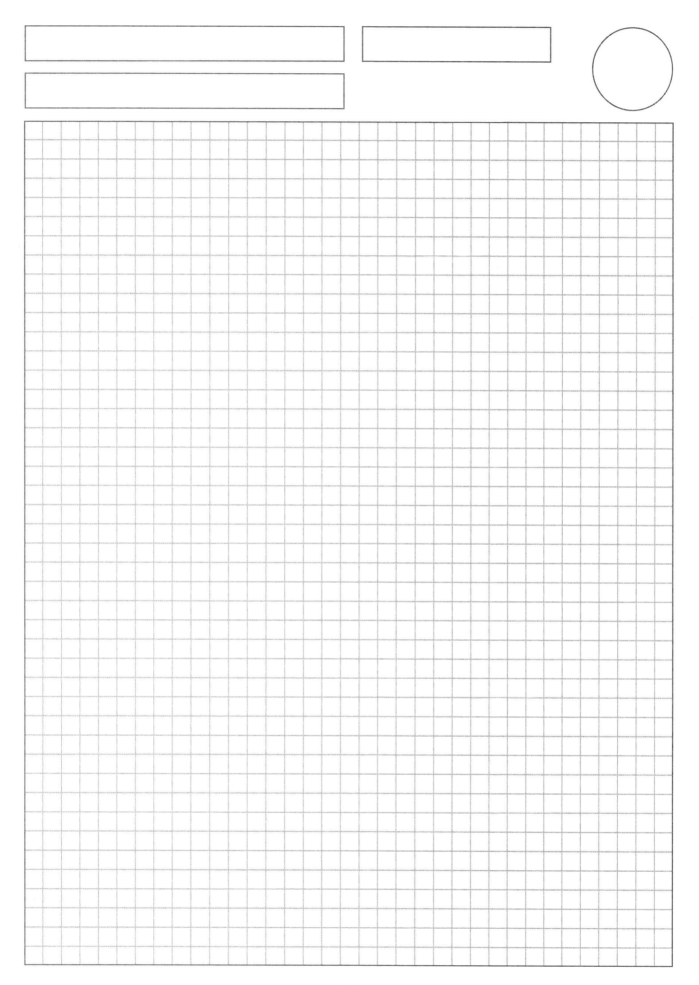

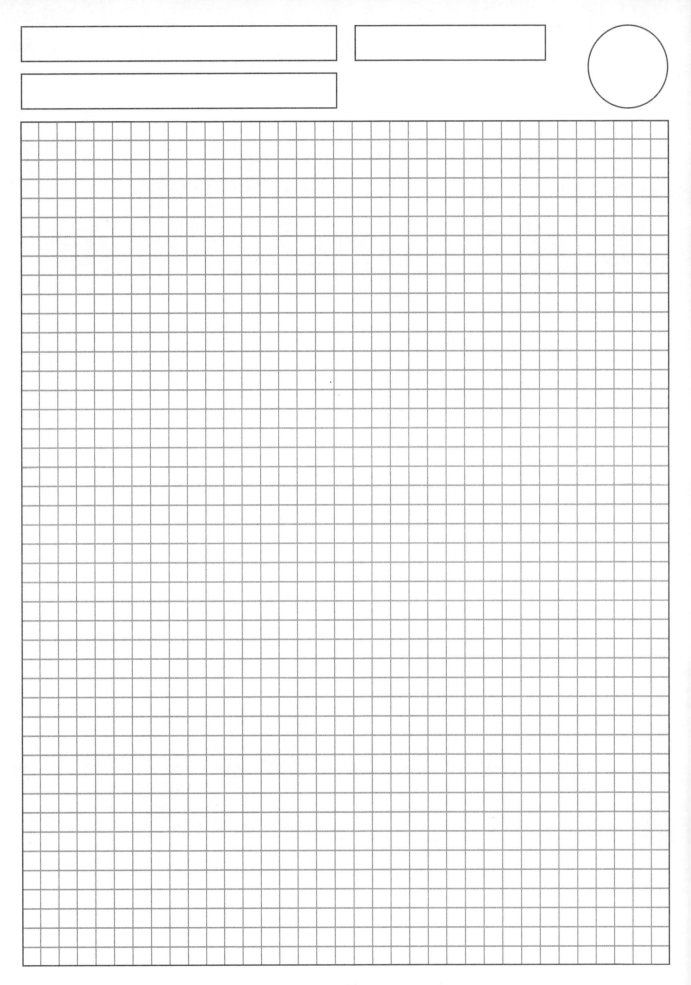

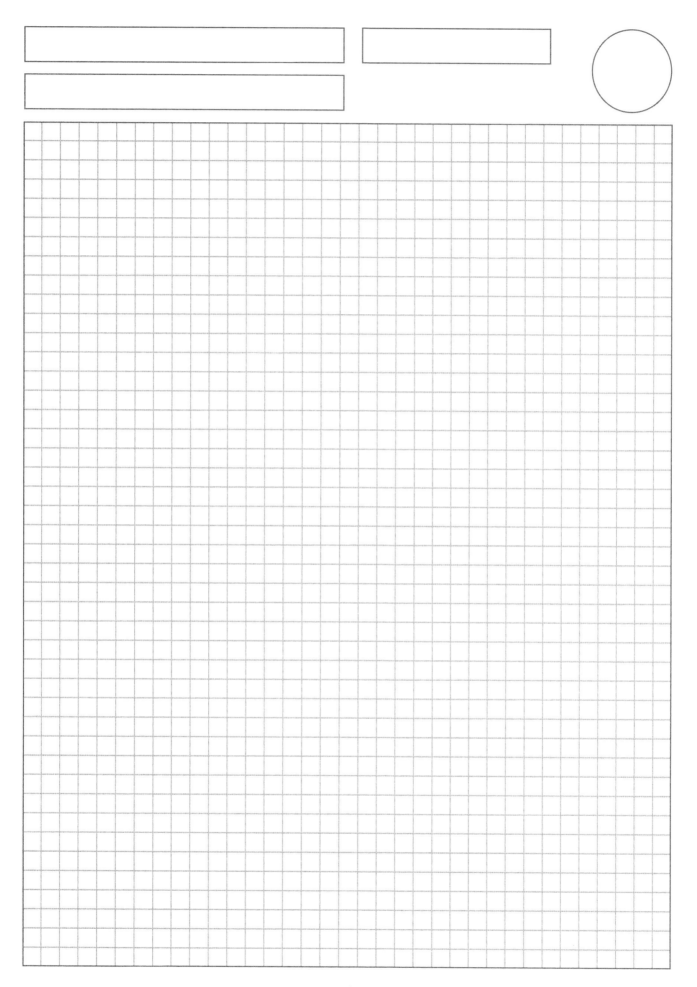

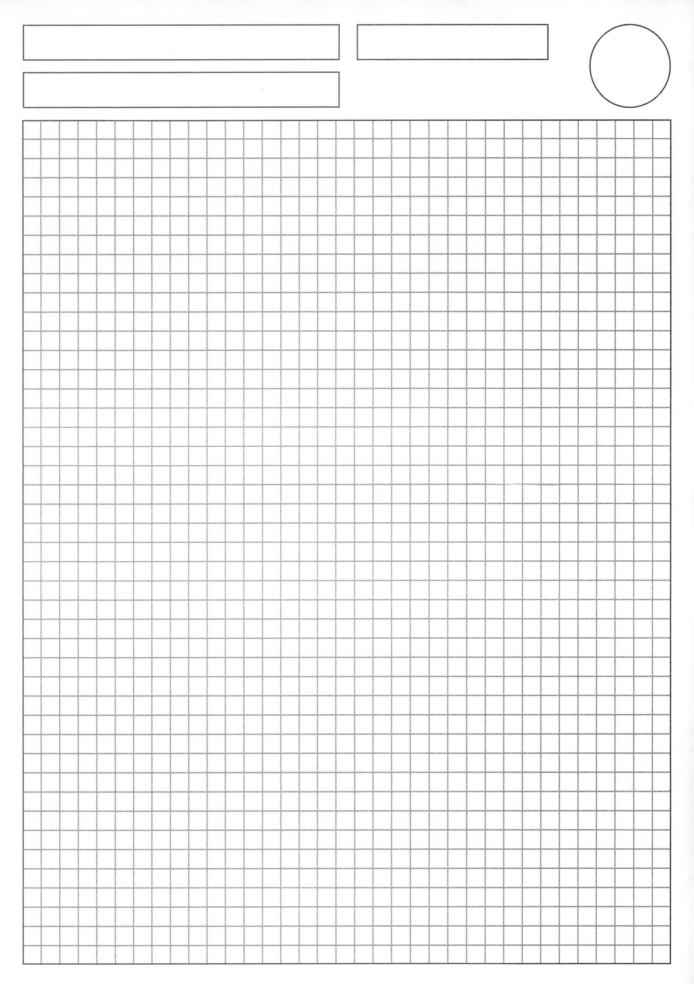

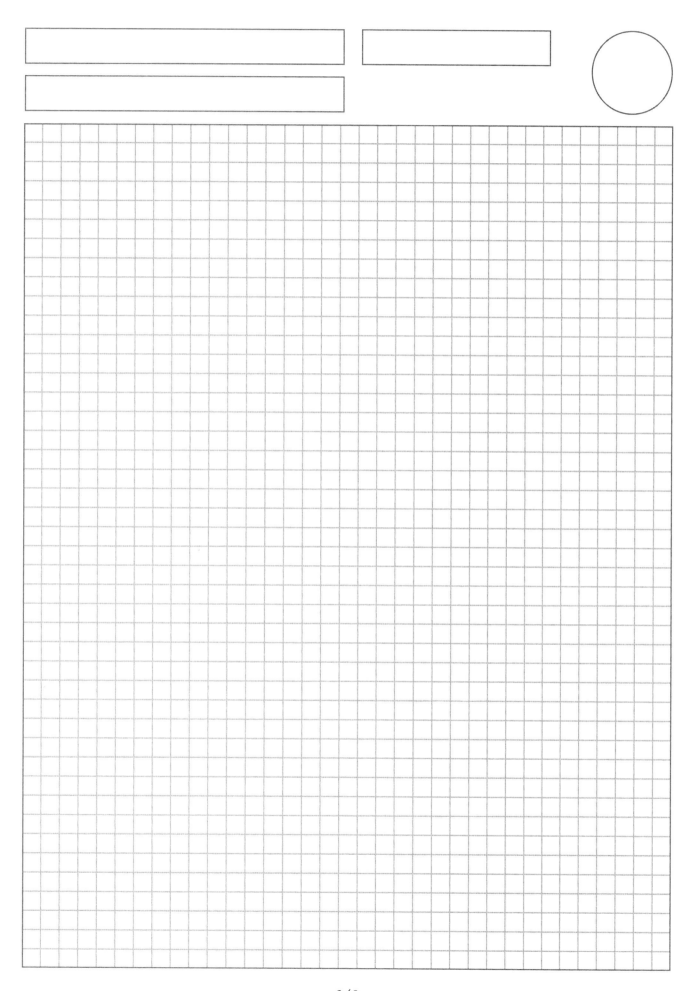

S10

SECTOR 10

SECTOR 10
FIRST RESPONDER OVERVIEW

THREAT ASSESSMENT SECTOR OVERVIEW

Sector:

Date:

Prepared by:

Situation:

Sector Overview:

Note: Make sure you print out map and directions to pertinent police precincts.

Police Departments:

PD Contact Information:

PD Response Times:

Crime Level:

Possible Threat Level:

Known Terror Threats:

Known Criminal Threats:

Note: Make sure you print out map and directions to all trauma centers. Always make the effort to proceed to a level 1 trauma center if the injury is life threatening.

Trauma Centers:

Trauma Center Level (I, II, III):

Response Times:

Weather Conditions:

Spring   Summer   Fall   Winter

RESPONSE RESOURCES
(Specific To This Sector)

Federal

- Department of Homeland Security (DHS)

  _____

  _____

- Federal Emergency Management Agency (FEMA)

  _____

  _____

- Federal Bureau of Investigation (FBI)

  _____

  _____

- Environmental Protection Agency (EPA)

  _____

  _____

- Health and Human Services (HHS)

  _____

  _____

State/Regional

- Emergency Management

  _____

  _____

- State Emergency Operations Center

  _____

  _____

- State Police

  _____

  _____

- National Guard

  _____

  _____

- Joint Terrorism Task Forces (JTTF)

  _____

  _____

> Note: Make sure you print out map and directions to pertinent police precincts. Always make the effort to proceed to a level 1 trauma center if the injury is life threatening.

Local First Responders

- Police

  _____

  _____

  - Special Weapons And Tactics (SWAT) Teams

    _____

  - Explosive Ordnance Disposal (EOD)

    _____

- Police

  _____

  _____

  - Special Weapons And Tactics (SWAT) Teams

    _____

  - Explosive Ordnance Disposal (EOD)

    _____

- Police

  _____

  _____

  - Special Weapons And Tactics (SWAT) Teams

    _____

  - Explosive Ordnance Disposal (EOD)

    _____

- Fire

  _____

  _____

  - Rescue / Emergency Medical Services

    _____

  - Hazardous Materials Response Teams

    _____

- Emergency Management

  _____

  _____

Note: Make sure you print out map and directions to all trauma centers. Always make the effort to proceed to a level 1 trauma center if the injury is life threatening.

Hospitals

- Level I Trauma Center

  _____

  _____

- Level II Trauma Center

  _____

  _____

RESPONSE RESOURCES (continued)
(Specific To This Sector)

- Urgent Care

  _____

  _____

- Other Medical Center

  _____

  _____

- Other Medical Center

  _____

  _____

Known Threats

- Crime

  _____

  _____

  _____

  _____

  _____

  _____

- Terror

  _____

  _____

  _____

  _____

  _____

  _____

_Note: If this sector is a special event or a vacation, take a screen shot
of the weather report and attach here_

SECTOR 10
VULNERABILITY MITIGATION

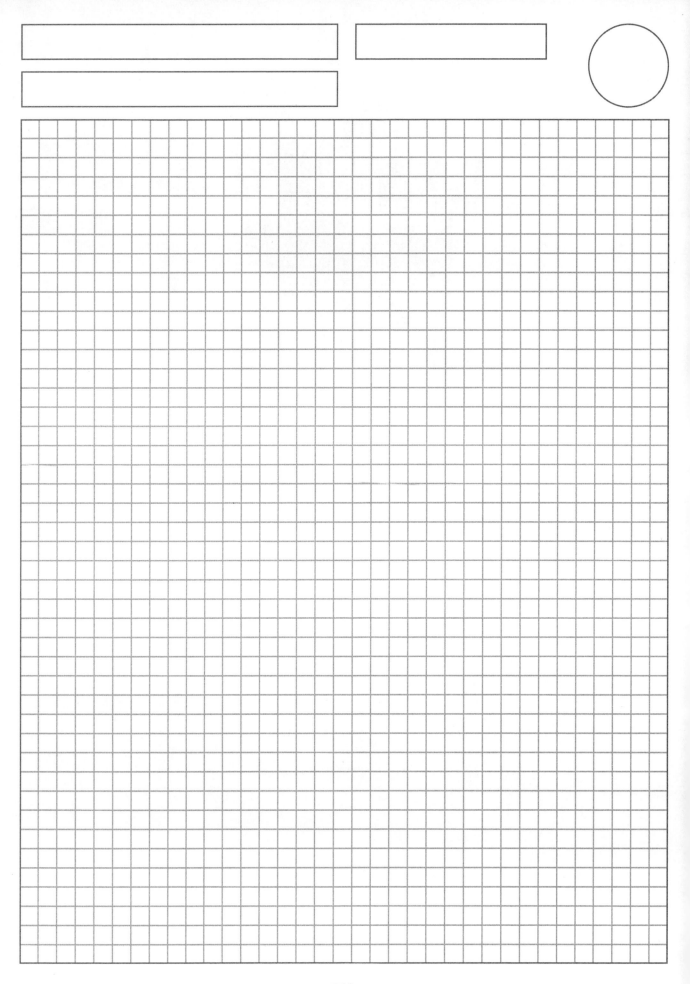

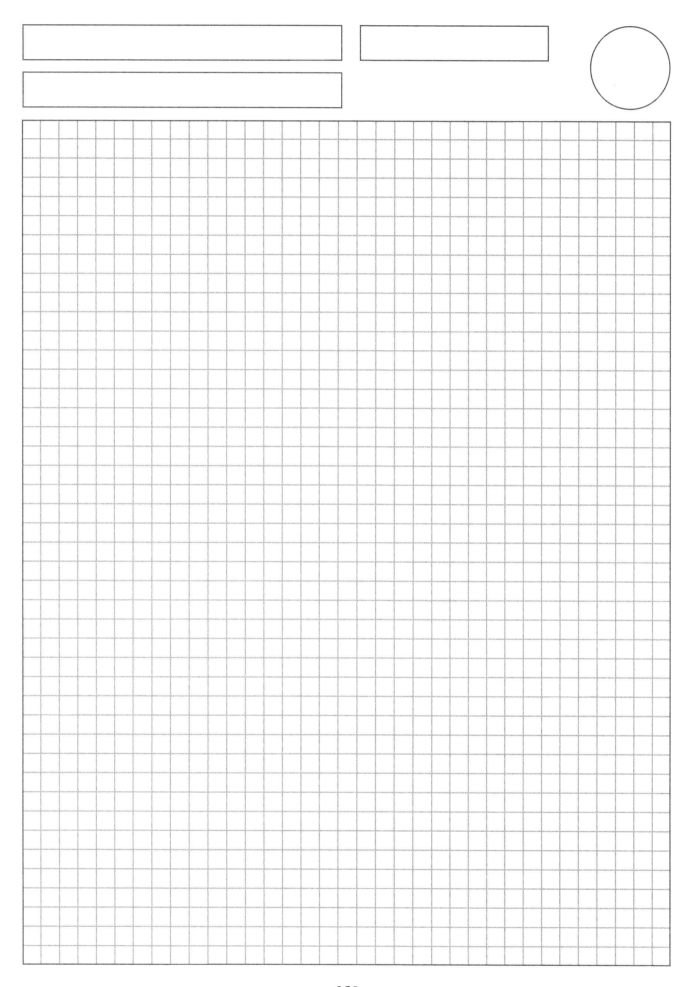

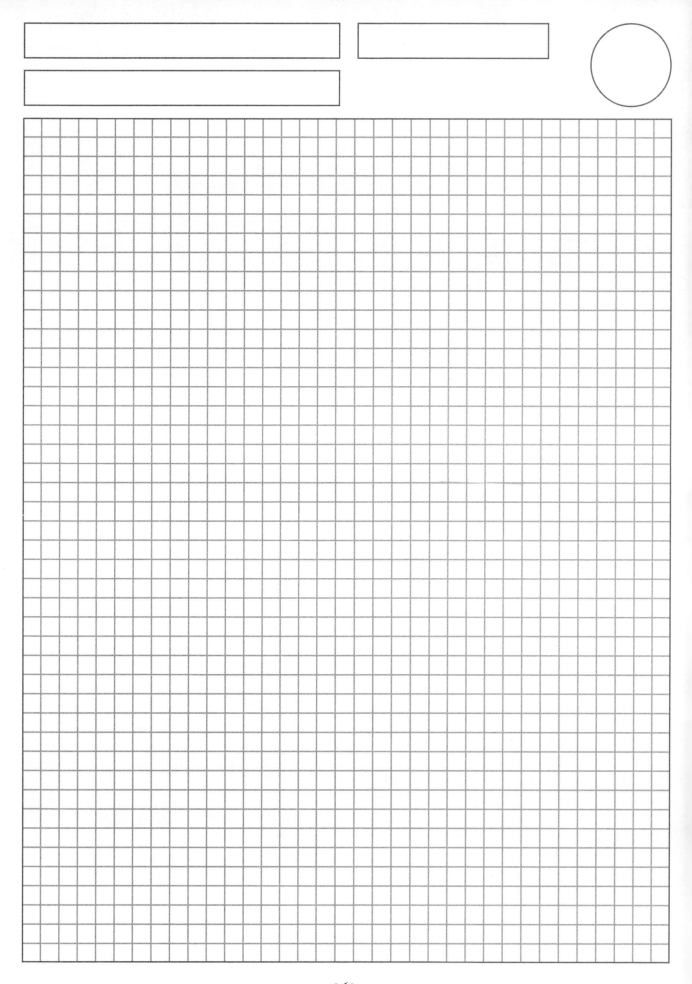

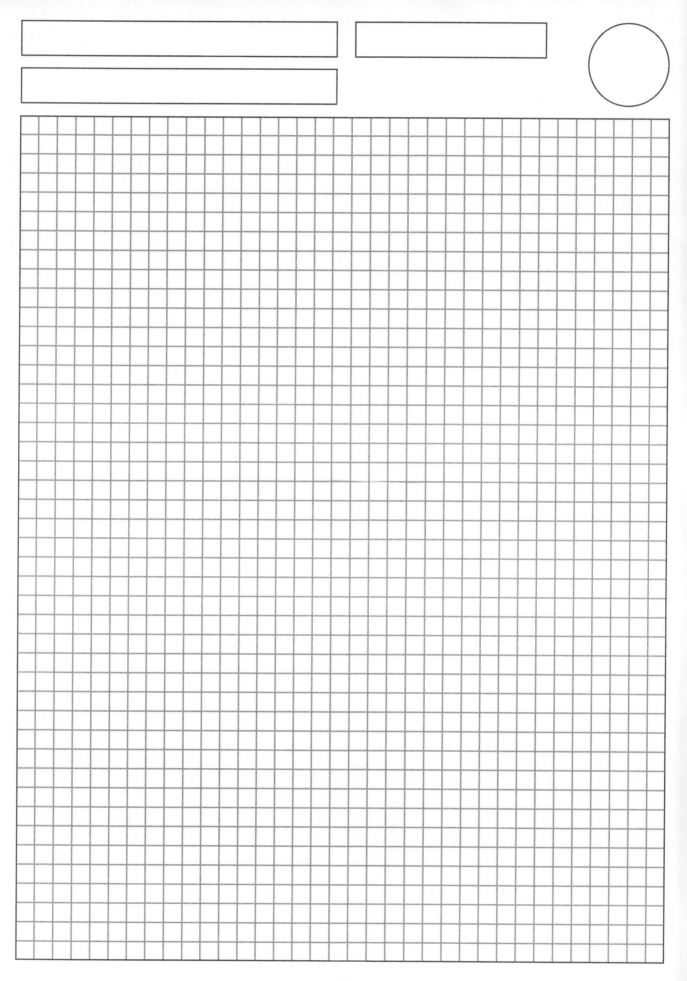

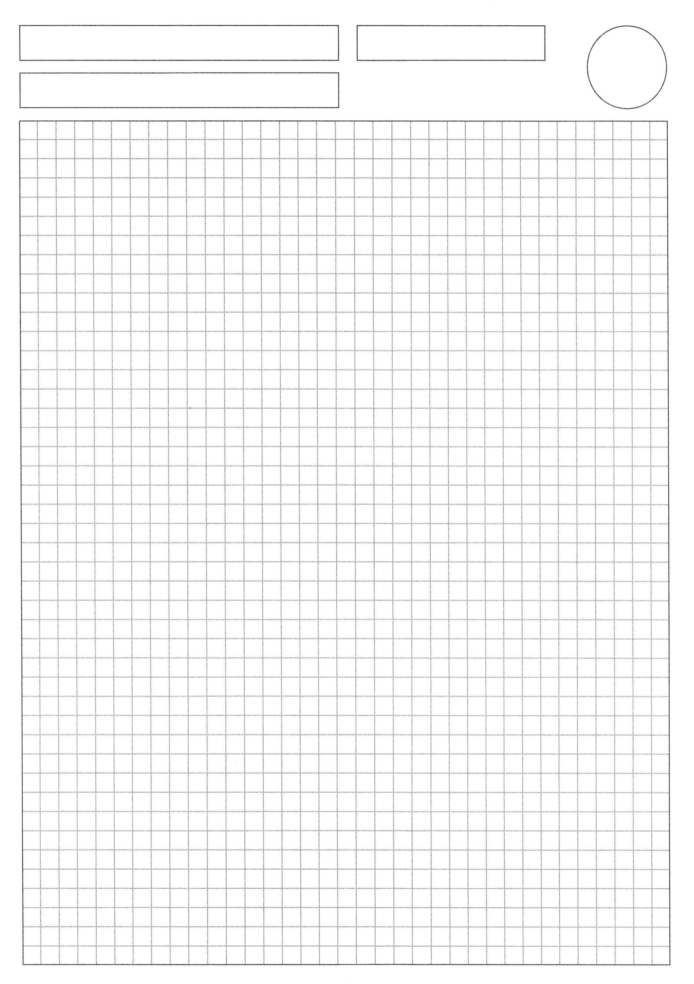

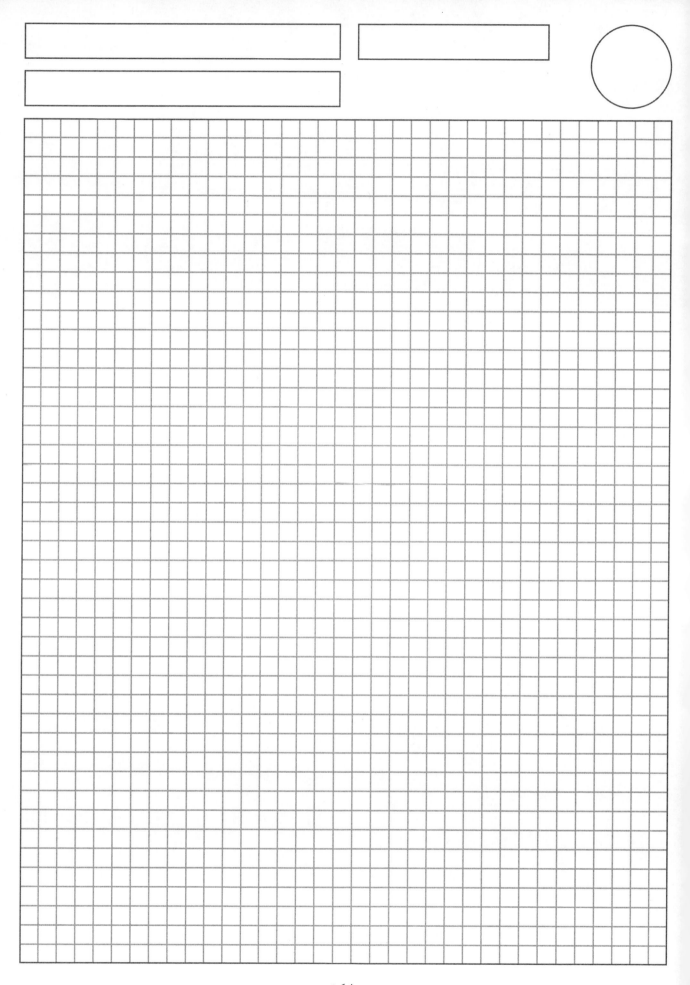

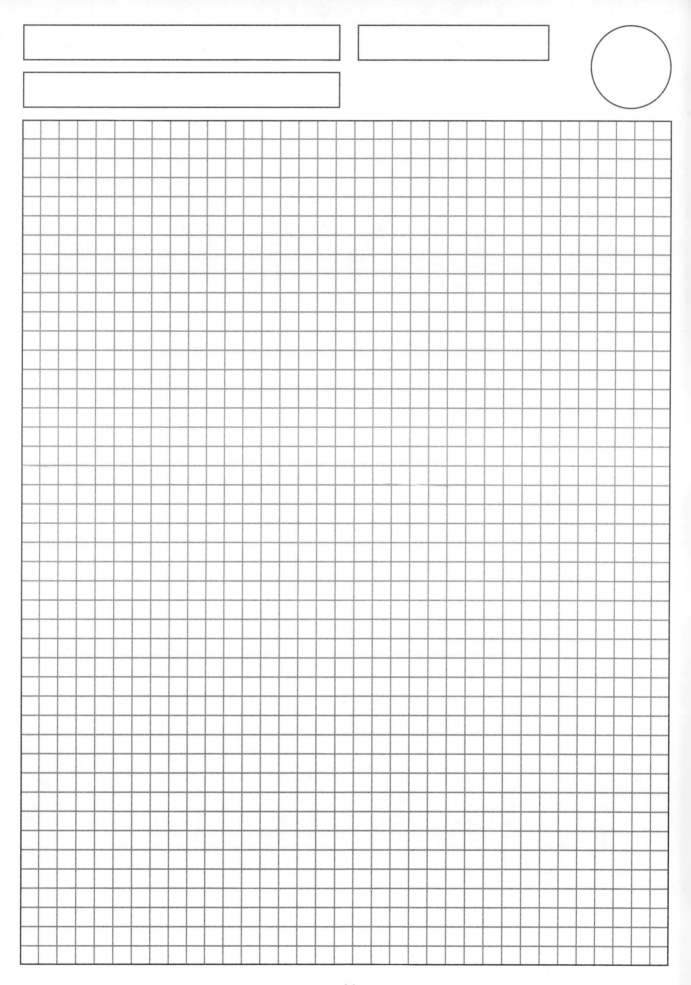

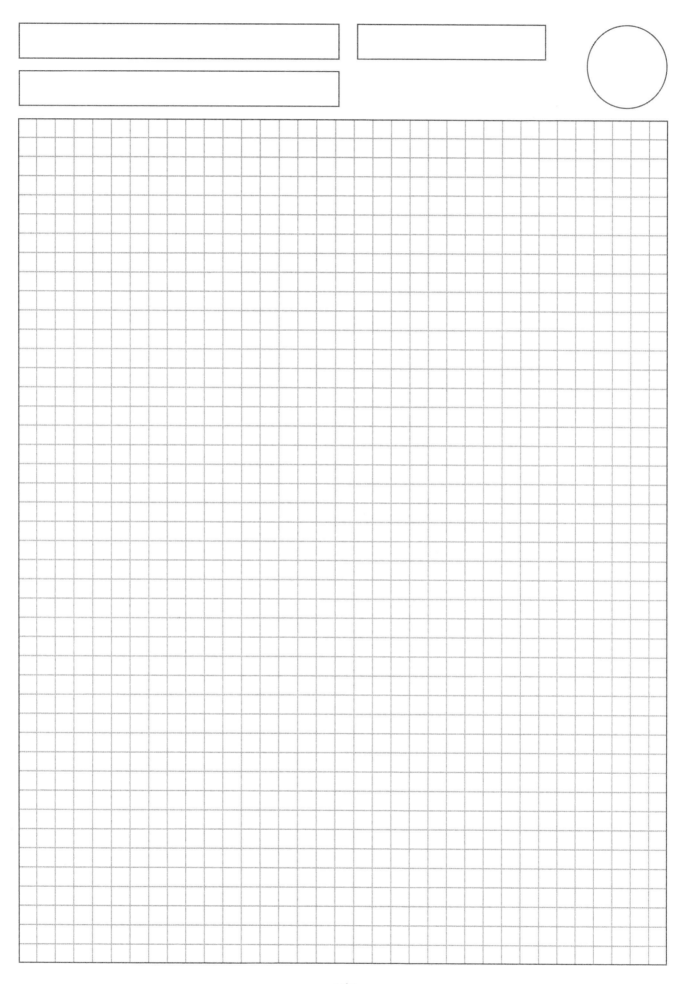

SECTOR 10

IMPLEMENTATION OF PHYSICAL

DEFENSE AND TECHNOLOGY

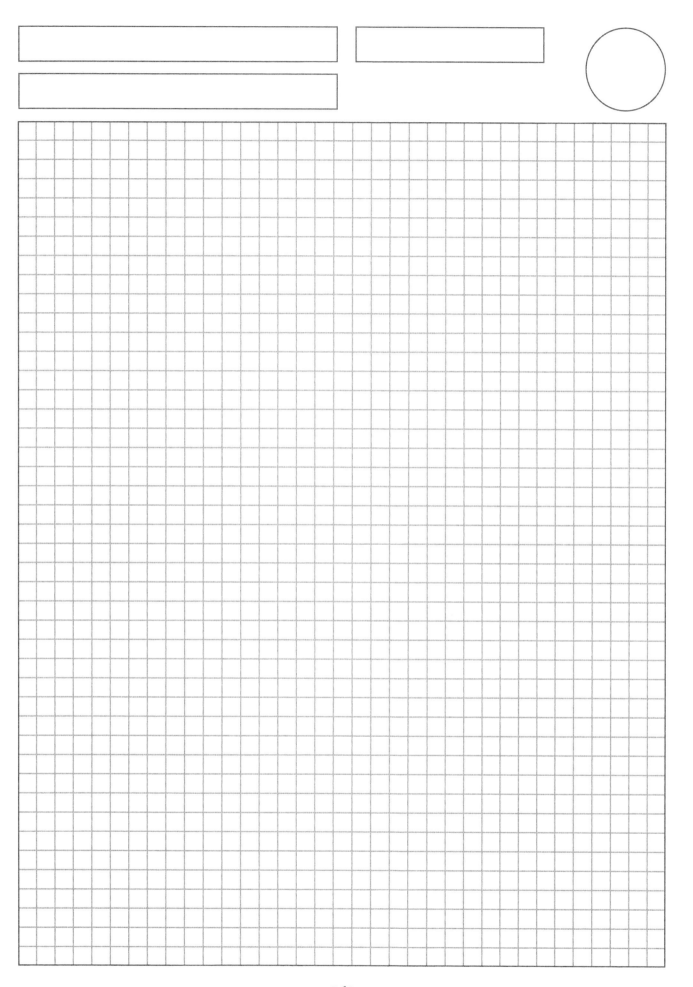

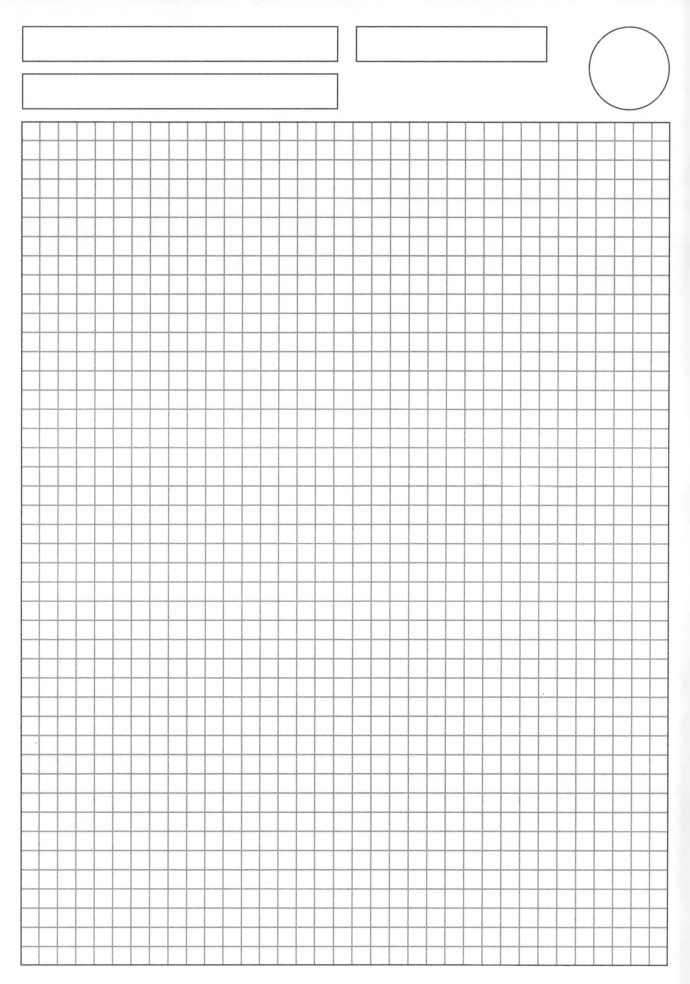

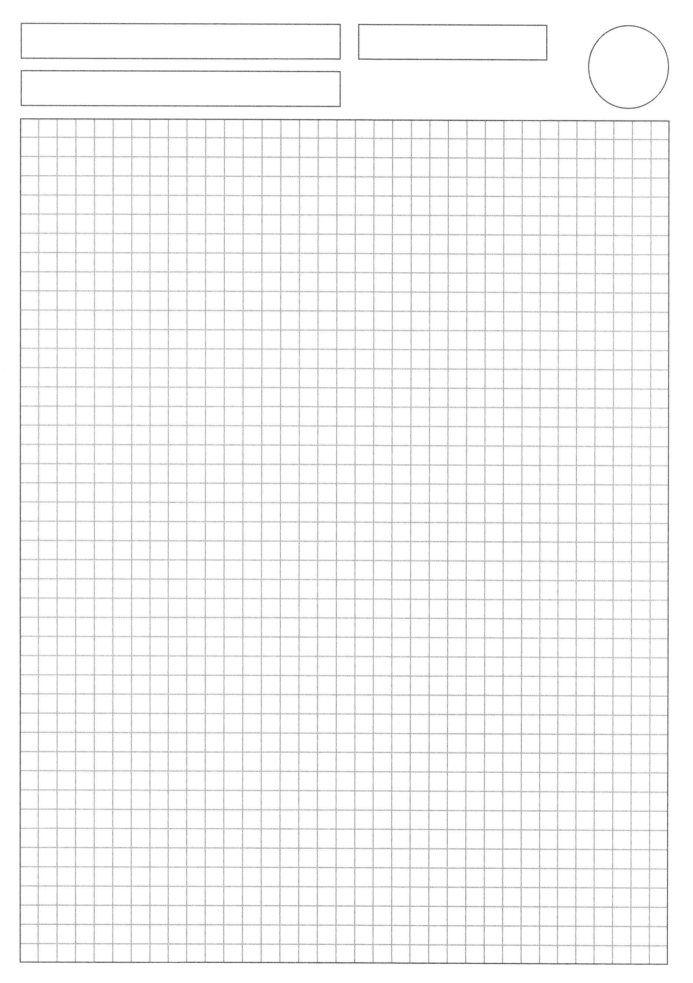

SECTOR 10
BEHAVIORS AND ATTACK
INDICATORS

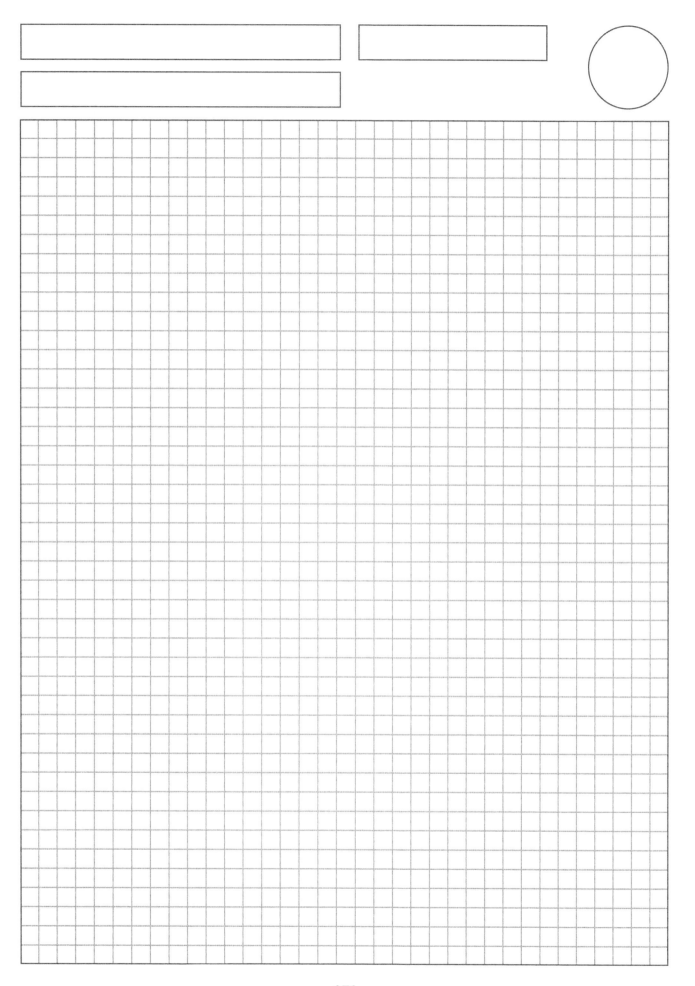

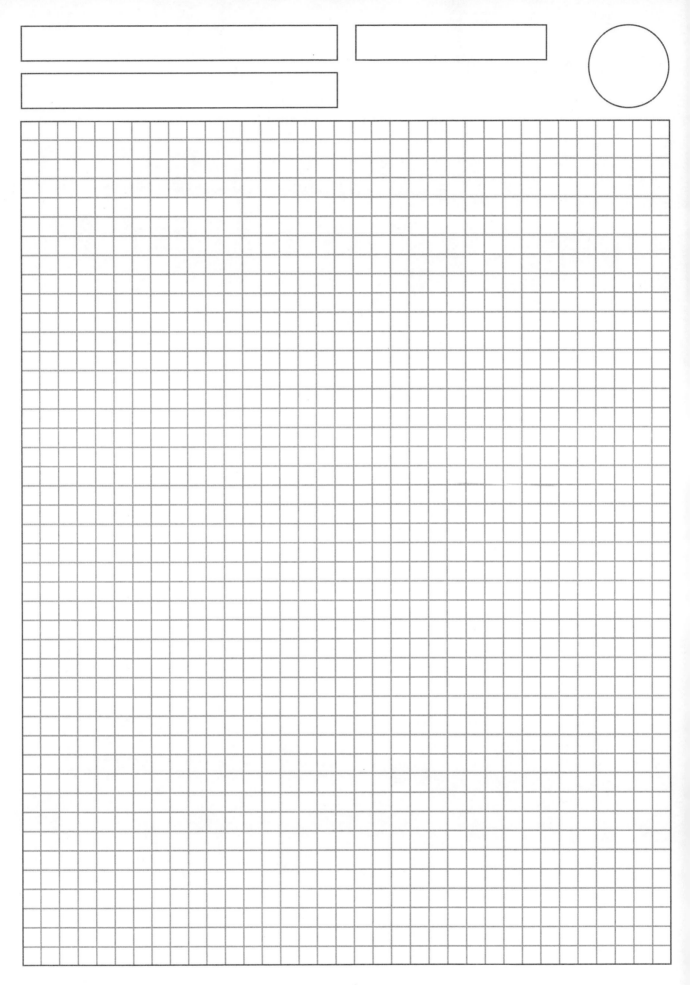

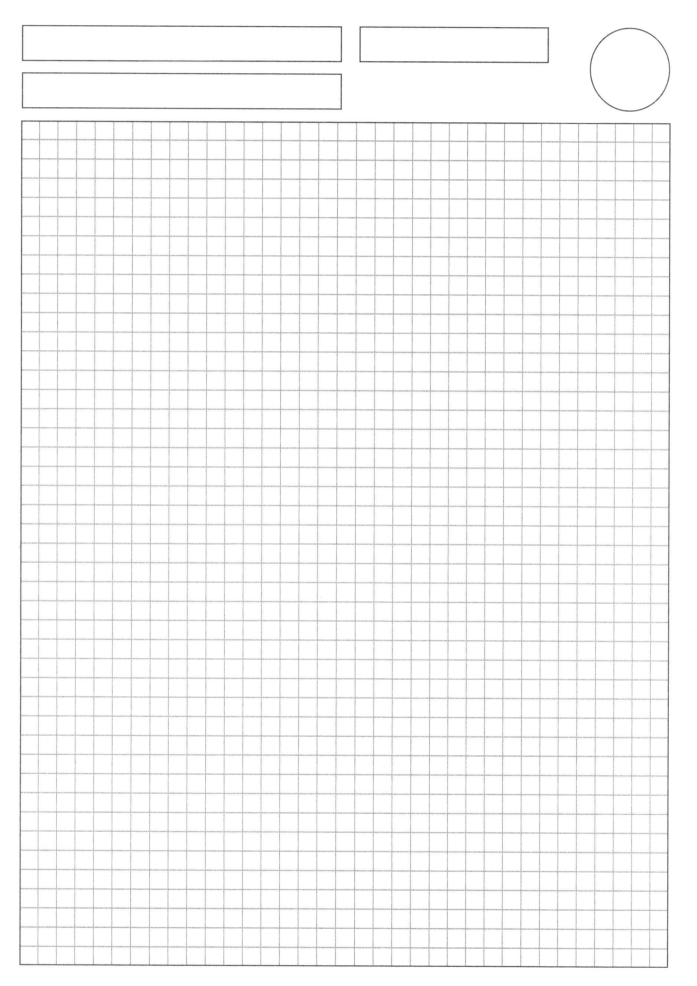

SECTOR 10
SHARED THREATS

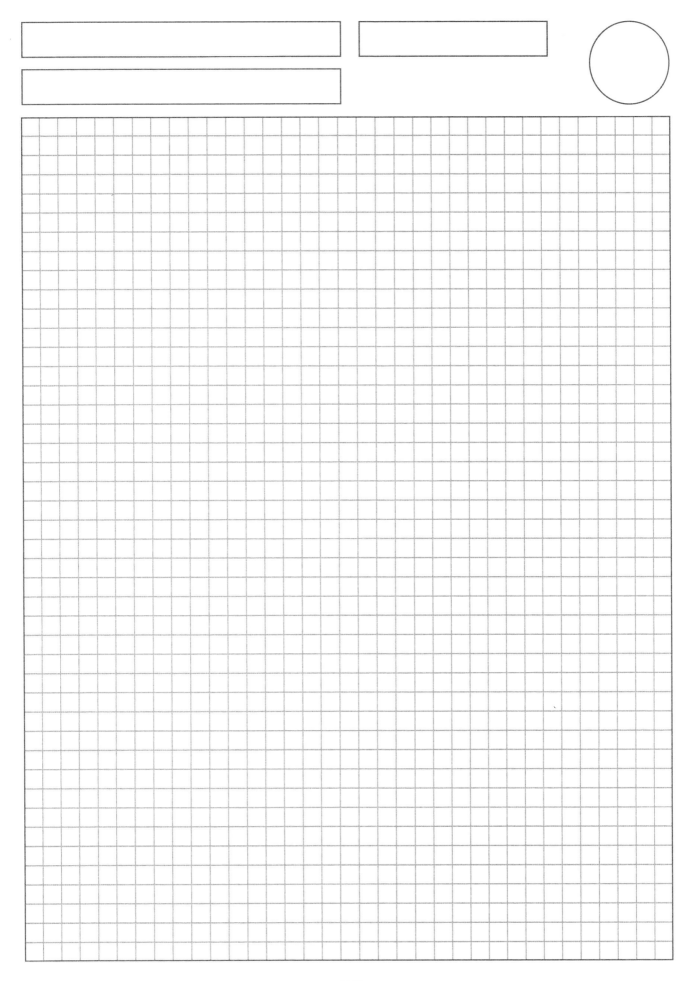

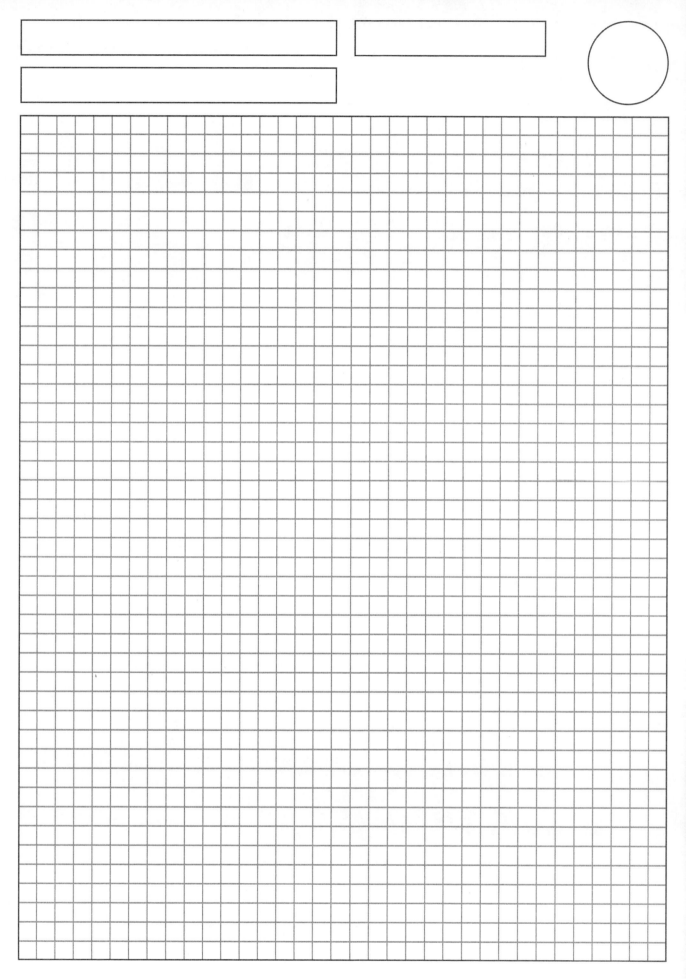

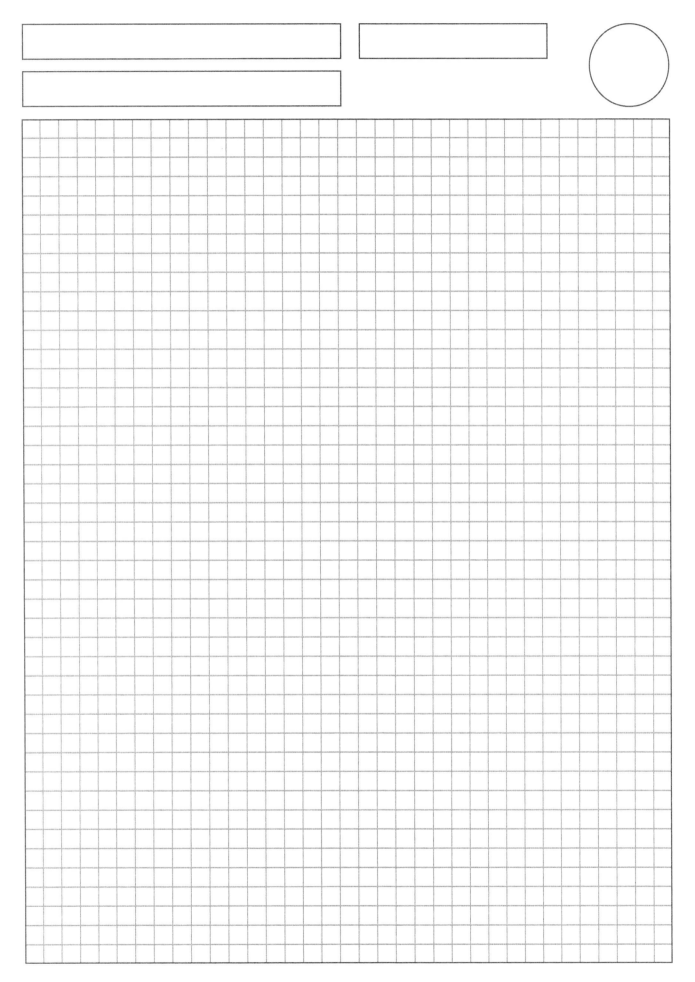

SECTOR 10
TACTICAL PLANS OF ACTION
(WHERE VULNERABILITIES CANNOT BE MITIGATED)

381

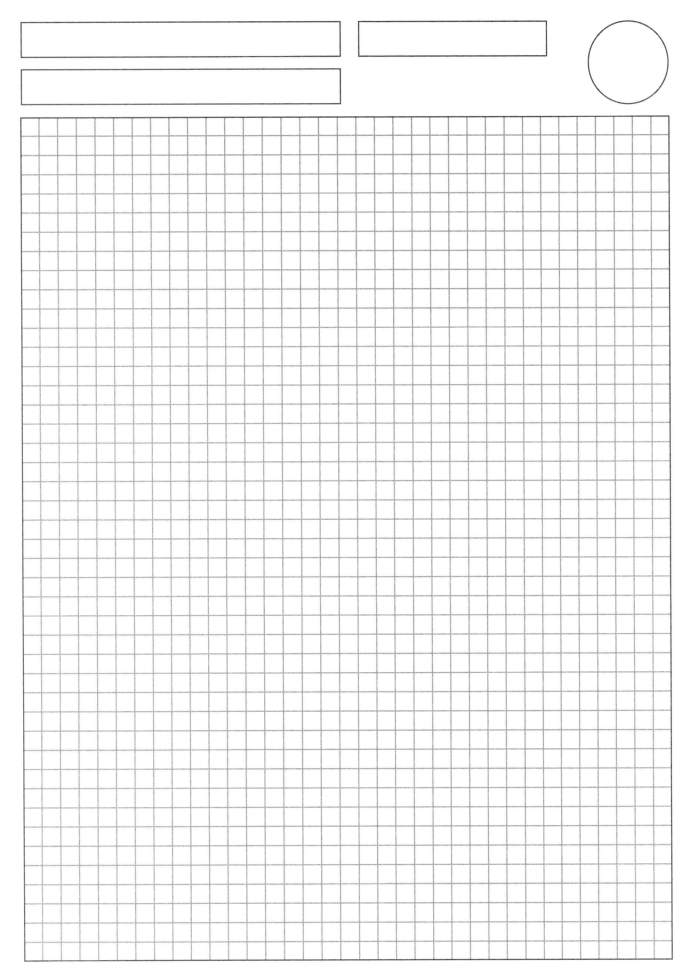

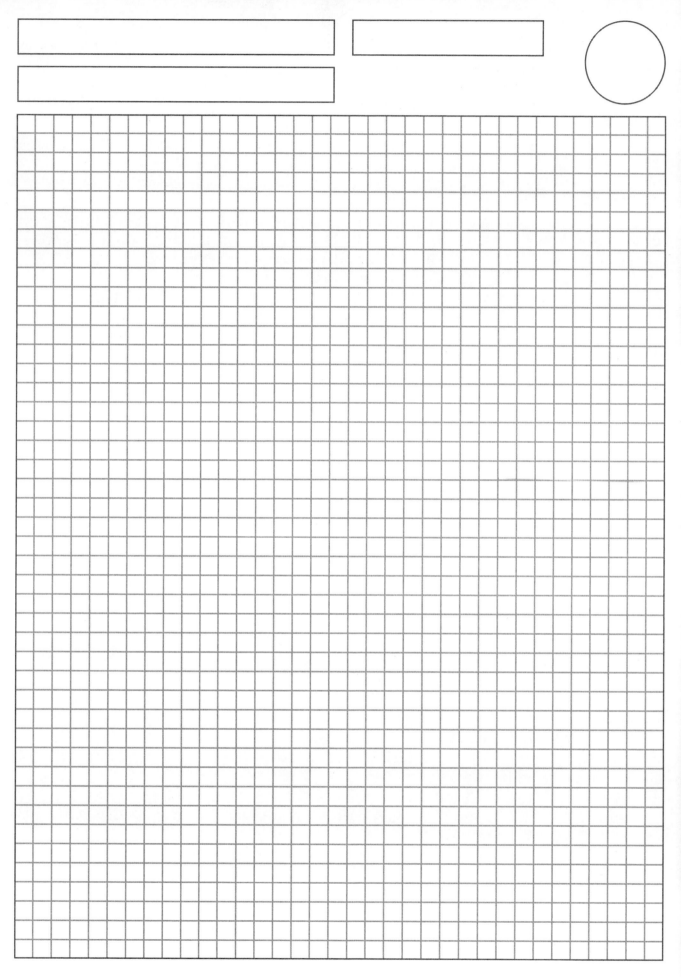

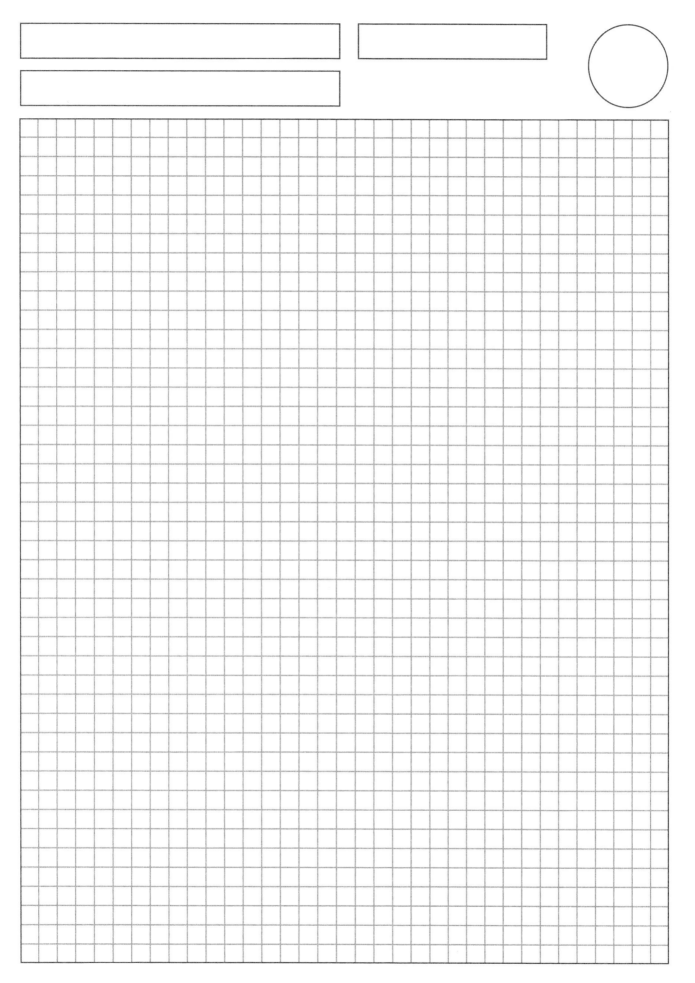

NEVER STOP ASSESSING YOUR ASSESSMENT

The key to staying safe lies in staying aware. Never assume you figured it all out, because as soon as you stop assessing, all the bad guys have to do is pick up their targeting where you stopped. Regardless of what society may tell you, safety is a personal endeavor that requires your involvement. Resting on the hopes that others will protect you, your family, your businesses or even your community is simply exercising learned helplessness.

If you have completed all three of the *Sheep No More* books, it is almost guaranteed that you will never be a victim of a violent attack as long as you incorporate the SOPs you have created. At the same time, you will now have a plan to act in areas where you were a sitting duck in the past.

It is time for you to start living a truly full life of awareness and freedom, forever vigilant and one step ahead of any attackers plans.

Jonathan T Gilliam

"For I know the plans I have for you," declares the Lord, "plans to prosper you and not to harm you, plans to give you hope and a future." — God

TO LEARN MORE GO TO
www.jonathanTGilliam.com

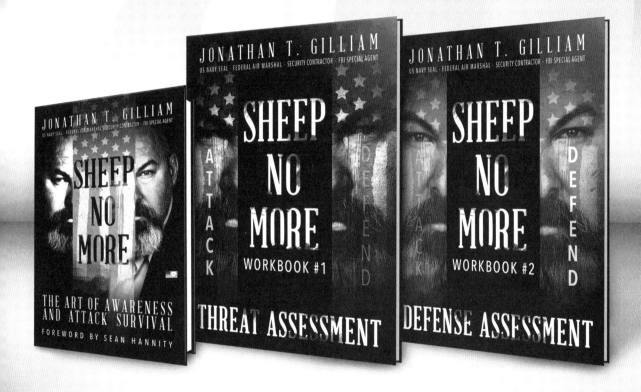

About the Author

Jonathan T. Gilliam is a bestselling Author and career public servant with over twenty years of service as a Navy SEAL, FBI Special Agent, Federal Air Marshal, Private Security Contractor, Police Officer, Public Speaker, Radio Host and Expert Media Commentator. Gilliam has extensive experience in crisis management, threat analysis and mitigation, small unit leadership, on-scene command, personal protection and special events/crisis management.